THE DEBATES IN
THE FEDERAL CONVENTION OF 1787
WHICH FRAMED THE CONSTITUTION
OF THE UNITED STATES OF AMERICA

REPORTED BY

JAMES MADISON

A Delegate from the State of Virginia

THE DEBATES IN
THE FEDERAL CONVENTION OF 1787
WHICH FRAMED THE CONSTITUTION
OF THE UNITED STATES OF AMERICA

REPORTED BY

JAMES MADISON

A Delegate from the State of Virginia

VOLUME ONE

GAILLARD HUNT AND JAMES BROWN SCOTT
EDITORS

I send you enclos'd the propos'd new Federal Constitution for these States. I was engag'd 4 Months of the last Summer in the Convention that form'd it. It is now sent by Congress to the several States for their Confirmation. If it succeeds, I do not see why you might not in Europe carry the Project of good Henry the 4th into Execution, by forming a Federal Union and One Grand Republick of all its different States & Kingdoms; by means of a like Convention; for we had many Interests to reconcile. (Benjamin Franklin to Mr. Grand, October 22, 1787. *Documentary History of the Constitution*, Vol. IV, pp. 341-342.)

PROMETHEUS BOOKS
BUFFALO, NEW YORK

K F
4 5/0
.U 54
1987
V I
July 1998

Published 1987 by Prometheus Books
700 East Amherst Street, Buffalo, New York 14215

Library of Congress Catalog Number: 86–63352
ISBN 0-87975-388-9

Printed in the United States of America

James Madison Memorial Committee

v

TABLE OF CONTENTS

---

[1] The Table of Contents to The Debates in the Federal Convention of 1787 is, with the exception of the first entry, the Session of Thursday, June 14, and the various items in the Appendix, reproduced from *Documentary History of the Constitution of the United States of America*, Vol. III (1900), pp. v-xix.

[Constitutional Convention Adjourns. End of volume one.]

PREFACE, 1987

This year marks the bicentennial of the Constitutional Convention in Philadelphia, sufficient reason for this anniversary edition of James Madison's *Journal* chronicling the events of that Pennsylvania summer during which the character of American democracy was ultimately defined. While Madison's account is not the only source of information concerning the framing of the nation's future, it is the primary source for information about the debates in the Convention. It is absolutely indispensable for citizens who are concerned to comprehend the principles at issue and the process of construction. In his volume titled *1787: The Grand Convention,* the well-known scholar Clinton Rossiter noted: "As one learns in comparing his notes with those of other self-appointed but only part-time scribes (Yates, Lansing, King, McHenry, Paterson, Hamilton, Pierce), the record he (Madison) left us is remarkably full, impartial, and accurate." Coupled with *The Federalist,* the *Journal* is the ideal textbook for any study of the Constitution. The celebrations of 1987 would be lamentably incomplete without the availability of a special printing of Mr. Madison's labors. The man whom we have come to honor as the "Father of the Constitution" offers fellow citizens of every generation a "narrative so unique as to render it a major treasure of the Republic."

It has now been several decades since scholars directed their skills to the primary documents penned by Madison. In 1977 Volume 10 of *The Papers of James Madison* published extensive excerpts from his writings but it noted that the "editors believe that it is beyond the scope of this present chronological series to reproduce the whole manuscript of JM's Federal Convention Debates" (p. 9). At some future time the editors may provide a newly edited and annotated edition of the *Journal.* Their interim decision to forego such an offering was clearly influenced by the already available publications of the Debates, of which they commented, "the most accurate are *Documentary History of the Constitution, III;* Farrand, *Records;* and *The Debates in the Federal Convention of 1787 which Framed the Constitution of the United States of America, Reported by James Madison,* ed. Gaillard Hunt and James Brown Scott (New York, 1920)." Reproduced here is the Hunt/Scott version, the most recent and most readable. It has the additional advantage of having been "read against the text" of the *Documentary History* (1900) and Farrand (1911).

The present edition includes all the Madison notes and remarks, along with a selection of additional data deemed useful for interpreting the events of that Summer.

A natural break in the *Journal* results from a Convention decision on July 2 to adjourn until July 5 that "time might be given to the Committee, and to such as chose to attend to the celebrations on the anniversary of Independence." That committee was to resolve the differences concerning representation in the two houses of Congress. On June 27 the Convention addressed the most thorny issue of the summer, "the rules of suffrage in the two branches." By July 2 the divisions were so acute that the Convention appointed the above mentioned committee "to devise and report some compromise." July 5 marked the beginning of the process that ultimately led to what modern scholars term the "Great Compromise," without which there would have been no Constitution of 1787.

In that debate Mr. Madison was a key figure, one whose views were not accepted when, on July 16 the "Great Compromise" was adopted by a state vote of 8 to 3. Yet, even as Madison expressed skepticism concerning the resolution of the struggle between the large and small states, he was prepared to write to Thomas Jefferson two days later about the progress in Philadelphia.

> The Convention continue to sit, and have been closely employed since the Commencement of the Session. I am still under the mortification of being restrained from disclosing any part of their proceeding. . . . I have taken lengthy notes of every thing that has yet passed, and mean to go on with the drudgery, if no indisposition obliges me to discontinue it. It is not possible to form any judgment of the future duration of the Session. I am led by sundry circumstances to guess that the residue of the work will not be very quickly dispatched. The public mind is very impatient for the event, and various reports are circulating which tend to inflame curiosity. I do not learn however that any discontent is expressed at the concealment; and have little doubt that the people will be as ready to receive as we shall be able to propose, a Government that will secure their liberties and happiness. (p. 105)

It is well known that Mr. Jefferson requested that his tombstone be inscribed with what he considered his chief accomplishments: writing the Virginia Statute on Religious Freedom, the founding of the University of Virginia, and the writing of the Declaration of Independence. In his later days Jefferson wrote to Madison, "Take care of me when I am dead." He was concerned for those testaments to his life that gave it substance and historic quality. Madison did not fail his most cherished friend. From 1826, the year of Jefferson's death, Rector Madison thrust

his energies into establishing the Charlottesville University as a monument to free, open scholarship. This practical genius had already trans-
lated the Virginia Statute into law in 1786 and would do the same for
the Declaration the following year. That friendship between two found-
ers, one that Dumas Malone has recently characterized as "one of the
greatest in history," changed the face of world history. In keeping alive
the Madison *Journal* a nation can care for him when he is dead.

One corrective to the notes by editor James Brown Scott does seem
necessary. Writing in 1918, Scott employed Supreme Court decisions,
particularly *State of Texas v. White* (1868) in order to alert readers to
the "separate and independent existence" of the states and to the belief
that there can "be no loss of separate and independent autonomy to the
States, through their union under the Constitution."

Today constitutional scholars would view the future differently
against the backdrop of the New Deal, massive social legislation, the
Warren Court and, most particularly, *Brown v. Board of Education*
(1954). The resulting struggles in the nation throughout the 1950s and
1960s brought forth vigorous states rights challenges to the prevailing
national mood. When the dust settled, interposition and militant state
sovereignty arguments collapsed; at present they offer merely echos of
a lost cause. As the political pendulum swings toward the right in the
1980s, the center has moved so dramatically that no serious attention is
any longer paid to those who would insist upon the "independent
autonomy" of the states. In the year 1987 citizens can understand even
more fully why Madison believed that the federal constitution would
"secure their liberties and happiness."

Robert S. Alley
University of Richmond
January 1987

INTRODUCTORY NOTE

I. MR. MADISON'S RECORD

There have been three prints from Madison's manuscript notes of the debates in the Convention which framed the Constitution of the United States—that in Volume III of the *Documentary History of the Constitution,* published in 1900 by the State Department which is the custodian of the original manuscript; that in Volumes III and IV of *The Writings of James Madison,* edited by Mr. Hunt, published in 1902 and printed separately in two volumes in 1908 (G. P. Putnam's Sons); and that published by the Yale University Press in 1911, Max Farrand, editor, as the chief part of Volumes I and II of the three volume edition of *The Records of the Federal Convention of 1787.* All of these works are reasonably accurate prints of the Madison record, while none is nor can be perfectly accurate. In the *Documentary History* and Professor Farrand's work an attempt is made to indicate in the printed page the alterations which Madison made in his manuscript. In the *Documentary History* this is done by the use of the caret, interlineations and the words " stricken out " to show the words through which Madison had drawn his pen. Mr. Farrand has made use of " angular brackets " to indicate additions made by Madison to his original notes and has added numerous footnotes to show what words were struck out by Madison. The inevitable result is that we have texts which are confusing or disagreeable to read. Even the special student who cares more for the form than the substance, and the suspicious investigator, who thinks that Madison may have made alterations in his original record so as to suppress or distort the truth or give a coloring to the facts, will not be satisfied with these attempts to visualize manuscript by print. He must, in fact, see the manuscript itself or a good photograph of it. None other than the special student would however, tolerate a photograph in this case, for the penmanship is not easy to read, and is so microscopic at times as to be a severe strain upon the eye.

The chief source of Madison's corrections of his notes was the official *Journal* of the Convention which was printed in 1819 and Yates's *Secret Proceedings and Debates of the Federal Convention* which appeared in 1821. Whenever Madison thought either of these records more correct than his he changed or added to his; but he noted more frequently errors in the official *Journal* itself. Yates's record he regarded as having little value. Nevertheless, he derived from it a few lesser motions which had escaped him.

Madison began the revision of his Notes after he retired from the Presidency in 1817 and had the manuscript copied under his own eye by his amanuensis, John C. Payne, Mrs. Madison's brother. On December 27, 1821, he wrote to John G. Jackson that he had set about arranging his papers "in earnest." On February 2, 1827, he wrote to Samuel Harrison Smith, who urged him to publish his record, that the world would not have long to wait for it. It was to be posthumous, he said, and Rufus King, William Few and himself were the only signers of the Constitution then surviving; "and of the lamps still burning, none can now be far from the socket," he added. King died a few months after this letter was written and Few in the following year. It is probable that the transcript was completed when Madison wrote, and the fact that it was being made caused a rumor to get abroad that he was writing a history of some sort, for he was obliged to deny to several correspondents that he had such a project.

At the end of the original manuscript of the debates in the Convention Madison wrote: "The few alterations and corrections made in these debates which are not in my handwriting, were dictated by me and made in my presence by John C. Payne." The entries made in Payne's hand are indeed few, and a careful examination fails to identify positively more than half-a-dozen, but when Payne wrote in small characters his writing resembled Madison's, and there were doubtless a few alterations made by him which can not be identified.

In Madison's will made in 1835 he says:

> In consideration of the particular and valuable aids received from my brother in law, John C. Payne and the affection which I bear him, I devise to him and his heirs two hundred and forty acres of land on which he lives.

The "particular and valuable aids," doubtless, were his services in revising the record of the debates and transcribing it for publication.

Madison died on June 28, 1836. In replying to the letter of condolence which the President, Andrew Jackson, sent to her, Mrs. Madison wrote (August 20, 1836):

> The best return I can make for the sympathy of my country is, to fulfil the sacred trust his confidence reposed in me— that of placing before it and the world what his pen prepared for their use—a legacy, the importance of which is deeply impressed on my mind.[1]

---

[1] *Executive Documents*, No. 8, 24th Congress, 2d Sess., Vol. I.

On November 15, 1836, she offered this legacy to the Government, and by act of March 3, 1837, the Government bought it for thirty thousand dollars. It was delivered to the Secretary of State, John Forsyth, by Mrs. Madison April 1, 1837, being described by her as: " the manuscript copy of the Debates in the Convention of 1787 and of the Debates &c in the Congress of the Confederation." In a letter of November 15, 1836, to President Jackson, she stated Mr. Madison's intention and gave a further description of the documents, saying:

> It was also intended to publish, with these debates, those taken by him in the Congress of the confederation in 1782, '3, and '7, of which he was then a member, and selections made by himself, and prepared under his eye, from his letters narrating the proceedings of that body during the periods of his service in it, prefixing the debates in 1776 on the declaration of independence by Thomas Jefferson, so as to embody all the memorials in that shape known to exist.[1]

These were " The Madison Papers." They comprised the original manuscripts and transcripts of them. Most of the transcripts, including the transcript of the debates in the Constitutional Convention, were made by Payne, but a few of the letters had been copied by Mrs. Madison herself. On July 9, 1838, a law was passed providing for the publication of " The Madison Papers." Henry D. Gilpin, Solicitor of the Treasury, was selected as the editor, and the joint committee of Senate and House on the Library ordered the withdrawal from the State Department of " one of the duplicate manuscript copies," which Mrs. Madison had deposited there. " The Madison Papers," being the debates and the other papers described by Mrs. Madison in her letter to the President, were published in three volumes in 1840 and from this edition several prints have since been made of the whole and of the debates separated from the other papers. The printer's copy for the publication of 1840 was returned to the joint Library Committee by the editor or printer, and the committee deposited it with the Librarian of Congress, instead of returning it to the Department of State whence it had come. It was not known until recently that this deposit was itself " one of the duplicate manuscript copies," which Mrs. Madison had deposited with the State Department. That part of it which concerns us, the debates in the Constitutional Convention, was Payne's transcript made under Madison's supervision; and Madison had himself gone over the transcript and had made a few additions and notes in his own hand. This printer's copy, therefore, has

---

[1] *Executive Documents,* No. 8, 24th Congress, 2d Sess., Vol. I.

more importance than commonly attaches to such material. It must, in fact, be considered when we are searching for an absolutely correct version of Madison's record. As, however, no transcript can be as correct as the original document which is transcribed, so the most correct version of the Madison record must be the original manuscript in Madison's own hand; but wherever Madison changed the transcript the change represents his final judgment and must be noticed in the interest of accuracy. Bringing the Payne transcript into comparison with the original record kept by Madison himself we have the last word in Madison's history of the Constitutional Convention.

In so far as any long text can be accurate the text which is printed here is believed to be accurate. Before it went to the printer it was collated with the original manuscript twice, each time by a different person. The galley proof was compared word for word with the original manuscript; the page proof was compared word for word by a different person with the original manuscript. The whole of the Payne transcript was read by the side of the Madison record to ascertain all variations and all corrections or additions which Madison made in the Payne transcript. With the exception of differences in spelling, abbreviation of words and punctuation, all variations between the two texts are stated in footnotes. The page proof was read against the text of the *Documentary History* and that of Professor Farrand in *The Records of the Federal Convention of 1787*, and the Madison manuscript was again consulted whenever a comparison showed any difference, however slight, in the three texts.

Finally, the foundry proof has, in the interest of accuracy, been read against Mr. Madison's original manuscript.

This is the first publication of the Madison record so compared.

GAILLARD HUNT.

WASHINGTON, D. C.,
November 11, 1918.

II. THE FEDERAL CONVENTION OF 1787 AN INTERNATIONAL CONFERENCE

The notes which James Madison made of the proceedings of the Federal Convention which met in Philadelphia, May 25th and adjourned September 17, 1787, were in fact, though not in form, the notes of the proceedings of an international conference, to use the language of today, or of a continental conference, as its members might have phrased it had they not preferred the term federal, as we apparently prefer constitutional, convention. Each preference is, however, correct according to the point of view of the observer. It was indeed a constitutional convention or conference, in the sense that it drafted a constitution of a more perfect Union of and for the States ratifying it; it was a federal convention or conference, in the sense that it proposed a draft for a federation of the States which the framers of the Constitution called a more perfect Union than that created by the Articles of Confederation, which the Constitution was to replace; it was a continental convention or conference in that it was composed of twelve of the thirteen States of the American continent; it was an international convention or conference, in that it was composed of official representatives of twelve of the thirteen " sovereign, free and independent " States of America, acting under instructions and meeting " for the sole and express purpose of revising the Articles of Confederation " in order to " render the federal Constitution adequate to the exigencies of government and the preservation of the Union."

The Union to be preserved had been composed but a short time previously of the thirteen American colonies, whose official representatives in the Continental Congress, on July 4, 1776, declared,

> That these United Colonies are, and of Right ought to be Free and Independent States; that they are Absolved from all Allegiance to the British Crown, and that all political connection between them and the State of Great Britain, is and ought to be totally dissolved; and that as Free and Independent States, they have full Power to levy War, conclude Peace, contract Alliances, establish Commerce, and to do all other Acts and Things which Independent States may of right do.

The official representatives in the Congress of the States thus declared to be free and independent drafted, and on November 15, 1777, approved Articles of Confederation, which, ratified by each of the thirteen States at various times, became effective on March 1, 1781, by the ratification of the State of Maryland, the last so to do. The contracting parties were thus the thirteen States declared to be free and independent by the Declaration of Independence; and the origin, the form and nature of the Union, its name and the relation of the States to one another and to the Confederation and perpetual Union, are thus stated in the caption and in the first three of the Articles of Confederation:[1]

> Articles of Confederation and perpetual Union between the states of Newhampshire, Massachusetts-bay, Rhodeisland and Providence Plantations, Connecticut, New-York, New-Jersey, Pennsylvania, Delaware, Maryland, Virginia, North-Carolina, South-Carolina and Georgia.
>
> Article I. The Stile of this confederacy shall be " The United States of America."
>
> Article II. Each state retains its sovereignty, freedom, and independence, and every Power, Jurisdiction and right, which is not by this confederation expressly delegated to the United States, in Congress assembled.
>
> Article III. The said states hereby severally enter into a firm league of friendship with each other, for their common defence, the security of their Liberties, and their mutual and general welfare, binding themselves to assist each other, against all force offered to, or attacks made upon them, or any of them, on account of religion, sovereignty, trade, or any other pretence whatever.

The " Confederation and perpetual Union between the States " not proving to be " adequate to the exigencies of government & the preservation of the Union," the Congress, on February 21, 1787, deemed it " expedient that on the second Monday in May next a Convention of delegates who shall have been appointed by the several states be held at Philadelphia for the sole and express purpose of revising the Articles of Confederation and reporting to Congress and the several legislatures such alterations and provisions therein as shall when agreed to in Congress and confirmed by the states render the federal constitution adequate to the exigencies of Government & the preservation of the Union."

Pursuant to this resolution, twelve of the thirteen " sovereign, free and independent " States sent official delegates to the convention to be held in Philadelphia for the revision of the Articles of Confed-

---

[1] *Journals of the Continental Congress*, Library of Congress edition, Vol. XIX (1912), p. 214.

eration, and succeeded with much good will, concession, and compromise, in drafting, instead of revising the Articles, a constitution and a scheme of government of a more perfect Union, which, submitted to the Congress of the Confederation, referred by it to the States, ratified in the course of 1787-88 by conventions in eleven of the States, became effective in accordance with the 7th Article of the Constitution, providing that " The Ratification of the Conventions of nine States, shall be sufficient for the Establishment of this Constitution between the States so ratifying the Same."

The government of the more perfect Union was to go into operation on March 4, 1789, and, in the course of that and of the subsequent year, the people of the States of North Carolina and of Rhode Island ratified the Constitution, thus making it the union of all thirteen of the original States of America.

In the leading case of *Ware* v. *Hylton* (3 Dallas, 199, 224), decided in 1796, Mr. Justice Chase took occasion to consider the course of events leading to the Declaration of Independence of the colonies, the result of that Declaration upon the colonies, and the relation of the States to one another before the Articles of Confederation became binding by the ratification of the State of Maryland, on March 1, 1781. In the course of his opinion that learned Justice said, under a sense of judicial responsibility:

In *June* 1776, the Convention of *Virginia formally* declared, that *Virginia* was a free, sovereign, and independent state; and on the 4th of *July*, 1776, following, the *United States*, in Congress assembled, declared the *Thirteen United Colonies* free and independent states; and that as *such*, they had full power to levy war, conclude peace, &c. I consider this as a declaration, not that the United Colonies *jointly*, in a *collective* capacity, were independent states, &c. but that *each* of them was a sovereign and independent state, that is, that *each* of them had a right to govern itself by its own authority, and its own laws, without any controul from any other power upon earth.

Before these solemn acts of separation from the Crown of *Great Britain*, the war between *Great Britain* and the United Colonies, *jointly*, and *separately*, was a *civil* war; but instantly on that great and ever memorable event, the war changed its *nature*, and became a PUBLIC war between *independent governments;* and immediately thereupon ALL the *rights* of *public* war (and all the other rights of an independent nation) attached to the government of *Virginia;* and all the *former political* connexion between *Great Britain* and *Virginia*, and also between their respective subjects, were totally dissolved; and not only the *two nations*, but all the subjects of each, were in a state of war; precisely as

in the present war between *Great Britain* and *France.* *Vatt. lib.*
3. c. 18. § 292. to 295. *lib.* 3. c. 5. § 70. 72. and 73

From the 4th of *July,* 1776, the *American* States were *de
facto,* as well as *de jure,* in the possession and actual exercise of
all the *rights* of independent governments. . . .

The Supreme Court of the United States, of which Mr. Justice
Chase was a member, apparently attaches great weight to this opinion in *Ware* v. *Hylton,* inasmuch as Mr. Justice Swayne, in deliver-
ing the unanimous opinion of this court in the case of *Hauenstein* v.
Lynham (100 U. S., 483, 489), decided in 1879, said:

> We have quoted from the opinion of Mr. Justice Chase in
> that case, . . . because it shows the views of a powerful legal
> mind at that early period, when the debates in the convention
> which framed the Constitution must have been fresh in the mem-
> ory of the leading jurists of the country.

It is proper to add, in this connection, that Mr. Justice Chase was a
signer of the Declaration of Independence.

It is also interesting to note, in this connection, that John Marshall
of Virginia, shortly to become and thereafter to remain, the great
Chief Justice of the Supreme Court, appeared in 1796 as counsel for
his State, in the case of *Ware* v. *Hylton,* and that in the course of his
argument he said:

> 1st. It has been conceded, that independent nations have, in
> general, the right of confiscation; and that *Virginia,* at the time
> of passing her law [1777], was an independent nation.

Speaking of the nature of the Confederation, the relations of the
States composing it both to themselves and to the Union, Mr. Chief
Justice Marshall observed, speaking for the Supreme Court of the
United States in *Sturges* v. *Crowninshield* (4 Wheaton, 122, 192),
decided in 1819:

> It must be recollected, that previous to the formation of the
> new constitution, we were divided into independent States, united
> for some purposes, but, in most respects, sovereign.

And in the later case of *Gibbons* v. *Ogden,* (9 Wheaton, 1, 187), decided in 1824, the same great jurist, recurring to this matter, again
remarked:

> As preliminary to the very able discussions of the constitution,
> which we have heard from the bar, and as having some influence
> on its construction, reference has been made to the political sit-
> uation of these States, anterior to its formation. It has been said,

that they were sovereign, were completely independent, and were connected with each other only by a league.   This is true.

As to the nature of the more perfect Union and the relation to it of the States whereof it is composed, Mr. Chief Justice Marshall solemnly declared, in the course of his opinion announcing and justifying the unanimous judgment of his brethren, in *McCulloch* v. *Maryland*, (4 Wheaton, 316, 410), decided in 1819, and which the late Professor Thayer considered the greatest of his cases:

> In America, the powers of sovereignty are divided between the government of the Union, and those of the States.   They are each sovereign, with respect to the objects committed to it, and neither sovereign with respect to the objects committed to the other.

And in the great and leading case of the *State of Texas* v. *White,* (7 Wallace, 700, 725), decided in 1868, Mr. Chief Justice Chase thus restated and elaborated in classic terms the views of his vigorous namesake, Mr. Justice Chase, and of his illustrious predecessor, Mr. Chief Justice Marshall:

> Under the Articles of Confederation each State retained its sovereignty, freedom, and independence, and every power, jurisdiction, and right not expressly delegated to the United States.   Under the Constitution, though the powers of the States were much restricted, still, all powers not delegated to the United States, nor prohibited to the States, are reserved to the States respectively, or to the people.   And we have already had occasion to remark at this term, that "the people of each State compose a State, having its own government, and endowed with all the functions essential to separate and independent existence," and that "without the States in union, there could be no such political body as the United States."   Not only, therefore, can there be no loss of separate and independent autonomy to the States, through their union under the Constitution, but it may be not unreasonably said that the preservation of the States, and the maintenance of their governments, are as much within the design and care of the Constitution as the preservation of the Union and the maintenance of the National government.   The Constitution, in all its provisions, looks to an indestructible Union, composed of indestructible States.

The international import of the Constitution of a more perfect Union was not lost upon Benjamin Franklin, the keenest, shrewdest, most sagacious and far-sighted observer of his day, who, shortly after the adjournment of the Federal Convention, was pleased to say in a letter to a friend in Europe:

> I send you enclos'd the propos'd new Federal Constitution for these States.   I was engag'd 4 Months of the last Summer

in the Convention that form'd it. It is now sent by Congress to the several States for their Confirmation.

And he was bold enough to suggest that:

> If it succeeds, I do not see why you might not in Europe carry the Project of good Henry the 4th into Execution, by forming a Federal Union and One Grand Republick of all its different States & Kingdoms; by means of a like Convention; for we had many Interests to reconcile.[1]

In view of the origin and nature of the Constitution drafted by official delegates of twelve of the thirteen " sovereign, free and independent " States of America, submitted to and ratified by the people of each of the several States in conventions assembled for that purpose, and binding only those States which had done so; and in view of the authoritative, conspicuous, and pertinent judgments of the Supreme Court of the United States regarding the nature and meaning of the Constitution thereof, it would appear that Madison's notes of the proceedings of that memorable and significant international conference from which there sprang " a more perfect Union . . . for the United States of America," are not only of interest to students of Federal Government, and to the good people of the United States, but also to students of International Law, and to the peoples of all the States forming the Society of Nations.

JAMES BROWN SCOTT.

WASHINGTON, D. C.,
November 11, 1918.

---

[1] Letter of October 22, 1787, to Mr. Grand. *Documentary History of the Constitution of the United States of America* (published by the Department of State of the United States), Vol. IV (1905), pp. 341-342.

PART I

ANTECEDENTS OF THE FEDERAL CONVENTION OF 1787

THE DECLARATION OF INDEPENDENCE—1776 [1]

In Congress, July 4, 1776

The unanimous Declaration of the thirteen united States of America

WHEN in the Course of human events, it becomes necessary for one people to dissolve the political bands which have connected them with another, and to assume among the powers of the earth, the separate and equal station to which the Laws of Nature and of Nature's God entitle them, a decent respect to the opinions of mankind requires that they should declare the causes which impel them to the separation.—We hold these truths to be self-evident, that all men are created equal, that they are endowed by their Creator with certain unalienable Rights, that among these are Life, Liberty and the pursuit of Happiness.—That to secure these rights, Governments are instituted among Men, deriving their just powers from the consent of the governed,—That whenever any Form of Government becomes destructive of these ends, it is the Right of the People to alter or to abolish it, and to institute new Government, laying its foundation on such principles and organizing its powers in such form, as to them shall seem most likely to effect their Safety and Happiness. Prudence, indeed, will dictate that Governments long established should not be changed for light and transient causes; and accordingly all experience hath shown, that mankind are more disposed to suffer, while evils are sufferable, than to right themselves by abolishing the forms to which they are accustomed. But when a long train of abuses and usurpations, pursuing invariably the same Object evinces a design to reduce them under absolute Despotism, it is their right, it is their duty, to throw off such Government, and to provide new Guards for their future security.—Such has been the patient sufferance of these Colonies; and such is now the necessity which constrains them to alter their former Systems of Government. The history of the present King of Great Britain is a history of repeated injuries and usurpations, all having in direct object the establishment of an absolute Tyranny over these States. To

---

[1] Printed from the facsimile of the engrossed copy of the original manuscript in the Library of the Department of State of the United States.

prove this, let Facts be submitted to a candid world.—He has refused his Assent to Laws, the most wholesome and necessary for
the public good.—He has forbidden his Governors to pass Laws
of immediate and pressing importance, unless suspended in their
operation till his Assent should be obtained; and when so suspended, he has utterly neglected to attend to them.—He has refused
to pass other Laws for the accommodation of large districts of people,
unless those people would relinquish the right of Representation in
the Legislature, a right inestimable to them and formidable to tyrants
only.—He has called together legislative bodies at places unusual,
uncomfortable, and distant from the depository of their public
Records, for the sole purpose of fatiguing them into compliance with
his measures.—He has dissolved Representative Houses repeatedly,
for opposing with manly firmness his invasions on the rights of the
people.—He has refused for a long time, after such dissolutions, to
cause others to be elected; whereby the Legislative powers, incapable
of Annihilation, have returned to the People at large for their exercise;
the State remaining in the mean time exposed to all the dangers of
invasion from without, and convulsions within.—He has endeavoured
to prevent the population of these States; for that purpose obstructing
the Laws for Naturalization of Foreigners; refusing to pass others to
encourage their migration hither, and raising the conditions of new
Appropriations of Lands.—He has obstructed the Administration of
Justice, by refusing his Assent to Laws for establishing Judiciary
powers.—He has made Judges dependent on his Will alone, for the
tenure of their offices, and the amount and payment of their salaries.
—He has erected a multitude of New Offices, and sent hither swarms
of Officers to harrass our people, and eat out their substance.—He
has kept among us, in times of peace, Standing Armies, without the
Consent of our legislatures.—He has affected to render the Military
independent of and superior to the Civil power.—He has combined
with others to subject us to a jurisdiction foreign to our constitution,
and unacknowledged by our laws; giving his Assent to their Acts of
pretended Legislation:—For quartering large bodies of armed troops
among us:—For protecting them, by a mock Trial, from punishment
for any Murders which they should commit on the Inhabitants of
these States:—For cutting off our Trade with all parts of the world:—
For imposing Taxes on us without our Consent:—For depriving us
in many cases, of the benefits of Trial by Jury:—For transporting
us beyond Seas to be tried for pretended offences:—For abolishing the
free System of English Laws in a neighbouring Province, establishing
therein an Arbitrary government, and enlarging its Boundaries so as

to render it at once an example and fit instrument for introducing the same absolute rule into these Colonies:—For taking away our Charters, abolishing our most valuable Laws, and altering fundamentally the Forms of our Governments:—For suspending our own Legislatures, and declaring themselves invested with power to legislate for us in all cases whatsoever.—He has abdicated Government here, by declaring us out of his Protection and waging War against us.—He has plundered our seas, ravaged our Coasts, burnt our towns, and destroyed the lives of our people.—He is at this time transporting large Armies of foreign Mercenaries to compleat the works of death, desolation and tyranny, already begun with circumstances of Cruelty & perfidy scarcely paralleled in the most barbarous ages, and totally unworthy the Head of a civilized nation.—He has constrained our fellow Citizens taken Captive on the high Seas to bear Arms against their Country, to become the executioners of their friends and Brethren, or to fall themselves by their Hands.—He has excited domestic insurrections amongst us, and has endeavoured to bring on the inhabitants of our frontiers, the merciless Indian Savages, whose known rule of warfare, is an undistinguished destruction of all ages, sexes and conditions. In every stage of these Oppressions We have Petitioned for Redress in the most humble terms: Our repeated Petitions have been answered only by repeated injury. A Prince, whose character is thus marked by every act which may define a Tyrant, is unfit to be the ruler of a free people. Nor have We been wanting in attentions to our Brittish brethren. We have warned them from time to time of attempts by their legislature to extend an unwarrantable jurisdiction over us. We have reminded them of the circumstances of our emigration and settlement here. We have appealed to their native justice and magnanimity, and we have conjured them by the ties of our common kindred to disavow these usurpations, which, would inevitably interrupt our connections and correspondence They too have been deaf to the voice of justice and of consanguinity. We must, therefore, acquiesce in the necessity, which denounces our Separation, and hold them, as we hold the rest of mankind, Enemies in War, in Peace Friends.—

WE, THEREFORE, the REPRESENTATIVES of the UNITED STATES OF AMERICA, in General Congress, Assembled, appealing to the Supreme Judge of the world for the rectitude of our intentions, do, in the Name, and by Authority of the good People of these Colonies, solemnly publish and declare, That these United Colonies are, and of Right ought to be FREE AND INDEPENDENT STATES; that they are Absolved from all Allegiance to the British Crown, and that all political connection between them and the State of Great Britain, is and ought to be totally dissolved; and that as Free and Independent States, they have full Power to levy War, conclude Peace, contract Alliances, establish Commerce, and to do all other Acts and Things which Independent States may of right do.—And for the support of this Declaration, with a firm reliance on the protection of Divine Providence, we mutually pledge to each other our Lives, our Fortunes and our sacred Honor.

JOHN HANCOCK.

New Hampshire
JOSIAH BARTLETT,
WM. WHIPPLE,
MATTHEW THORNTON

Massachusetts Bay
SAML. ADAMS,
JOHN ADAMS,
ROBT. TREAT PAINE,
ELBRIDGE GERRY.

Rhode Island
STEP. HOPKINS,
WILLIAM ELLERY.

Connecticut
ROGER SHERMAN,
SAM'EL HUNTINGTON,
WM. WILLIAMS,
OLIVER WOLCOTT.

New York
WM. FLOYD,
PHIL. LIVINGSTON,
FRANS. LEWIS,
LEWIS MORRIS.

New Jersey
RICHD. STOCKTON,
JNO. WITHERSPOON,
FRAS. HOPKINSON,
JOHN HART,
ABRA. CLARK.

Pennsylvania
ROBT. MORRIS,
BENJAMIN RUSH,
BENJA. FRANKLIN,
JOHN MORTON,
GEO. CLYMER,
JAS. SMITH,
GEO. TAYLOR,
JAMES WILSON,
GEO. ROSS.

Delaware
CAESAR RODNEY,
GEO. READ,
THO. M'KEAN.

Maryland
SAMUEL CHASE,
WM. PACA,
THOS. STONE,
CHARLES CARROLL of Carrollton.

Virginia
GEORGE WYTHE,
RICHARD HENRY LEE,
TH. JEFFERSON,
BENJA. HARRISON,
THS. NELSON, JR.,
FRANCIS LIGHTFOOT LEE,
CARTER BRAXTON.

North Carolina
WM. HOOPER,
JOSEPH HEWES,
JOHN PENN.

South Carolina
EDWARD RUTLEDGE,
THOS. HEYWARD, JUNR.,
THOMAS LYNCH, JUNR.,
ARTHUR MIDDLETON.

Georgia
BUTTON GWINNETT,
LYMAN HALL,
GEO. WALTON.

NOTE.—Mr. Ferdinand Jefferson, Keeper of the Rolls in the Department of State, at Washington, says: "The names of the signers are spelt above as in the facsimile of the original, but the punctuation of them is not always the same; neither do the names of the States appear in the facsimile of the original. The names of the signers of each State are grouped together in the facsimile of the original, except the name of Matthew Thornton, which follows that of Oliver Wolcott."—*Revised Statutes of the United States*, 2d Edition, 1878, page 6.

ARTICLES OF CONFEDERATION [1]

MARCH 1, 1781

To all to whom these Presents shall come, we the under signed Delegates of the States affixed to our Names, send greeting.

Whereas the Delegates of the United States of America, in Congress assembled, did, on the 15th day of November, in the Year of Our Lord One thousand Seven Hundred and Seventy seven, and in the Second Year of the Independence of America, agree to certain articles of Confederation and perpetual Union between the States of New-hampshirē, Massachusetts-bay, Rhodeisland and Providence Plantations, Connecticut, New York, New Jersey, Pennsylvania, Delaware, Maryland, Virginia, North-Carolina, South-Carolina and Georgia in the words following, viz. " Articles of Confederation and perpetual Union between the states of Newhampshire, Massachusetts-bay, Rhodeisland and Providence Plantations, Connecticut, New-York, New-Jersey, Pennsylvania, Delaware, Maryland, Virginia, North-Carolina, South-Carolina and Georgia.

Article I. The Stile of this confederacy shall be " The United States of America."

Article II. Each state retains its sovereignty, freedom, and independence, and every Power, Jurisdiction and right, which is not by this confederation expressly delegated to the United States, in Congress assembled.

Article III. The said states hereby severally enter into a firm league of friendship with each other, for their common defence, the security of their Liberties, and their mutual and general welfare, binding themselves to assist each other, against all force offered to, or at-

---

[1] *Journals of the Continental Congress*, Library of Congress edition, Vol. XIX (1912), p. 214.

The Articles of Confederation were agreed to by the Congress, November 15, 1777. They were, as appears from the list of signatures affixed to these Articles, signed at different times by the delegates of the different American States. On March 1, 1781, the delegates from Maryland, the last of the States to take action, " did, in behalf of the said State of Maryland, sign and ratify the said articles, by which act the Confederation of the United States of America was completed, each and every of the Thirteen United States, from New Hampshire to Georgia, both included, having adopted and confirmed, and by their delegates in Congress, ratified the same." *Ibid.*, p. 214.

tacks made upon them, or any of them, on account of religion, sovereignty, trade, or any other pretence whatever.

Article IV. The better to secure and perpetuate mutual friendship and intercourse among the people of the different states in this union, the free inhabitants of each of these states, paupers, vagabonds and fugitives from justice excepted, shall be entitled to all privileges and immunities of free citizens in the several states; and the people of each state shall have free ingress and regress to and from any other state, and shall enjoy therein all the privileges of trade and commerce, subject to the same duties, impositions and restrictions as the inhabitants thereof respectively, provided that such restriction shall not extend so far as to prevent the removal of property imported into any state, to any other state, of which the Owner is an inhabitant; provided also that no imposition, duties or restriction shall be laid by any state, on the property of the united states, or either of them.

If any Person guilty of, or charged with treason, felony, or other high misdemeanor in any state, shall flee from Justice, and be found in any of the united states, he shall, upon demand of the Governor or executive power, of the state from which he fled, be delivered up and removed to the state having jurisdiction of his offence.

Full faith and credit shall be given in each of these states to the records, acts and judicial proceedings of the courts and magistrates of every other state.

Article V. For the more convenient management of the general interests of the united states, delegates shall be annually appointed in such manner as the legislature of each state shall direct, to meet in Congress on the first Monday in November, in every year, with a power reserved to each state, to recal its delegates, or any of them, at any time within the year, and to send others in their stead, for the remainder of the Year.

No state shall be represented in Congress by less than two, nor by more than seven Members; and no person shall be capable of being a delegate for more than three years in any term of six years; nor shall any person, being a delegate, be capable of holding any office under the united states, for which he, or another for his benefit receives any salary, fees or emolument of any kind.

Each state shall maintain its own delegates in a meeting of the states, and while they act as members of the committee of the states.

In determining questions in the united states in Congress assembled, each state shall have one vote.

Freedom of speech and debate in Congress shall not be impeached or questioned in any Court, or place out of Congress, and the members of congress shall be protected in their persons from arrests and imprisonments, during the time of their going to and from, and attendance on congress, except for treason, felony, or breach of the peace.

Article VI.   No state, without the Consent of the united states in congress assembled, shall send any embassy to, or receive any embassy from, or enter into any conference, agreement, alliance or treaty with any King prince or state; nor shall any person holding any office of profit or trust under the united states, or any of them, accept of any present, emolument, office or title of any kind whatever from any king, prince or foreign state; nor shall the united states in congress assembled, or any of them, grant any title of nobility.

No two or more states shall enter into any treaty, confederation or alliance whatever between them, without the consent of the united states in congress assembled, specifying accurately the purposes for which the same is to be entered into, and how long it shall continue.

No state shall lay any imposts or duties, which may interfere with any stipulations in treaties, entered into by the united states in congress assembled, with any king, prince or state, in pursuance of any treaties already proposed by congress, to the courts of France and Spain.

No vessels of war shall be kept up in time of peace by any state, except such number only, as shall be deemed necessary by the united states in congress assembled, for the defence of such state, or its trade; nor shall any body of forces be kept up by any state, in time of peace, except such number only, as in the judgment of the united states, in congress assembled, shall be deemed requisite to garrison the forts necessary for the defence of such state; but every state shall always keep up a well regulated and disciplined militia, sufficiently armed and accoutred, and shall provide and constantly have ready for use, in public stores, a due number of field pieces and tents, and a proper quantity of arms, ammunition and camp equipage.

No state shall engage in any war without the consent of the united states in congress assembled, unless such state be actually invaded by enemies, or shall have received certain advice of a resolution being formed by some nation of Indians to invade such state, and the danger is so imminent as not to admit of a delay till the united states in congress assembled can be consulted: nor shall any state grant commissions to any ships or vessels of war, nor letters of marque or reprisal, except it be after a declaration of war by the united states in congress assembled, and then only against the kingdom or state and the subjects thereof, against which war has been so declared, and under such regulations as shall be established by the united states in congress assembled, unless such state be infested by pirates, in which case vessels of war may be fitted out for that occasion, and kept so long as the danger shall continue, or until the united states in congress assembled, shall determine otherwise.

Article VII. When land-forces are raised by any state for the common defence, all officers of or under the rank of colonel, shall be appointed by the legislature of each state respectively, by whom such forces shall be raised, or in such manner as such state shall direct, and all vacancies shall be filled up by the State which first made the appointment.

Article VIII. All charges of war, and all other expences that shall be incurred for the common defence or general welfare, and allowed by the united states in congress assembled, shall be defrayed out of a common treasury, which shall be supplied by the several states in proportion to the value of all land within each state, granted to or surveyed for any Person, as such land and the buildings and improvements thereon shall be estimated according to such mode as the united states in congress assembled, shall from time to time direct and appoint.

The taxes for paying that proportion shall be laid and levied by the authority and direction of the legislatures of the several states within the time agreed upon by the united states in congress assembled.

Article IX. The united states in congress assembled, shall have the sole and exclusive right and power of determining on peace and war, except in the cases mentioned in the sixth article—of sending and receiving ambassadors—entering into treaties and alliances, provided that no treaty of commerce shall be made whereby the legislative power of the respective states shall be restrained from imposing such imposts and duties on foreigners, as their own people are subjected to, or from prohibiting the exportation or importation of any species of goods or commodities whatsoever—of establishing rules for deciding in all cases, what captures on land or water shall be legal, and in what manner prizes taken by land or naval forces in the service of the united states shall be divided or appropriated—of granting letters of marque and reprisal in times of peace—appointing courts for the trial of piracies and felonies committed on the high seas and establishing courts for receiving and determining finally appeals in all cases of captures, provided that no member of congress shall be appointed a judge of any of the said courts.

The united states in congress assembled shall also be the last resort on appeal in all disputes and differences now subsisting or that hereafter may arise between two or more states concerning boundary, jurisdiction or any other cause whatever; which authority shall always be exercised in the manner following. Whenever the legislative or executive authority or lawful agent of any state in controversy with another shall present a petition to congress stating the matter in question and praying for a hearing, notice thereof shall be given by order of congress to the legislative or executive authority of the other state in controversy, and a day assigned for the appearance of the parties by their lawful agents, who shall then be directed to appoint by joint consent, commissioners or judges to constitute a court for hearing and determining the matter in question: but if they cannot agree, congress shall name three persons out of each of the united states, and from the list of such persons each party shall alternately strike out one, the petitioners beginning, until the number shall be reduced to thirteen; and from that number not less than seven, nor more than nine names as congress shall direct, shall in the presence of congress be drawn out by lot, and the persons whose names shall be so drawn or any five of them, shall be commissioners or judges, to hear and finally determine the controversy, so always as a major part of the judges who shall hear the cause shall agree in the determination: and if either party shall neglect to attend at the day appointed, without showing reasons, which congress shall judge sufficient, or being present shall refuse to strike, the congress shall proceed to nominate three persons out of each state, and the secretary of congress shall strike in behalf of such party absent or refusing; and the judgment and sentence of the court to be appointed, in the manner before prescribed, shall be final and conclusive; and if any of the parties shall refuse to submit to the authority of such court, or to appear or defend their claim or cause, the court shall nevertheless proceed to pronounce sentence, or judgment, which shall in like manner be final and decisive, the judgment or sentence and other proceedings being in either case transmitted to congress, and lodged among the acts of congress for the security of the parties concerned: provided that every commissioner, before he sits in judgment, shall take an oath to be administred by one of the judges of the supreme or superior court of the state, where the cause shall be tried, " well and truly to hear and determine the matter in question, according to the best of his judgment, without favour, affection or hope of reward:"

provided also, that no state shall be deprived of territory for the benefit of the united states.

All controversies concerning the private right of soil claimed under different grants of two or more states, whose jurisdictions as they may respect such lands, and the states which passed such grants are adjusted, the said grants or either of them being at the same time claimed to have originated antecedent to such settlement of jurisdiction, shall on the petition of either party to the congress of the united states, be finally determined as near as may be in the same manner as is before prescribed for deciding disputes respecting territorial jurisdiction between different states.

The united states in congress assembled shall also have the sole and exclusive right and power of regulating the alloy and value of coin struck by their own authority, or by that of the respective states—fixing the standard of weights and measures throughout the united states—regulating the trade and managing all affairs with the Indians, not members of any of the states, provided that the legislative right of any state within its own limits be not infringed or violated—establishing or regulating post-offices from one state to another, throughout all the united states, and exacting such postage on the papers passing thro' the same as may be requisite to defray the expences of the said office—appointing all officers of the land forces, in the service of the united states, excepting regimental officers—appointing all the officers of the naval forces, and commissioning all officers whatever in the service of the united states—making rules for the government and regulation of the said land and naval forces, and directing their operations.

The united states in congress assembled shall have authority to appoint a committee, to sit in the recess of congress, to be denominated " A Committee of the States," and to consist of one delegate from each state; and to appoint such other committees and civil officers as may be necessary for managing the general affairs of the united states under their direction—to appoint one of their number to preside, provided that no person be allowed to serve in the office of president more than one year in any term of three years; to ascertain the necessary sums of Money to be raised for the service of the united states, and to appropriate and apply the same for defraying the public expences—to borrow money, or emit bills on the credit of the united states, transmitting every half year to the respective states an account of the sums of money so borrowed or emitted,—to build and equip a navy—to agree upon the number of land forces, and to make requisitions from each state for its quota, in proportion to the number of white inhabitants in such state; which requisition shall be binding, and thereupon the legislature of each state shall appoint the regimental officers, raise the men and cloath, arm and equip them in a soldier like manner, at the expence of the united states; and the officers and men so cloathed, armed and equipped shall march to the place appointed, and within the time agreed on by the united states in congress assembled: But if the united states in congress assembled shall, on consideration of circumstances judge proper that any state should not raise men, or should raise a smaller number than its quota, and that any other state should raise a greater number of men than the quota thereof, such extra number shall be raised, officered, cloathed, armed and equipped in the same manner as the quota of such state, unless the legislature of such state shall judge that such extra number cannot be safely spared out of the same, in which case they shall raise officer, cloath, arm and equip as many of such extra number as they judge can be safely spared. And the officers and men so cloathed, armed and equipped, shall march to the place appointed, and within the time agreed on by the united states in congress assembled.

The united states in congress assembled shall never engage in a war, nor grant letters of marque and reprisal in time of peace, nor enter into any treaties or alliances, nor coin money, nor regulate the value thereof, nor ascertain the sums and expences necessary for the defence and welfare of the united states, or any of them, nor emit bills, nor borrow money on the credit of the united states, nor appropriate money, nor agree upon the number of vessels of war, to be built or purchased, or the number of land or sea forces to be raised, nor appoint a commander in chief of the army or navy, unless nine states assent to the same: nor shall a question on any other point, except for adjourning from day to day be determined, unless by the votes of a majority of the united states in congress assembled.

The congress of the united states shall have power to adjourn to any time within the year, and to any place within the united states, so that no period of adjournment be for a longer duration than the space of six Months, and shall publish the Journal of their proceedings monthly, except such parts thereof relating to treaties, alliances or military operations, as in their judgment require secrecy; and the yeas and nays of the delegates of each state on any question shall be entered on the Journal, when it is desired by any delegate; and the delegates of a state, or any of them, at his or their request shall be furnished with a transcript of the said Journal, except such parts as are above excepted, to lay before the legislatures of the several states.

Article X. The committee of the states, or any nine of them, shall be authorized to execute, in the recess of congress, such of the powers of congress as the united states in congress assembled, by the consent of nine states, shall from time to time think expedient to vest them with; provided that no power be delegated to the said committee, for the exercise of which, by the articles of confederation, the voice of nine states in the congress of the united states assembled is requisite.

Article XI. Canada acceding to this confederation, and joining in the measures of the united states, shall be admitted into, and entitled to all the advantages of this union: but no other colony shall be admitted into the same, unless such admission be agreed to by nine states.

Article XII. All bills of credit emitted, monies borrowed and debts contracted by, or under the authority of congress, before the assembling of the united states, in pursuance of the present confederation, shall be deemed and considered as a charge against the united states, for payment and satisfaction whereof the said united states, and the public faith are hereby solemnly pledged.

Article XIII. Every state shall abide by the determinations of the united states in congress assembled, on all questions which by this confederation are submitted to them. And the Articles of this confederation shall be inviolably observed by every state, and the union shall be perpetual; nor shall any alteration at any time hereafter be made in any of them; unless such alteration be agreed to in a congress of the united states, and be afterwards confirmed by the legislatures of every state.

And Whereas it hath pleased the Great Governor of the World to incline the hearts of the legislatures we respectively represent in congress, to approve of, and to authorize us to ratify the said articles of confederation and perpetual union. Know Ye that we the undersigned delegates, by virtue of the power and authority to us given for that purpose, do by these presents, in the name and in behalf of our respective constituents, fully and entirely ratify and confirm each and every of the said articles of confederation and perpetual union, and all and singular the matters and things therein contained: And we do further solemnly plight and engage the faith of our respective constituents, that they shall abide by the determinations of the united states in congress assembled, on all questions, which by the said confederation are submitted to them. And that the articles thereof shall be inviolably observed by the states we respectively represent, and that the union shall be perpetual. In Witness whereof we have here-unto set our hands in Congress. Done at Philadelphia in the state of Pennsylvania the ninth day of July, in the Year of our Lord one Thousand seven Hundred and Seventy-eight, and in the third year of the independence of America.

Josiah Bartlett,
John Wentworth, junr
   August 8th, 1778, } On the part & behalf of the State of New Hampshire.

John Hancock,
Samuel Adams,
Elbridge Gerry,
Francis Dana,
James Lovell,
Samuel Holten, } On the part and behalf of the State of Massachusetts Bay.

William Ellery,
Henry Marchant,
John Collins, } On the part and behalf of the State of Rhode-Island and Providence Plantations.

Roger Sherman,
Samuel Huntington,
Oliver Wolcott,
Titus Hosmer,
Andrew Adams, } On the part and behalf of the State of Connecticut.

Jas Duane,
Fra: Lewis,
Wm Duer,
Gouvr Morris, } On the part and behalf of the State of New York.

Jno Witherspoon,
Nathl Scudder, } On the Part and in Behalf of the State of New Jersey, November 26th, 1778.

Robert Morris,
Daniel Roberdeau,
Jon. Bayard Smith,
William Clingan,
Joseph Reed,
   22d July, 1778, } On the part and behalf of the State of Pennsylvania.

Thos McKean,
   Feby 22d, 1779,
John Dickinson,
   May 5th, 1779,
Nicholas Van Dyke, } On the part & behalf of the State of Delaware.

John Hanson,
   March 1, 1781,
Daniel Carroll, do } On the part and behalf of the State of Maryland.

Richard Henry Lee,
John Banister,
Thomas Adams,
Jno Harvie,
Francis Lightfoot Lee, } On the Part and Behalf of the State of Virginia.

| John Penn,
   July 21st, 1778,
Corn^s Harnett,
Jno Williams, | } On the part and behalf of the State of North Carolina. |

John Penn,
   July 21st, 1778,
Corn^s Harnett,
Jno Williams,
} On the part and behalf of the State of North
Carolina.

Henry Laurens,
William Henry Drayton,
Jno Mathews,
Richd Hutson,
Thos Heyward, jun^r.
} On the part and on behalf of the State of South
Carolina.

Jno Walton,
   24th July, 1778,
Edwd Telfair,
Edwd Langworthy,
} On the part and behalf of the State of Georgia.[1]

---

[1] The proceedings of this day with respect to the signing of the Articles of Confederation, the Articles themselves and the signers are entered in the *Papers of the Continental Congress*, No. 9 (History of the Confederation), but not in the Journal itself. The Articles are printed here from the original roll in the Bureau of Rolls and Library, Department of State.

LIST OF DELEGATES APPOINTED BY THE STATES REP-
RESENTED IN THE FEDERAL CONVENTION [1]

From		*Attended*
New Hampshire.	1. John Langdon,	July 23, 1787
	John Pickering,	
	2. Nicholas Gilman,	July 23,
	Benjamin West.	
Massachusetts.	*Francis Dana,*	
	Elbridge Gerry,	May 29,
	3. Nathaniel Gorham,	May 28,
	4. Rufus King,	May 25,
	Caleb Strong,	May 28,
Rhode Island.	[No appointment.]	
Connecticut.	5. Wm. Sam. Johnson,	June 2,
	6. Roger Sherman,	May 30,
	Oliver Elsworth,	May 29,
New York.	Robert Yates,	May 25,
	7. Alexander Hamilton,	do.
	John Lansing,	June 2,
New Jersey.	8. William Livingston,	June 5,
	9. David Brearley,	May 25,
	William C. Houston,	do.
	10. William Patterson,	do.
	John Neilson.	
	Abraham Clark.	
	11. Jonathan Dayton,	June 21,
Pennsylvania.	12. Benjamin Franklin,	May 28,
	13. Thomas Mifflin,	do.
	14. Robert Morris,	May 25,
	15. George Clymer,	May 28,
	16. Thomas Fitzsimons,	May 25,
	17. Jared Ingersoll,	May 28,

[1] Reprinted from *Journal, Acts and Proceedings of the Convention which formed the Constitution of the United States,* John Quincy Adams, Editor (1819), pp. 13-15.

For a more elaborate list including the names of delegates who were elected but declined, and fuller and revised details of attendance, see *The Records of the Federal Convention of 1787,* Max Farrand, Editor, Vol. III (1901), pp. 557-559, 586-590.

From		*Attended*
	18. James Wilson,	May 25,
	19. Gouverneur Morris,	do.
Delaware.	20. George Read,	do.
	21. Gunning Bedford, jr.	May 28,
	22. John Dickinson,	do.
	23. Richard Basset,	May 25,
	24. Jacob Broom,	do.
Maryland.	25. James M'Henry,	May 29,
	26. Daniel of St. Thomas Jenifer,	June 2,
	27. Daniel Carroll,	July 9,
	John Francis Mercer,	Aug. 6,
	Luther Martin,	June 9,
Virginia.	28. George Washington,	May 25,
	Patrick Henry,	(declined.)
	Edmund Randolph,	May 25,
	29. John Blair,	do.
	30. James Madison, jr	do.
	George Mason,	do.
	George Wythe,	do.
	James M'Clurg, (in the room of P. Henry)	do.
North Carolina.	*Richard Caswell,*	(resigned.)
	Alexander Martin,	May 25,
	William R. Davie,	do.
	31. William Blount, (in the room of R. Caswell)	June 20,
	Willie Jones,	(declined.)
	32. Richard D. Spaight,	May 25,
	33. Hugh Williamson, (in the room of W. Jones)	May 25,
South Carolina.	34. John Rutledge,	do.
	35. Charles C. Pinckney,	do.
	36. Charles Pinckney,	do.
	37. Pierce Butler,	do.
Georgia.	38. William Few,	do.
	39. Abraham Baldwin,	June 11,
	William Pierce,	May 31,
	George Walton.	
	William Houstoun,	June 1,
	Nathaniel Pendleton.	

Those with numbers before their names, signed the Constitution.. 39
Those in Italicks, never attended............................ 10
Members who attended, but did not sign the Constitution..... 16

——

65

PART II
THE FEDERAL CONVENTION OF 1787

PREFACE TO DEBATES IN THE CONVENTION [1]

A Sketch Never Finished nor Applied. [2]

As the weakness and wants of man naturally lead to an association of individuals, under a common authority, whereby each may have the protection of the whole against danger from without, and enjoy in safety within, the advantages of social intercourse, and an exchange of the necessaries & comforts of life: in like manner feeble communities, independent of each other, have resorted to a Union, less intimate, but with common Councils, for the common safety agst powerful neighbors, and for the preservation of justice and peace among themselves. Ancient history furnishes examples of these confederal [3] associations, tho' with a very imperfect account, of their structure, and of the attributes and functions of the presiding Authority. There are examples of modern date also, some of them still existing, the modifications and transactions of which are sufficiently known.

It remained for the British Colonies, now United States, of North America, to add to those examples, one of a more interesting character than any of them: which led to a system without a [4] example ancient or modern, a system founded on popular rights, and so combing. a federal form with the forms of individual Republics, as may

---

[1] The proposed Preface has been printed from Madison's original manuscript in the Department of State. There is a transcript of the Preface in an unknown hand in the Library of Congress, which was sent to the printer and from which Henry D. Gilpin printed *The Papers of James Madison*, 3 volumes (1840). The text of the Preface as here printed has been read with the printer's copy thereof and important differences noted.

In the Preface, Madison referred in passing to documents which he evidently intended to embody in a finished draft which, unfortunately, he never completed. The matter referred to has been placed in footnotes or reference has been made to other pages of the present volume.

Footnotes bearing star or dagger instead of figures to indicate their order, are Madison's own notes and have been placed above the line. The editors' notes and indications of differences between the Madison manuscript and the transcript of the Preface have been numbered and placed below the line.

[2] These are the words which Madison wrote at the head of this document after he had scratched out the phrase "Preface to Debates in the Convention of 1787." It is a very rough and uneven draft, full of insertions and deletions. The last few pages are in Mrs. Madison's hand, having been written from her husband's dictation when his hands were crippled with rheumatism. A few words in the draft were written by John C. Payne (Mrs. Madison's brother) at Madison's direction. The date of the draft was between 1830 and 1836.

[3] The word "confederate" is substituted in the transcript for "confederal."

[4] The word "an" is substituted in the transcript for "a."

1

enable each to supply the defects of the other and obtain the advantages of both.[1]

Whilst the Colonies enjoyed the protection of the parent Country as it was called, against foreign danger; and were secured by its superintending controul, against conflicts among themselves, they continued independent of each other, under a common, tho' limited dependence, on the parental Authority. When however the growth of the offspring in strength and in wealth, awakened the jealousy and tempted the avidity of the parent, into schemes of usurpation & exaction, the obligation was felt by the former of uniting their counsels and efforts to avert the impending calamity.

As early as the year 1754, indications having been given of a design in the Brittish Government to levy contributions on the Colonies, without their consent; a meeting of Colonial deputies took place at Albany, which attempted to introduce a compromising substitute, that might at once satisfy the British requisitions, and save their own rights from violation. The attempt had no other effect, than by bringing these rights into a more conspicuous view, to invigorate the attachment to them, on [2] one side; and to nourish the haughty & encroaching spirit on the other.

In 1774. The progress made by G. B. in the open assertion of her pretensions, and in [3] the apprehended purpose of otherwise maintaining them than by Legislative enactments and declarations, had been such that the Colonies did not hesitate to assemble, by their deputies, in a formal Congress, authorized to oppose to the British innovations whatever measures might be found best adapted to the occasion; without however losing sight of an eventual reconciliation.

The dissuasive measures of that Congress, being without effect, another Congress was held in 1775, whose pacific efforts to bring about a change in the views of the other party, being equally unavailing, and the commencement of actual hostilities having at length put an end to all hope of reconciliation; the Congress finding moreover that the popular voice began to call for an entire & perpetual dissolution of the political ties which had connected them with G. B., proceeded on the memorable 4th of July, 1776 to declare the 13 Colonies, Independent States.[4]

During the discussions of this solemn Act, a Committee consisting of a member from each colony had been appointed to prepare &

---

[1] In place of "the advantages of both" the transcript reads "that advantage of both."
[2] The word "the" is here inserted in the transcript.
[3] The word "in" is omitted in the transcript.
[4] The words "Independent States" are italicized in the transcript.

digest a form of Confederation, for the future management of the common interests, which had hitherto been left to the discretion of Congress, guided by the exigences of the contest, and by the known intentions or occasional instructions of the Colonial Legislatures.

It appears that as early as the 21ˢᵗ of July 1775, A plan entitled " Articles of Confederation & *perpetual* Union of the Colonies " had been sketched by Docʳ Franklin, the plan being on that day submitted by him to Congress; and tho' not copied into their Journals remaining on their files in his handwriting. But notwithstanding the term " perpetual " observed in the title, the articles provided expressly for the event of a return of the Colonies to a connection with G. Britain.

This sketch became a basis for the plan reported by the Comᵉ on the 12 of July, now also remaining on the files of Congress, in the handwriting of Mʳ Dickinson. The plan, tho' dated after the Declaration of Independence, was probably drawn up before that event; since the name of *Colonies,* not *States* is used throughout the draught. The plan reported, was debated and amended from time to time, till the 17ᵗʰ of November 1777, when it was agreed to by Congress, and proposed to the Legislatures of the States, with an explanatory and recommendatory letter. The ratifications of these by their Delegates in Congᵉ duly authorized took place at successive dates; but were not compleated till March 1.[1] 1781. when Maryland who had made it a prerequisite that the vacant lands acquired from the British Crown should be a Common fund, yielded to the persuasion that a final & formal establishment of the federal Union & Govᵗ would make a favorable impression not only on other foreign Nations, but on G. B. herself.

The great difficulty experienced in so framing the fedˡ system as to obtain the unanimity required for its due sanction, may be inferred. from the long interval, and recurring discussions, between the commencement and completion of the work; from the changes made during its progress; from the language of Congˢ when proposing it to the States, wᶜʰ dwelt on the impracticability of devising a system acceptable to all of them; from the reluctant assent given by some; and the various alterations proposed by others; and by a tardiness in others again which produced a special address to them from Congˢ enforcing the duty of sacrificing local considerations and favorite opinions to to the public safety, and the necessary harmony: Nor was the assent of some of the States finally yielded without strong protests against par-

---

[1] The phrase "the first of March" is substituted in the transcript for " March 1."

ticular articles, and a reliance on future amendments removing their objections.

It is to be recollected, no doubt, that these delays might be occasioned in some degree, by an occupation of the public Councils both general & local, with the deliberations and measures, essential to a Revolutionary struggle; But there must have been a balance for these causes, in the obvious motives to hasten the establishment of a regular and efficient Gov^t; and in the tendency of the crisis to repress opinions and pretensions, which might be inflexible in another state of things.

The principal difficulties which embarrassed the progress, and retarded the completion of the plan of Confederation, may be traced to 1.[1] the natural repugnance of the parties to a relinquishment of power: 2[1] a natural jealousy of its abuse in other hands than their own: 3[1] the rule of suffrage among parties unequal in size, but equal in sovereignty. 4 the ratio of contributions in money and in troops, among parties,[2] whose inequality in size did not correspond with that of their wealth, or of their military or free population. 5.[3] the selection and definition of the powers, at once necessary to the federal head, and safe to the several members.

To these sources of difficulty, incident to the formation of all such Confederacies, were added two others one of a temporary, the other of a permanent nature. The first was the case of the Crown lands, so called because they had been held by the British Crown, and being ungranted to individuals when its authority ceased, were considered by the States within whose charters or asserted limits they lay, as devolving on them; whilst it was contended by the others, that being wrested from the dethroned authority, by the equal exertion of all, they resulted of right and in equity to the benefit of all. The lands being of vast extent and of growing value, were the occasion of much discussion & heart-burning; & proved the most obstinate of the impediments to an earlier consummation of the plan of federal Gov^t The State of Maryland the last that acceded to it held out as already noticed, till March 1,[4] 1781, and then yielded only to the hope that by giving a stable & authoritative character to the Confederation, a successful termination of the Contest might be accelerated. The dispute was happily compromised by successive surrenders of portions of the

---

[1] The figures 1, 2, and 3 are changed to "first," "secondly" and "thirdly" in the transcript.

[2] The phrase "unequal in size, but equal in sovereignty. 4 the ratio of contributions in money and in troops, among parties" is erroneously omitted in the transcript.

[3] The figure 5 is changed to "fourthly" in the transcript.

[4] In the transcript the date reads "the first of March, 1781.

territory by the States having exclusive claims to it, and acceptances of them by Congress.

The other source of dissatisfaction was the peculiar situation of some of the States, which having no convenient ports for foreign commerce, were subject to be taxed by their neighbors, thro whose ports, their commerce was carryed on. New Jersey, placed between Phil? & N. York, was likened to a cask tapped at both ends; and N. Carolina, between Virg? & S. Carolina to a patient bleeding at both arms. The Articles of Confederation provided no remedy for the complaint: which produced a strong protest on the part of N. Jersey; and never ceased to be a source of dissatisfaction & discord, until the new Constitution, superseded the old.

But the radical infirmity of the " art? of Confederation " was the dependance of Cong? on the voluntary and simultaneous compliance with its Requisitions, by so many independant Communities, each consulting more or less its particular interests & convenience and distrusting the compliance of the others. Whilst the paper emissions of Cong? continued to circulate they were employed as a sinew of war, like gold & silver. When that ceased to be the case, the fatal defect of the political System was felt in its alarming force. The war was merely kept alive and brought to a successful conclusion by such foreign aids and temporary expedients as could be applied; a hope prevailing with many, and a wish with all, that a state of peace, and the sources of prosperity opened by it, would give to the Confederacy in practice, the efficiency which had been inferred from its theory.

The close of the war however brought no cure for the public embarrasments. The States relieved from the pressure of foreign danger, and flushed with the enjoyment of independent and sovereign power; [instead of a diminished disposition to part with it,] persevered in omissions and in measures incompatible with their relations to the Federal Gov? and with those among themselves;

Having served as a member of Cong? through the period between Mar. 1780 & the arrival of peace in 1783, I had become intimately acquainted with the public distresses and the causes of them. I had observed the successful opposition to every attempt to procure a remedy by new grants of power to Cong? I had founnd moreover that despair of success hung over the compromising provision [1] of April 1783 for the public necessities which had been so elaborately planned, and so impressively recommended to the States.* Sympathizing, under this

* See address of Congress.[2]

---

[1] The word "principle" is substituted for "provision" in the transcript.
[2] This footnote is omitted in the transcript.

aspect of affairs, in the alarm of the friends of free Gov^t, at the threatened danger of an abortive result to the great & perhaps last experiment in its favour, I could not be insensible to the obligation to co-operate [1] as far as I could in averting the calamity. With this view I acceded to the desire of my fellow Citizens of the County that I should be one of its representatives in the Legislature, hoping that I might there best contribute to inculcate the critical posture to which the Revolutionary cause was reduced, and the merit of a leading agency of the State in bringing about a rescue of the Union and the blessings of liberty a [2] staked on it, from an impending catastrophe.

It required but little time after taking my seat in the House of Delegates in May 1784 to discover that, however favorable the general disposition of the State might be towards the Confederacy the Legislature retained the aversion of its predecessors to transfers of power from the State to the Gov^t of the Union; notwithstanding the urgent demands of the Federal Treasury; the glaring inadequacy of the authorized mode of supplying it, the rapid growth of anarchy in the Fed^l System, and the animosity kindled among the States by their conflicting regulations.

The temper of the Legislature & the wayward course of its proceedings may be gathered from the Journals of its Sessions in the years 1784 & 1785.

The failure however of the varied propositions in the Legislature, for enlarging the powers of Congress, the continued failure of the efforts of Cong^s to obtain from them the means of providing for the debts of the Revolution; and of countervailing the commercial laws of G. B. a source of much irritation & ag^st which the separate efforts of the States were found worse than abortive; these Considerations with the lights thrown on the whole subject, by the free & full discussion it had undergone led to an [3] general acquiescence in the Resol^n passed, on the 21. of Jany 1786. which proposed & invited a meeting of Deputies from all the States to '' insert the Resol (See Journal.)1.[4]

The resolution had been brought forward some weeks before on the failure of a proposed grant of power to Congress to collect a revenue from commerce, which had been abandoned by its friends in consequence of material alterations made in the grant by a Committee of the whole. The Resolution tho introduced by Mr Tyler an influ-

---

[1] The word "aid" is substituted in the transcript for "co-operate."
[2] The word "a" is omitted in the transcript.
[3] The word "a" is substituted in the transcript for "an."
[4] The phrase "to 'insert the Resol. (See Journal.) 1 " is omitted in the transcript which substitutes the words "as follows: " and inserts the resolution which is printed in this volume at page xlvii.

encial member, who having never served in Congress, had more the ear of the House than those whose services there exposed them to an imputable bias, was so little acceptable that it was not then persisted in. Being now revived by him, on the last day of the Session, and being the alternative of adjourning without any effort for the crisis in the affairs of the Union, it obtained a general vote; less however with some of its friends from a confidence in the success of the experiment than from a hope that it might prove a step to a more comprehensive & adequate provision for the wants of the Confederacy

It happened also that Commissioners who had been [1] appointed by Virg.ª & Mary.ᵈ to settle the jurisdiction on waters dividing the two States had, apart from their official reports, recommended a uniformity in the regulations of the 2 States on several subjects & particularly on those having relation to foreign trade. It apeared at the same time that Mary.ᵈ had deemed a concurrence of her neighbors Pen.ª & Delaware indispensable in such a case, who for like reasons would require that of their neighbors. So apt and forceable an illustration of the necessity of a uniformity throughout all the States could not but favour the passage of a Resolution which proposed a Convention having that for its object.

The commissioners appointed by the Legisl: & who attended the Convention were E. Randolph the Attorney of the State, S.ᵗ Geo: Tucker & J. M.[2] The designation of the time & place for its meeting to be proposed and communicated to the States having been left to the Com.ʳˢ they named for the time early [3] September and for the place the City of Annapolis avoiding the residence of Cong.ˢ and large Commercial Cities as liable to suspicions of an extraneous influence.

Altho the invited Meeting appeared to be generally favored, five States only assembled; some failing to make appointments, and some of the individuals appointed not hastening their attendance, the result in both cases being ascribed mainly, to a belief that the time had not arrived for such a political reform, as might be expected from a further experience of its necessity.

But in the interval between the proposal of the Convention and the time of its meeting, such had been the advance of public opinion in the desired direction, stimulated as it had been by the effect of the contemplated object, of the meeting, in turning the genal attention to the Critical State of things, and in calling forth the sentiments and exertions of the most enlightened & influencial patriots,

---

[1] The phrase "who had been" is omitted in the transcript.
[2] James Madison.
[3] In place of the word "early" the transcript reads "the first Monday in."

that the Convention thin as it was did not scruple to decline the limited task assigned to it and to recommend to the States a Convention with powers adequate to the occasion. Nor was it [1] unnoticed that the commission of the N. Jersey Deputation, had extended its object to a general provision for the exigencies of the Union. A recommendation for this enlarged purpose was accordingly reported by a Com.ᵉ to whom the subject had been referred. It was drafted by Col: H.[2] and finally agreed to unanimously [3] in the following form. Insert it.[4]

The recommendation was well rec.ᵈ by the Legislature of Virg.ᵃ which happened to be the *first* that *acted* on it, and the example of her compliance was made as conciliatory and impressive as possible. The Legislature were unanimous or very nearly so on the occasion, and [5] as a proof of the magnitude & solemnity attached to it, they placed Gen.ˡ W. at the head of the Deputation from the State; and as a proof of the deep interest he felt in the case he overstepped the obstacles to his acceptance of the appointment.

The law complying with the recommendation from Annapolis was in the terms following: [6]

A resort to a General Convention to remodel the Confederacy, was not a new idea. It had entered at an early date into the conversations and speculations of the most reflecting & foreseeing observers of the inadequacy of the powers allowed to Congress. In a pamphlet published in May 81 at the seat of Cong.ˢ Pelatiah Webster an able tho' not conspicuous Citizen, after discussing the fiscal system of the U. States, and suggesting among other remedial provisions [7] including a national Bank remarks that " the Authority of Cong.ˢ at present is very inadequate to the performance of their duties; and this indicates the necessity of their calling a *Continental Convention* for the express purpose of ascertaining, defining, enlarging, and limiting, the duties & powers of their Constitution." [8]

---

[1] The words " had it been " are substituted in the transcript for the words "was it."

[2] Alexander Hamilton.

[3] The word " unanimously " is omitted in the transcript.

[4] Madison's direction " Insert it " is omitted in the transcript, and there is inserted the text of the proceedings and recommendation of the Annapolis Convention for which see, *ante*, pages xlviii-lii. The transcript text begins with the words " To the Honorable," and concludes with the paragraph beginning " Though your Commissioners," etc.

[5] The word " and " is omitted in the transcript.

[6] The text of this law of October 16, 1786 (printed *ante* pages lxviii-lxix) is inserted in the transcript beginning with the words " Whereas, the Commissioners," etc. and ending with the words ". . . States in the Union."

[7] The word " one " is here inserted in the transcript.

[8] Madison was in error. The pamphlet was written by William Barton.

On the 1. day of Ap! 1783, Col. Hamilton, in a debate in Cong?
observed that [1]

He alluded probably to [see Life of Schuyler in Longacre [2]
It does not appear however that his expectation had been fulfilled.]

In a letter to J. M. from R. H. Lee then President of Cong? dated
Nov! 26, 1784 He says [3]

The answer of J. M. remarks [4]

[5] In 1785, Noah Webster whose pol. & other valuable writings had
made him known to the public, in one of his publications of American
policy brought into view the same resort for supplying the defects
of the Fed! System [see his life in Longacre]

The proposed & expected Convention at Annapolis the first of a

---

See Gaillard Hunt, "Pelatiah Webster and the Constitution," in *The Nation*,
December 28, 1911.

[1] The following is supplied in the transcript: "he wished instead of them
[partial Conventions] to see a general Convention take place; and that he
should soon, in pursuance of instructions from his constituents, propose to Congress a plan for that purpose, the object [of which] would be to strengthen the
Federal Constitution."—See *The Writings of James Madison*, Hunt, Editor,
Vol. I (1900), pp. 438, 439.

[2] The phrase "[see Life of Schuyler in Longacre]" is omitted in the transcript and the following quoted matter is substituted: "the resolutions introduced by General Schuyler in the Senate, and passed unanimously by the
Legislature of New York in the summer of 1782, declaring, that the Confederation was defective, in not giving Congress power to provide a revenue for itself,
or in not investing them with funds from established and productive sources;
and that it would be advisable for Congress to recommend to the States to call
a general Convention to revise and amend the Confederation."

The sketch is of Hamilton, not Schuyler, for which see *The National Portrait Gallery of Distinguished Americans*, conducted by Longacre and Herring,
Vol. II (1835), p. 7.

[3] The following sentence is supplied in the transcript: "It is by many here
suggested as a very necessary step for Congress to take, the calling on the
States to form a Convention for the sole purpose of revising the Confederation,
so far as to enable Congress to execute with more energy, effect and vigor the
powers assigned to it, than it appears by experience that they can do under the
present state of things." The letter referred to is among the Madison papers in
the Manuscript Division of the Library of Congress.

[4] The transcript here inserts the following: "I hold it for a maxim, that
the Union of the States is essential to their safety against foreign danger and
internal contention; and that the perpetuity and efficacy of the present system
cannot be confided in. The question, therefore, is, in what mode, and at what
moment, the experiment for supplying the defects ought to be made."—See,
also, *The Writings of James Madison*, Hunt, Editor, Vol. II (1901), pp. 99,
100.

[5] The paragraph beginning "In 1785" reads as follows in the transcript:
"In the winter of 1784-5, Noah Webster, whose political and other valuable
writings had made him known to the public, proposed, in one of his publications, 'a new system of government which should act, not on the States, but
directly on individuals, and vest in Congress full power to carry its laws into
effect.'"

See, also, *The National Portrait Gallery of Distinguished Americans*, conducted by Longacre and Herring, Vol. II (1835), p. 4.

general character that appears to have been realized, & the state of the public mind awakened by it had attracted the particular attention of Cong? and favored the idea there of a Convention with fuller powers for amending the Confederacy.[1]

It does not appear that in any of these cases, the reformed system was to be otherwise sanctioned than by the Legislative auth? of the States; nor whether or how far, a change was to be made in the structure of the Depository of Federal powers.

The act of Virg? providing for the Convention at Philad?, was succeeded by appointments from[2] other States as their Legislatures were assembled, the appointments being selections from the most experienced & highest standing Citizens. Rh. I. was the only exception to a compliance with the recommendation from Annapolis, well known to have been swayed by an obdurate adherence to an advantage which her position gave her of taxing her neighbors thro' their consumption of imported supplies, an advantage which it was foreseen would be taken from her by a revisal of the " Articles of Confederation

As the pub. mind had been ripened for a salutary Reform of the pol. System, in the interval between the proposal & the meeting, of Com?? at Annapolis, the interval between the last event, and the meeting of Dep? at Phil? had continued to develop more & more the necessity & the extent of a Systematic provision for the preservation and Gov? of the Union; among the ripening incidents was the Insurrection of Shays,[3] in Mass?? against her Gov?; which was with difficulty suppressed, notwithstanding the influence on the insurgents of an apprehended interposition of the Fed? troops.

At the date of the Convention, the aspect & retrospect of the pol: condition of the U. S. could not but fill the pub. mind with a gloom which was relieved only by a hope that so select a Body would devise an adequate remedy for the existing and prospective evils so impressively demanding it

It was seen that the public debt rendered so sacred by the cause in which it had been incurred remained without any provision for its payment. The reiterated and elaborate efforts of Cong. to procure from the States a more adequate power to raise the means of payment had failed. The effect of the ordinary requisitions of Congress had

---

[1] In the transcript after the word " Confederacy " the following footnote is inserted: " The letters of Wm. Grayson, March 22d, 1786, and of James Monroe, of April 28th, 1786, both then members, to Mr. Madison, state that a proposition for such a Convention had been made."

[2] The word " the " is inserted in the transcript after " from."

[3] The final " s " is crossed off the word " Shays " in the transcript.

only displayed the inefficiency [1] of the auth? making them; none of the States having duly complied with them, some having failed altogether or nearly so; and [2] in one instance, that of N. Jersey [3] a compliance was expressly [4] refused; nor was more yielded to the expostulations of members of Cong? deputed to her Legislature, than a mere repeal of the law, without a compliance. [see letter of Grayson to J. M.[5]

The want of Auth? in Cong? to regulate Commerce had produced in Foreign nations particularly G. B. a monopolizing policy injurious to the trade of the U. S. and destructive to their navigation; the imbecilicity and anticipated dissolution of the Confederacy extinguish? all apprehensions of a Countervailing policy on the part of the U. States

The same want of a general power over Commerce, led to an exercise of the power separately, by the States, wch not only proved abortive, but engendered rival, conflicting and angry regulations. Besides the vain attempts to supply their respective treasuries by imposts, which turned their commerce into the neighbouring ports, and to co-erce a relaxation of the British monopoly of the W. Ind? navigation, which was attempted by Virg? [see the Journal of   ] [6] the States having ports for foreign commerce, taxed & irritated the adjoining States, trading thro' them, as N. Y. Pen? Virg? & S. Carolina. Some of the States, as Connecticut, taxed imports [7] as from Mass?

---

[1] The transcript substitutes the word "inefficacy" for the word "inefficiency" but the Gilpin edition prints the word as in the original notes.

[2] In the transcript the word "and" is crossed out and the word "which" written above it.

[3] After the word "Jersey," reference is made in the transcript to the following footnote: "A letter of Mr. Grayson to Mr. Madison of March 22d, 1786, relating the conduct of New Jersey states this fact. Editor."

[4] The word "expressly" is italicized in the transcript.

[5] The phrase " [see letter of Grayson to J. M." is omitted in the transcript. An extract from the letter referred to reads as follows: "The Antients were surely men of more candor than we are; they contended openly for an abolition of debts in so many words, while we strive as hard for the same thing under the decent & specious pretense of a circulating medium. . . . There has been some serious thoughts in the minds of some of the members of Congress to recommend to the States the meeting of a general Convention, to consider, of an alteration of the Confederation, & there is a motion to this effect now under consideration: it is contended that the present Confederation is utterly inefficient, and that if it remains much longer in it's present state of imbecility we shall be one of the most contemptible nations on the face of the earth."— Letter from William Grayson to James Madison, March 22, 1786. The Madison Papers (manuscript), Library of Congress.

[6] In the transcript the footnote "See the Journal of her Legislature" is substituted for the phrase in brackets. The allusion is to the act of the Virginia Assembly passed January 21, 1786, imposing a tonnage tax of 5s. on vessels of foreigners.

[7] After the word "imports" down to the sentence beginning, "In sundry instances," the transcript reads "from others, as from Mass., which complained in a letter to the Executive of Virginia, and doubtless to those of other States."

higher than imports even from G. B. of wch Mass^{ts} complained to Virg^a and doubtless to other States. [See letter of J. M.^{1} In sundry instances as of N. Y. N. J. P^a & Mary^d [see   ] ^{2} the navigation laws treated the Citizens ^{3} other States as aliens.

In certain cases the auth^y of the Confederacy was disregarded, as in violations not only of the Treaty of peace; but of Treaties with France & Holland, which were complained of to Cong^s

In other cases the Fed^l Auth^y was violated by Treaties & wars with Indians, as by Geo: by troops raised & kept up with^t the consent of Cong^s as by Mass^{ts} by compacts with^t the consent of Cong^s as between Pen^a and N. Jersey, and between Virg^a & Mary^d From the Legisl: Journals of Virg^a it appears, that a vote refusing to apply for a sanction of Cong^s was followed by a vote agst the communication of the Compact to Cong^s

In the internal administration of the States a violation of Contracts had become familiar in the form of depreciated paper made a legal tender, of property substituted for money, of Instalment laws, and of the occlusions of the Courts of Justice; although evident that all such interferences affected the rights of other States, relatively creditor,^{4} as well as Citizens Creditors within the State

Among the defects which had been severely felt was that of a uniformity in cases requiring it, as laws of naturalization,^{5} bankruptcy, a Coercive authority operating on individuals and a guaranty of the internal tranquility of the States.

As natural consequences ^{6} of this distracted and disheartening condition of the union, the Fed^l Auth^y had ceased to be respected abroad, and dispositions ^{7} shewn there, particularly in G. B., to take advantage of its imbecility, and to speculate on its approaching downfall; at home it had lost all confidence & credit; the unstable and unjust career of the States had also forfeited the respect & confidence essential to order and good Gov^t, involving a general decay of confidence & credit between man & man. It was found moreover, that those least partial to popular Gov^t, or most distrustful of its efficacy were yielding to anticipations, that from an increase of the confusion a Gov^t might result mcre congenial with their taste or their opinions;

---

^{1} The facts are given in Madison's letter to Jefferson, January 22, 1786. *The Writings of James Madison*, Hunt, Editor, Vol. II (1901), p. 218.
^{2} Madison's direction " [see   ] " is omitted in the transcript.
^{3} The word " of " is inserted in the transcript after " Citizens."
^{4} The word " creditor " is plural in the transcript.
^{5} The word " and " is inserted in the transcript after " naturalization."
^{6} The words " a natural consequence " are substituted in the transcript for " natural consequences."
^{7} The word " were " is inserted in the transcript after " dispositions."

whilst those most devoted to the principles and forms of Republics, were alarmed for the cause of liberty itself, at stake in the American Experiment, and anxious for a system that w^d avoid the inefficacy of a mere confederacy without passing into the opposite extreme of a consolidated gov^t it was known that there were individuals who had betrayed a bias towards Monarchy [see Knox to G. W. & him to Jay] (Marshall's life [1]) and there had always been some not unfavorable to a partition of the Union into several Confederacies; either from a better chance of figuring on a Sectional Theatre, or that the Sections would require stronger Gov^{ts}, or by their hostile conflicts lead to a monarchical consolidation. The idea of a [2] dismemberment had recently made its appearance in the Newspapers.

Such were the defects, the deformities, the diseases and the ominous prospects, for which the Convention were to provide a remedy, and which ought never to be overlooked in expounding & appreciating the Constitutional Charter the remedy that was provided.

As a sketch on paper, the earliest perhaps of a Constitutional Gov^t for the Union [organized into the regular Departments with physical means operating on individuals] to be sanctioned by *the people of the States*, acting in their original & sovereign character, was contained in [3] a letter of Apl. 8. 1787 from J. M. to Govr Randolph, a copy of the letter is here inserted.

The feature in the letter [4] which vested in the general Authy. a negative on the laws of the States, was suggested by the negative in the head of the British Empire, which prevented collisions between the parts & the whole, and between the parts themselves. It was supposed that the substitution, of an elective and responsible authority for an hereditary and irresponsible one, would avoid the appearance even of a departure from the principle of [5] Republicanism. But altho' the subject was so viewed in the Convention, and the votes on it were more than once equally divided, it was finally & justly abandoned see note

---

[1] This direction in Madison's notes is omitted in the transcript. His reference was to *The Life of George Washington*, by John Marshall, Vol. V (1807), pp. 91 *et seq.* For the text of the correspondence in question, see Appendix to Debates, I, Nos. 1, 2 and 3, pp. 585-588.

[2] The word "a" is omitted in the transcript.

[3] The phrase beginning with the words "a letter" down to the end of the paragraph is changed in the transcript to read as follows: "the letters of James Madison to Thomas Jefferson of the nineteenth of March; to Governor Randolph of the eighth of April; and to General Washington of the sixteenth of April, 1787, for which see these respective dates."

For the material portions of these letters see Appendix to Debates, II, Nos. 1, 2 and 3, pp. 589-595.

[4] The words "the letter" have been changed to "these letters" in the transcript.

[5] The words "the principle of" are omitted in the transcript.

for   for this erasure substitute the amend: marked * for this page [1]
[as, apart from other objections, it was not practicable among so many
states, increasing in number, and enacting, each of them, so many
laws. Instead of the proposed negative, the objects of it were left
as finally provided for in the Constitution.] [2]

On the arrival of the Virginia Deputies at Philad: it occurred to
them that from the early and prominent part taken by that State in
bringing about the Convention some initiative step might be expected
from them. The Resolutions introduced by Governor Randolph were
the result of a Consultation on the subject; with an understanding
that they left all the Deputies entirely open to the lights of discussion,
and free to concur in any alterations or modifications which their reflections and judgments might approve. The Resolutions as the
Journals shew became the basis on which the proceedings of the Convention commenced, and to the developments, variations and modifications of which the plan of Gov: proposed by the Convention may be
traced.

The curiosity I had felt during my researches into the History of
the most distinguished Confederacies, particularly those of antiquity,
and the deficiency I found in the means of satisfying it more especially
in what related to the process, the principles, the reasons, & the anticipations, which prevailed in the formation of them, determined me
to preserve as far as I could an exact account of what might pass in
the Convention whilst executing its trust, with the magnitude of
which I was duly impressed, as I was with [3] the gratification promised
to future curiosity by an authentic exhibition of the objects, the opinions, & the reasonings from which the new System of Gov: was to
receive its peculiar structure & organization. Nor was I unaware of
the value of such a contribution to the fund of materials for the History of a Constitution on which would be staked the happiness of a
people great even in its infancy, and possibly the cause of Liberty
throught the world.

In pursuance of the task I had assumed I chose a seat in front of
the presiding member, with the other members on my right & left
hands. In this favorable position for hearing all that passed, I noted
in terms legible & in abreviations & marks intelligible to myself what
was read from the Chair or spoken by the members; and losing not
a moment unnecessarily between the adjournment & reassembling of

---

[1] The words "see note for   for this erasure substitute the amend:
marked * for this page" are omitted in the transcript.
[2] The passage enclosed in brackets is copied from the transcript. The
original notes appear to have been lost since Gilpin's edition.
[3] The word "by" is substituted in the transcript for "with."

the Convention I was enabled to write out my daily notes [see page 18-[1] during the session or within a few finishing days after its close—see pa. 18 [2] in the extent and form preserved in my own hand on my files.

In the labour & correctness of doing [3] this, I was not a little aided by practice & by a familiarity with the style and the train of observation & reasoning which characterized the principal speakers. It happened, also that. I was not absent a single day, nor more than a cassual fraction of an hour in any day, so that I could not have lost a single speech, unless a very short one. Insert the Remark on the — slip of paper marked A [4]

[It may be proper to remark, that, with a very few exceptions, the speeches were neither furnished, nor revised, nor sanctioned, by the speakers, but written out from my notes, aided by the freshness of my recollections. A further remark may be proper, that views of the subject might occasionally be presented in the speeches and proceedings, with a latent reference to a compromise on some middle ground, by mutual concessions. The exceptions alluded to were,— first, the sketch furnished by Mr. Randolph of his speech on the introduction of his propositions, on the twenty-ninth day of May; secondly, the speech of Mr. Hamilton, who happened to call on me when putting the last hand to it, and who acknowledged its fidelity, without suggesting more than a very few verbal alterations which were made; thirdly, the speech of Gouverneur Morris on the second day of May, which was communicated to him on a like occasion, and who acquiesced in it without even a verbal change. The correctness of his language and the distinctness of his enunciation were particularly favorable to a reporter. The speeches of Doctor Franklin, excepting a few brief ones, were copied from the written ones read to the Convention by his colleague, Mr. Wilson, it being inconvenient to the Doctor to remain long on his feet.] [5]

Of the ability & intelligence of those who composed the Convention, the debates & proceedings may be a test; as the character of the work which was the offspring of their deliberations must be tested by the experience of the future, added to that of the nearly half century which has passed.[6]

---

[1] Madison's direction " [see page 18-" is omitted in the transcript.
[2] Madison's direction " see pa. 18 " is omitted in the transcript.
[3] The word " doing " is omitted in the transcript.
[4] Madison's direction " Insert the Remark," etc. is omitted in the transcript.
[5] The passage enclosed in brackets is copied from the transcript. The original notes appear to have been lost since Gilpin's edition.
[6] The phrase " of the nearly half century " is changed to " of nearly half a century " in the transcript.

But whatever may be the judgment pronounced on the competency of the architects of the Constitution, or whatever may be the destiny, of the edifice prepared by them, I feel it a duty to express my profound & solemn conviction, derived from my intimate opportunity of observing & appreciating the views of the Convention, collectively & individually, that there never was an assembly of men, charged with a great & arduous trust, who were more pure in their motives, or more exclusively or anxiously [devoted to the object committed to them, than were the members of the Federal Convention of 1787, to the object of devising and proposing a constitutional system which would best supply the defects of that which it was to replace, and best secure the permanent liberty and happiness of their country.] [1]

---

[1] The passage enclosed in brackets is copied from the transcript. The original notes appear to have been lost since Gilpin's edition.

[1] Monday May 14th 1787 was the day fixed for the meeting of the deputies in Convention for revising the federal system of Government. On that day a small number only had assembled. Seven States were not convened till,

Friday 25 of May, when the following members [2] appeared to wit: see Note A.[3]

viz,[3] From *Massachussetts* Rufus King. *N. York* Robert Yates,[4] Alex! Hamilton. *N. Jersey,* David Brearly, William Churchill Houston,[4] William Patterson. *Pennsylvania,* Robert Morris, Thomas Fitzsimmons, James Wilson,[4] Govurneur Morris. *Delaware,* George Read, Richard Basset,[4] Jacob Broome. *Virginia,* George Washington, Edmund Randolph, John Blair, James Madison, George Mason, George Wythe, [4] James M:Clurg. *N. Carolina,* Alexander Martin, William Richardson Davie, Richard Dobbs Spaight,[4] Hugh Williamson. *S. Carolina,* John Rutlidge, Charles Cotesworth Pinckney, Charles Pinckney,[4] Pierce Butler. *Georgia,* William Few.

M: ROBERT MORRIS informed the members assembled that by the instruction & in behalf, of the deputation of Pen! he proposed George Washington Esq! late Commander in chief for president of the Convention.[5] M: JN? RUTLIDGE seconded the motion; expressing his confidence that the choice would be unanimous, and observing that the presence of Gen! Washington forbade any observations on the occasion which might otherwise be proper.

General WASHINGTON was accordingly unanimously elected by

---

[1] The text of the present edition of Madison's Debates has been read against the manuscript of the transcript in the Library of Congress, and every difference between Madison's original manuscript and the transcript has been noted except typographical differences such as capitalization, spelling (including abbreviation of words and figures), punctuation and paragraphing.

The word "Debates" is used as a heading in the transcript.

[2] Madison is not uniform in the spelling of proper names, but the correct form in each instance is to be found in the credentials of the delegates, pp. lvi-lxxxii.

[3] The words "to wit: see Note A. viz," are omitted in the transcript.

[4] The word "and" is here inserted in the transcript.

[5] The paragraph in brackets beginning with the words "The nomination" and ending with the word "house" (page 18) is printed as a footnote in the transcript with reference mark after the word "Convention."

ballot, and conducted to the Chair by M: R. Morris and M: Rutlidge; from which in a very emphatic manner he thanked the Convention for the honor they had conferred on him, reminded them of the novelty of the scene of business in which he was to act, lamented his want of better qualifications, and claimed the indulgence of the House towards the involuntary errors which his inexperience might occasion.

[1] [The nomination came with particular grace from Penna. as Doc: Franklin alone could have been thought of as a competitor. The Doc: was himself to have made the nomination of General Washington, but the state of the weather and of his health confined him to his house.]

M: WILSON moved that a Secretary be appointed, and nominated M: Temple Franklin.

Col HAMILTON nominated Major Jackson.

On the ballot Maj: Jackson had 5 votes & M: Franklin 2 votes.

On reading the credentials of the deputies it was noticed that those from Delaware were prohibited from changing the article in the Confederation establishing an equality of votes among the States.

The appointment of a Committee, consisting of Mess:² Wythe, Hamilton & C. Pinckney, on the motion of M: C. PINCKNEY,[2] to prepare standing rules & orders was the only remaining step taken on this day.

MONDAY MAY 28.[3]—

[4] From Mass:² Nat: Gorham & Caleb Strong. From Connecticut Oliver Elseworth. From Delaware, Gunning Bedford. From Maryland James M°Henry. From Penn: B. Franklin, George Clymer, Th: Mifflin & Jared Ingersol took their seats.

M: WYTHE from the Committee for preparing rules made a report which employed the deliberations of this day.

M: KING objected to one of the rules in the Report authorising any member to call for the yeas & nays and have them entered on the minutes. He urged that as the acts of the Convention were not to bind the Constituents, it was unnecessary to exhibit this evidence of the votes; and improper as changes of opinion would be frequent

---

[1] See footnote [5] on page 17.
[2] The phrase "on the motion of Mr. C. Pinckney" is transposed in the transcript so that it reads: "The appointment of a Committee, on the motion of Mr. C. Pinckney, consisting," etc.
[3] The year "1787" is here inserted in the transcript.
[4] The words "In Convention" are here inserted in the transcript.

in the course of the business & would fill the minutes with contradictions.

Col. MASON seconded the objection; adding that such a record of the opinions of members would be an obstacle to a change of them on conviction; and in case of its being hereafter promulged must furnish handles to the adversaries of the Result of the Meeting.

The proposed rule was rejected nem. contradicente. The standing rules * ¹ agreed to were as follow: [see the Journal & copy here the printed rules] ²

[viz. ³ A House to do business shall consist of the Deputies of not less than seven States; and all questions shall be decided by the greater number of these which shall be fully represented: but a less number than seven may adjourn from day to day.

Immediately after the President shall have taken the chair, and the members their seats, the minutes of the preceding day shall be read by the Secretary.

Every member, rising to speak, shall address the President; and whilst he shall be speaking, none shall pass between them, or hold discourse with another, or read a book, pamphlet or paper, printed or manuscript—and of two members rising ⁴ at the same time, the President shall name him who shall be first heard.

A member shall not speak oftener than twice, without special leave, upon the same question; and not the second time, before every other, who had been silent, shall have been heard, if he choose to speak upon the subject.

A motion made and seconded, shall be repeated, and if written, as it shall be when any member shall so require, read aloud by the

* Previous to the arrival of a majority of the States, the rule by which they ought to vote in the Convention had been made a subject of conversation among the members present. It was pressed by Governeur Morris and favored by Robert Morris and others from Pennsylvania, that the large States should unite in firmly refusing to the small states an equal vote, as unreasonable, and as enabling the small States to negative every good system of Government, which must in the nature of things, be founded on a violation of that equality. The members from Virginia, conceiving that such an attempt might beget fatal altercations between the large & small States, and that it would be easier to prevail on the latter, in the course of the deliberations, to give up their equality for the sake of an effective Government, than on taking the field of discussion to disarm themselves of the right & thereby throw themselves on the mercy of the large States, discountenanced & stifled the project.

---

¹ Madison's footnote reference mark after the word "rules" is placed in the transcript after the word "him" (page 20) thus placing the footnote at the end of the rules instead of at the beginning.

² Madison's direction is omitted from the transcript and the word "Rules" is inserted.

³ The word "viz." is omitted in the transcript.

⁴ The words "to speak" are inserted in the transcript after "rising."

Secretary, before it shall be debated; and may be withdrawn at any time, before the vote upon it shall have been declared.

Orders of the day shall be read next after the minutes, and either discussed or postponed, before any other business shall be introduced.

When a debate shall arise upon a question, no motion, other than to amend the question, to commit it, or to postpone the debate shall be received.]

[A question which is complicated, shall, at the request of any member, be divided, and put separately on [1] the propositions, of which it is compounded.

The determination of a question, altho' fully debated, shall be postponed, if the deputies of any State desire it until the next day.

A writing which contains any matter brought on to be considered, shall be read once throughout for information, then by paragraphs to be debated, and again, with the amendments, if any, made on the second reading; and afterwards, the question shall be put on [1] the whole, amended, or approved in its original form, as the case shall be.

[2] Committees shall be appointed by ballot; and [2] the members who have the greatest number of ballots, altho' not a majority of the votes present, shall [3] be the Committee— When two or more members have an equal number of votes, the member standing first on the list in the order of taking down the ballots, shall be preferred.

A member may be called to order by any other member, as well as by the President; and may be allowed to explain his conduct or expressions supposed to be reprehensible.— And all questions of order shall be decided by the President without appeal or debate.

Upon a question to adjourn for the day, which may be made at any time, if it be seconded, the question shall be put without a debate.

When the House shall adjourn, every member shall stand in his place, until the President pass him.][4]

A letter from sundry persons of the State of Rho. Island addressed to the Honorable [5] The Chairman of the General Convention was presented to the Chair by M: Gov: MORRIS, and being read, was ordered to lie on the table for further consideration. [For the letter see Note in the Appendix][6]

---

[1] The word "upon" is substituted for "on" in the transcript.
[2] The word "that" is here inserted in the transcript.
[3] The word "shall" is omitted in the transcript.
[4] See footnote [1] on page 19.
[5] The words "the Honorable" are omitted in the transcript.
[6] The footnote in the transcript reads as follows: "For the letter, see Appendix No. blank." The text referred to is printed in the Appendix to Debates, III, p. 595.

M? BUTLER moved that the House provide agst interruption of business by absence of members, and against licentious publications of their proceedings—to which was added by—M? SPAIGHT—a motion to provide that on the one hand the House might not be precluded by a vote upon any question, from revising the subject matter of it, when they see cause, nor, on the other hand, be led too hastily to rescind a decision, which was the result of mature discussion.— Whereupon it was ordered that these motions be referred to [1] the consideration of the Committee appointed to draw up the standing rules and that the Committee make report thereon.

Adj^d till tomorrow [2] 10. OClock.

TUESDAY MAY 29. [3]

John Dickenson, and Elbridge Gerry, the former from Delaware, the latter from Mass^{ts} took their seats. The following rules were added, on the report of M? Wythe from the Committee [see the Journal]—[4]

Additional rules. [see preceding page][4]

That no member be absent from the House, so as to interrupt the representation of the State, without leave.

That Committees do not sit whilst the House shall be or ought to be, sitting.

That no copy be taken of any entry on the journal during the sitting of the House without leave of the House.

That members only be permitted to inspect the journal.

That nothing spoken in the House be printed, or otherwise published or communicated without leave.

That a motion to reconsider a matter which had [5] been determined by a majority, may be made, with leave unanimously given, on the same day on which the vote passed; but otherwise not without one day's previous notice: in which last case, if the House agree to the reconsideration, some future day shall be assigned for the [6] purpose.

M? C. PINKNEY moved that a Committee be appointed to superintend the Minutes.

---

[1] The word "for" is substituted in the transcript for the word "to."
[2] The word "at" is here inserted in the transcript.
[3] The words "In Convention" are here inserted in the transcript.
[4] Madison's directions "[see the Journal]—" and "[see preceding page]" are omitted in the transcript as are also the words "Additional rules."
[5] The word "has" is substituted in the transcript for "had."
[6] The word "that" is substituted in the transcript for "the."^{i}

M⁺ Gov⁺ MORRIS objected to it. The entry of the proceedings of the Convention belonged to the Secretary as their impartial officer. A committee might have an interest & bias in moulding the entry, according to their opinions and wishes.

The motion was negatived, 5 noes, 4 ays.

M⁺ RANDOLPH then opened the main business.

[Here insert his speech [1] including his resolutions.] [2]

(M⁺ R. Speech A. to be inserted Tuesday May 29) [2]

He expressed his regret, that it should fall to him, rather than those, who were of longer standing in life and political experience, to open the great subject of their mission. But, as the convention had originated from Virginia, and his colleagues supposed that some proposition was expected from them, they had imposed this task on him.

He then commented on the difficulty of the crisis, and the necessity of preventing the fulfilment of the prophecies of the American downfal.

He observed that in revising the fœderal system we ought to inquire 1.[3] into the properties, which such a government ought to possess, 2.[3] the defects of the confederation, 3.[3] the danger of our situation & 4.[3] the remedy.

1. The Character of such a government ought to secure 1.[3] against foreign invasion: 2.[3] against dissentions between members of the Union, or seditions in particular states: 3.[3] to procure to the several States, various blessings, of which an isolated situation was incapable: 4.[3,4] to be able to defend itself against incroachment: & 5.[3] to be paramount to the state constitutions.

2. In speaking of the defects of the confederation he professed a high respect for its authors, and considered them, as having done all that patriots could do, in the then infancy of the science, of constitutions, & of confederacies,—when the inefficiency of requisitions was unknown—no commercial discord had arisen among any states—no rebellion had appeared as in Mass⁺ˢ—foreign debts had not become urgent—the havoc of paper money had not been foreseen—treaties had not been violated—and perhaps nothing better could be obtained from the jealousy of the states with regard to their sovereignty.

---

[1] The speech is in Randolph's handwriting.
[2] Madison's direction is omitted in the transcript.
[3] The figures indicated by the reference mark [3] are changed in the transcript to " first," " secondly," " thirdly," etc.
[4] The words " it should " are here inserted in the transcript.

He then proceeded to enumerate the defects: 1.[1] that the confederation produced no security against foreign invasion; congress not being permitted to prevent a war nor to support it by their own authority—Of this he cited many examples; most of which tended to shew, that they could not cause infractions of treaties or of the law of nations, to be punished: that particular states might by their conduct provoke war without controul; and that neither militia nor draughts being fit for defence on such occasions, inlistments only could be successful, and these could not be executed without money.

2.[1] that the fœderal government could not check the quarrels between states, nor a rebellion in any, not having constitutional power nor means to interpose according to the exigency:

3.[1] that there were many advantages, which the U. S. might acquire, which were not attainable under the confederation—such as a productive impost—counteraction of the commercial regulations of other nations—pushing of commerce ad libitum—&c &c.

4.[1] that the fœderal government could not defend itself against the[2] incroachments from the states.

5.[1] that it was not even paramount to the state constitutions, ratified, as it was in may of the states.

3. He next reviewed the danger of our situation,[3] appealed to the sense of the best friends of the U. S.—the prospect of anarchy from the laxity of government every where; and to other considerations.

4. He then proceeded to the remedy; the basis of which he said must be the republican principle

He proposed as conformable to his ideas the following resolutions, which he explained one by one [Here insert ye Resolutions annexed].[4]

RESOLUTIONS PROPOSED BY M[r] RANDOLPH IN CONVENTION
MAY 29, 1787.[4]

1. Resolved that the Articles of Confederation ought to be so corrected & enlarged as to accomplish the objects proposed by their institution; namely, " common defence, security of liberty and general welfare."

2. Res[d] therefore that the rights of suffrage in the National Legislature ought to be proportioned to the Quotas of contribution, or to

---

[1] The figures indicated by the reference mark [1] are changed in the transcript to " First," " Secondly," etc.
[2] The word " the " is crossed out in the transcript.
[3] The word " and " is here inserted in the transcript.
[4] This direction and the heading are omitted in the transcript.

the number of free inhabitants, as the one or the other rule may seem best in different cases.

3. Res^d that the National Legislature ought to consist of two branches.

4. Res^d that the members of the first branch of the National Legislature ought to be elected by the people of the several States every   for the term of   ; to be of the age of years at least, to receive liberal stipends by which they may be compensated for the devotion of their time to [1] public service; to be ineligible to any office established by a particular State, or under the authority of the United States, except those beculiarly belonging to the functions of the first branch, during the term of service, and for the space of   after its expiration; to be incapable of re-election for the space of   after the expiration of their term of service, and to be subject to recall.

5. Resol^d that the members of the second branch of the National Legislature ought to be elected by those of the first, out of a proper number of persons nominated by the individual Legislatures, to be of the age of   years at least; to hold their offices for a term sufficient to ensure their independency; [2] to receive liberal stipends, by which they may be compensated for the devotion of their time to [3] public service; and to be ineligible to any office established by a particular State, or under the authority of the United States, except those peculiarly belonging to the functions of the second branch, during the term of service, and for the space of   after the expiration thereof.

6. Resolved that each branch ought to possess the right of originating Acts; that the National Legislature ought to be impowered to enjoy the Legislative Rights vested in Congress by the Confederation & moreover to legislate in all cases to which the separate States are incompetent, or in which the harmony of the United States may be interrupted by the exercise of individual Legislation; to negative all laws passed by the several States, contravening in the opinion of the National Legislature the articles of Union; [4] and to call forth the force of the Union agst any member of the Union failing to fulfill its duty under the articles thereof.

7. Res^d that a National Executive be instituted; to be chosen by

---

[1] The word "the" is here inserted in the transcript.
[2] The word "independency" is changed to "independence" in the transcript.
[3] The word "the" is here inserted in the transcript.
[4] The phrase "or any treaty subsisting under the authority of the Union" is here added in the transcript.

the National Legislature for the term of   years,[1] to receive
punctually at stated times, a fixed compensation for the services
rendered, in which no increase or[2] diminution shall be made so as
to affect the Magistracy, existing at the time of increase or diminution, and to be ineligible a second time; and that besides a general
authority to execute the National laws, it ought to enjoy the Executive rights vested in Congress by the Confederation.

8. Res^d that the Executive and a convenient number of the
National Judiciary, ought to compose a Council of revision with
authority to examine every act of the National Legislature before
it shall operate, & every act of a particular Legislature before a
Negative thereon shall be final; and that the dissent of the said
Council shall amount to a rejection, unless the Act of the National
Legislature be again passed, or that of a particular Legislature be
again negatived by   of the members of each branch.

9. Res^d that a National Judiciary be established to consist of
one or more supreme tribunals, and of inferior tribunals to be chosen
by the National Legislature, to hold their offices during good behaviour; and to receive punctually at stated times fixed compensation for their services, in which no increase or diminution shall be
made so as to affect the persons actually in office at the time of such
increase or diminution. that the jurisdiction of the inferior tribunals shall be to hear & determine in the first instance, and of the
supreme tribunal to hear and determine in the dernier resort, all
piracies & felonies on the high seas, captures from an enemy; cases
in which foreigners or citizens of other States applying to such jurisdictions may be interested, or which respect the collection of the
National revenue; impeachments of any National officers, and questions which may involve the national peace and harmony.

10. Resolv^d that provision ought to be made for the admission of
States lawfully arising within the limits of the United States, whether
from a voluntary junction of Government & Territory or otherwise,
with the consent of a number of voices in the National legislature
less than the whole.

11. Res^d that a Republican Government & the territory of each
State, except in the instance of a voluntary junction of Government
& territory, ought to be guarantied by the United States to each
State

12. Res^d that provision ought to be made for the continuance of
Congress and their authorities and privileges, until a given day after

---

[1] The word " years " is omitted in the transcript.
[2] The word " or " is changed to " nor " in the transcript.

the reform of the articles of Union shall be adopted, and for the completion of all their engagements.

13. Res.ᵈ that provision ought to be made for the amendment of the Articles of Union whensoever it shall seem necessary, and that the assent of the National Legislature ought not to be required thereto.

14. Res.ᵈ that the Legislative Executive & Judiciary powers within the several States ought to be bound by oath to support the articles of Union

15. Res.ᵈ that the amendments which shall be offered to the Confederation, by the Convention ought at a proper time, or times, after the approbation of Congress to be submitted to an assembly or assemblies of Representatives, recommended by the several Legislatures to be expressly chosen by the people, to consider & decide thereon.[1]

He concluded with an exhortation, not to suffer the present opportunity of establishing general peace, harmony, happiness and liberty in the U. S. to pass away unimproved.[*]

It was then Resolved—That the House will tomorrow resolve itself into a Committee of the Whole House to consider of the state of the American Union.—and that the propositions moved by M.ʳ Randolph be referred to the said Committee.

M.ʳ CHARLES PINKNEY laid before the house the draught of a federal Government which he had prepared, to be agreed upon between the free and independent States of America.[3]—M.ʳ P. plan[4] ordered

[*] This Abstract of the speech was furnished to J. M. by M.ʳ Randolph and is in his handwriting.   [2] As a report of it from him had been relied on, it was omitted by J. M.

---

[1] The fifteen resolutions, constituting the "Virginia Plan," are in Madison's handwriting.
[2] This sentence is omitted in the transcript.
[3] Robert Yates, a delegate from New York, gives the following account of Pinckney's motion: "Mr. C. Pinkney, a member from South-Carolina, then added, that he had reduced his ideas of a new government to a system, which he read, and confessed that it was grounded on the same principle as of the above resolutions." (*Secret Proceedings of the Federal Convention* (1821), p. 97.)
[4] The words, "Mr. P. plan," are omitted in the transcript, and what purports to be the plan itself is here inserted.
Madison himself did not take a copy of the draft nor did Pinckney furnish him one, as he did a copy of his speech which he later delivered in the Convention and which is printed as a part of the debates (session of Monday, June 25), *infra*, pp. 155-161, and Madison's note, p. 161.   Many years later, in 1818, when John Quincy Adams, then Secretary of State, was preparing the Journal of the Convention for publication, he wrote to Pinckney, requesting a copy of his plan, and, in compliance with this request, Pinckney sent him what purported to be the draft, but which appears to have been a copy of the report of the Committee of Detail of August 6, 1787, with certain alterations and additions.   The alleged draft and Pinckney's letter transmitting it were written upon paper bearing the water-mark, "Russell & Co. 1797."
The Pinckney draft was not debated; it was neither used in the Committee of the Whole nor in the Convention.   It was however referred to the Committee

that the same be referred to the Committee of the Whole appointed to consider the state of the American Union.
adjourned.

WEDNESDAY MAY 30.

Roger Sherman (from Connecticut) took his seat.

The House went into Committee of the Whole on the State of the Union. Mᵣ Gorham was elected to the Chair by Ballot.

The propositions of Mᵣ RANDOLPH which had been referred to the Committee being taken up. He moved on the suggestion of Mᵣ G. Morris, that the first of his propositions to wit " Resolved that the articles of Confederation ought to be so corrected & enlarged, as to accomplish the objects proposed by their institution; namely, common defence, security of liberty & general welfare: [1]—should be postponed, in order to consider the 3 following:

1. that a Union of the States merely federal will not accomplish the objects proposed by the articles of Confederation, namely common defence, security of liberty, & genᶫ welfare.

2. that no treaty or treaties among the whole or part of the States, as individual Sovereignties, would be sufficient.

3. that a *national* Government ought to be established consisting of a *supreme* Legislative, Executive & Judiciary.

The motion for postponing was seconded by Mᵣ Govᵣ MORRIS and unanimously agreed to.

Some verbal criticisms were raised agˢᵗ the first proposition, and it was agreed on motion of Mᵣ BUTLER seconded by Mᵣ RANDOLPH, to pass on to the third, which underwent a discussion, less however on its general merits than on the force and extent of the particular terms *national* & *supreme*.

Mᵣ CHARLES PINKNEY wished to know of Mᵣ Randolph whether he meant to abolish the State Governᵗˢ altogether. Mᵣ R. replied that

---

of Detail, which appears to have made some use of it, as extracts from it have been identified by J. Franklin Jameson and an outline of it discovered by Andrew C. McLaughlin, among the papers and in the handwriting of James Wilson, a delegate from Pennsylvania, deposited with the Pennsylvania Historical Society.

For the main features of this plan as reconstructed by Professor McLaughlin according to Professor Jameson's and his own discoveries, see Appendix to Debates, IV, No. 1, 596-598.

For the text of the Pinckney plan submitted to John Quincy Adams and printed by him in the Journal of the Convention, for Madison's observations upon it and for further details concerning it, see Appendix to Debates, IV, Nos. 3 and 4, pp. 600-607.

[1] The resolution is italicized in the transcript.

he meant by these general propositions merely to introduce the particular ones which explained the outlines of the system he had in view.

Mʳ BUTLER said he had not made up his mind on the subject, and was open to the light which discussion might throw on it. After some general observations he concluded with saying that he had opposed the grant of powers to Congˢ heretofore, because the whole power was vested in one body. The proposed distribution of the powers into [1] different bodies changed the case, and would induce him to go great lengths.

Genˡ PINKNEY expressed a doubt whether the act of Congˢ recommending the Convention, or the Commissions of the Deputies to it, could [2] authorise a discussion of a System founded on different principles from the federal Constitution.

Mʳ GERRY seemed to entertain the same doubt.

Mʳ Govʳ MORRIS explained the distinction between a *federal* and *national, supreme,* Govᵗ; the former being a mere compact resting on the good faith of the parties; the latter having a compleat and *compulsive* operation. He contended that in all Communities there must be one supreme power, and one only.

Mʳ MASON observed that the present confederation was not only [3] deficient in not providing for coercion & punishment agˢᵗ delinquent States; but argued very cogently that punishment could not in the nature of things be executed on the States collectively, and therefore that such a Govᵗ was necessary as could directly operate on individuals, and would punish those only whose guilt required it.

Mʳ SHERMAN who took his seat today,[4] admitted that the Confederation had not given sufficient power to Congˢ and that additional powers were necessary; particularly that of raising money which he said would involve many other powers. He admitted also that the General & particular jurisdictions ought in no case to be concurrent. He seemed however not [5] be disposed to make too great inroads on the existing system; intimating as one reason, that it would be wrong to lose every amendment, by inserting such as would not be agreed to by the States.

It was moved by Mʳ READ [6] 2ᵈᵉᵈ by Mʳ Chˢ COTESWORTH PINKNEY,

---

[1] The word "with" is substituted in the transcript for "into."

[2] The word "would" is substituted in the transcript for "could."

[3] The words "not only" are transposed in the transcript, which reads as follows: "Mr. Mason observed, not only that the present Confederation was deficient." . . .

[4] The phrase "who took his seat today" is omitted in the transcript.

[5] The word "to" is here inserted in the transcript.

[6] The word "and" is here inserted in the transcript.

to postpone the 3ᵈ proposition last offered by Mᵣ Randolph viz that a national Government ought to be established consisting of a supreme Legislative Executive and Judiciary,'' in order to take up the following—viz. ''Resolved that in order to carry into execution the Design of the States in forming this Convention, and to accomplish the objects proposed by the Confederation a more effective Government consisting of a Legislative, Executive and Judiciary ought to be established.'' The motion to postpone for this purpose was lost:

Yeas ¹ Massachussetts, Connecticut, Delaware, S. Carolina—¹ 4
Nays.² N. Y. Pennsylvania, Virginia, North Carolina—² 4.

On the question as moved by Mᵣ Butler, on the third proposition it was resolved in Committee of the whole that a national governᵗ ought to be established consisting of a supreme Legislative Executive & Judiciary.'' Massᵗˢ being ay—Connect.—no. N. York divided [Col. Hamilton ay Mᵣ Yates no] Penᵃ ay. Delaware ay. Virgᵃ ay. N. C. ay. S. C. ay.³

[Note E] ⁴

Resol: 2. of Mᵣ R's proposition towit—see May 29.⁴

The following Resolution, being the 2ᵈ of those proposed by Mᵣ Randolph was taken up, viz—'' that the rights of suffrage in the National Legislature ought to be proportioned to the quotas of contribution, or to the number of free inhabitants, as the one or the other rule may seem best in different cases.'' ⁵

Mᵣ MADISON observing that the words '' *or to the number of free inhabitants,*'' might occasion debates which would divert the Committee from the general question whether the principle of representation should be changed, moved that they might be struck out.

Mᵣ KING observed that the quotas of contribution which would alone remain as the measure of representation, would not answer, because waving every other view of the matter, the revenue might hereafter be so collected by the general Govᵗ that the sums respectively drawn from the States would not appear; and would besides be continually varying.

Mᵣ MADISON admitted the propriety of the observation, and that some better rule ought to be found.

---

¹ The word "Yeas" is omitted in the transcript and the word "aye" inserted before the figure "4."

² The word "Nays" is omitted in the transcript and the word "no" inserted before the figure "4."

³ In the transcript the vote reads: "Massachusetts, Pennsylvania, Delaware, Virginia, North Carolina, South Carolina, aye—6; Connecticut, no—1; New York, divided (Colonel Hamilton, aye, Mr. Yates, no)."

⁴ Madison's direction is omitted in the transcript.

⁵ The resolution is italicized in the transcript.

Col. HAMILTON moved to alter the resolution so as to read " that the rights of suffrage in the national Legislature ought to be proportioned to the number of free inhabitants. M̃ SPAIGHT 2^{ded} the motion.

It was then moved that the Resolution be postponed, which was agreed to.

M̃ RANDOLPH and M̃ MADISON then moved the following resolution—" that the rights of suffrage in the national Legislature ought to be proportioned."

It was moved and 2^{ded} to amend it by adding " and not according to the present system "—which was agreed to.

It was then moved and 2^{ded} to alter the resolution so as to read " that the rights of suffrage in the national Legislature ought not to be according to the present system."

It was then moved & 2^{ded} to postpone the Resolution moved by M̃ Randolph & M̃ Madison, which being agreed to:

M̃ MADISON, moved, in order to get over the difficulties, the following resolution—" that the equality of suffrage established by the articles of Confederation ought not to prevail in the national Legislature, and that an equitable ratio of representation ought to be substituted." This was 2^{ded} by M̃ Goṽ MORRIS, and being generally relished, would have been agreed to; when,

M̃ REED moved that the whole clause relating to the point of Representation be postponed; reminding the Com̃ that the deputies from Delaware were restrained by their commission from assenting to any change of the rule of suffrage, and in case such a change should be fixed on, it might become their duty to retire from the Convention.

M̃ Goṽ MORRIS observed that the valuable assistance of those members could not be lost without real concern, and that so early a proof of discord in the Convention as a secession of a State, would add much to the regret; that the change proposed was however so fundamental an article in a national Goṽ that it could not be dispensed with.

M̃ MADISON observed that whatever reason might have existed for the equality of suffrage when the Union was a federal one among sovereign States, it must cease when a national Goverm̃ should be put into the place. In the former case, the acts of Cong̃ depended so much for their efficacy on the cooperation of the States, that these had a weight both within & without Congress, nearly in proportion to their extent and importance. In the latter case, as the acts of the Geñ Goṽ would take effect without the intervention of the State legislatures, a vote from a small State w^d have the same efficacy & importance as a vote from a large one, and there was the same reason for different numbers of representatives from different States, as from Counties of different extents within particular States. He suggested as an expedient for at once taking the sense of the members on this point and saving the Delaware deputies from embarrassment, that the question should be taken in Committee, and the clause on report to the House be postponed without a question there. This however did not appear to satisfy Mr Read.

By several it was observed that no just construction of the Act of Delaware, could require or justify a secession of her deputies, even if the resolution were to be carried thro' the House as well as the Committee. It was finally agreed however that the clause should be postponed: it being understood that in the event the proposed change of representation would certainly be agreed to, no objection or difficulty being started from any other quarter than from Delaware.

The motion of Mr Read to postpone being agreed to,

The Committee then rose. The Chairman reported progress, and the House having resolved to resume the subject in Committee to-morrow,

Adjourned to 10 OClock.

THURSDAY MAY 31 [1]

William Pierce from Georgia took his seat.

In Committee of the whole on Mr Randolph's propositions.

The 3^d Resolution "that the national Legislature ought to consist of two branches" was agreed to without debate or dissent, except that of Pennsylvania, given probably from complaisance to Doc^r Franklin who was understood to be partial to a single House of Legislation.

Resol: 4.[2] first clause "that the members of the first branch of the National Legislature ought to be elected by the people of the several States" being taken up,

Mr SHERMAN opposed the election by the people, insisting that it ought to be by the State Legislatures. The people he said, im-

---

[1] The year " 1787 " is here inserted in the transcript.
[2] The transcript changes " Resol: 4." to " The fourth Resolution."

mediately should have as little to do as may be about the Government. They want information and are constantly liable to be misled.

M: GERRY. The evils we experience flow from the excess of democracy. The people do not want virtue, but are the dupes of pretended patriots. In Mass:ᵗˢ it had been fully confirmed by experience that they are daily misled into the most baneful measures and opinions by the false reports circulated by designing men, and which no one on the spot can refute. One principal evil arises from the want of due provision for those employed in the administration of Governm: It would seem to be a maxim of democracy to starve the public servants. He mentioned the popular clamour in Mass:ᵗˢ for the reduction of salaries and the attack made on that of the Gov: though secured by the spirit of the Constitution itself. He had he said been too republican heretofore: he was still however republican, but had been taught by experience the danger of the levilling spirit.

M: MASON, argued strongly for an election of the larger branch by the people. It was to be the grand depository of the democratic principle of the Gov: It was, so to speak, to be our House of Commons—It ought to know & sympathise with every part of the community; and ought therefore to be taken not only from different parts of the whole republic, but also from different districts of the larger members of it, which had in several instances particularly in Virg:ᵃ, different interests and views arising from difference of produce, of habits &c &c. He admitted that we had been too democratic but was afraid we s:ᵈ incautiously run into the opposite extreme. We ought to attend to the rights of every class of the people. He had often wondered at the indifference of the superior classes of society to this dictate of humanity & policy; considering that however affluent their circumstances, or elevated their situations, might be, the course of a few years, not only might but certainly would, distribute their posterity throughout the lowest classes of Society. Every selfish motive therefore, every family attachment, ought to recommend such a system of policy as would provide no less carefully for the rights and happiness of the lowest than of the highest orders of Citizens.

M: WILSON contended strenuously for drawing the most numerous branch of the Legislature immediately from the people. He was for raising the federal pyramid to a considerable altitude, and for that reason wished to give it as broad a basis as possible. No government could long subsist without the confidence of the people. In a republican Government this confidence was peculiarly essential.

He also thought it wrong to increase the weight of the State Legislatures by making them the electors of the national Legislature. All interference between the general and local Governm.ts should be obviated as much as possible. On examination it would be found that the opposition of States to federal measures had proceded much more from the officers of the States, than from the people at large.

M.r Madison considered the popular election of one branch of the National Legislature as essential to every plan of free Government. He observed that in some of the States one branch of the Legislature was composed of men already removed from the people by an intervening body of electors. That if the first branch of the general legislature should be elected by the State Legislatures, the second branch elected by the first—the Executive by the second together with the first; and other appointments again made for subordinate purposes by the Executive, the people would be lost sight of altogether; and the necessary sympathy between them and their rulers and officers, too little felt. He was an advocate for the policy of refining the popular appointments by successive filtrations, but thought it might be pushed too far. He wished the expedient to be resorted to only in the appointment of the second branch of the Legislature, and in the Executive & judiciary branches of the Government. He thought too that the great fabric to be raised would be more stable and durable, if it should rest on the solid foundation of the people themselves, than if it should stand merely on the pillars of the Legislatures.

M.r Gerry did not like the election by the people. The maxims taken from the British constitution were often fallacious when applied to our situation which was extremely different. Experience he said had shewn that the State legislatures drawn immediately from the people did not always possess their confidence. He had no objection however to an election by the people if it were so qualified that men of 'honor & character might not be unwilling to be joined in the appointments. He seemed to think the people might nominate a certain number out of which the State legislatures should be bound to choose.

M.r Butler thought an election by the people an impracticable mode.

On the question for an election of the first branch of the national Legislature by the people,

Mass.ts ay. Connec.t div.d N. York ay. N. Jersey no. Pen.a ay. Delaw.e div.d V.a ay. N. C. ay. S. C. no. Georg.a ay.

The remaining Clauses of Resolution 4th.[1] relating to the qualifications of members of the National Legislature,[1] being posp^d nem. con., as entering too much into detail for general propositions;

The Committee proceeded to Resolution 5.[2] " that the second, [or senatorial] branch of the National Legislature ought to be chosen by the first branch out of persons nominated by the State Legislatures."

Mr SPAIGHT contended that the 2^d branch ought to be chosen by the State Legislatures and moved an amendment to that effect.

Mr BUTLER apprehended that the taking so many powers out of the hands of the States as was proposed, tended to destroy all that balance and security of interests among the States which it was necessary to preserve; and called on Mr Randolph the mover of the propositions, to explain the extent of his ideas, and particularly the number of members he meant to assign to this second branch.

Mr RAND^f observed that he had at the time of offering his propositions stated his ideas as far as the nature of general propositions required; that details made no part of the plan, and could not perhaps with propriety have been introduced. If he was to give an opinion as to the number of the second branch, he should say that it ought to be much smaller than that of the first; so small as to be exempt from the passionate proceedings to which numerous assemblies are liable. He observed that the general object was to provide a cure for the evils under which the U. S. laboured; that in tracing these evils to their origin every man had found it in the turbulence and follies of democracy: that some check therefore was to be sought for ag^st this tendency of our Governments: and that a good Senate seemed most likely to answer the purpose.

Mr KING reminded the Committee that the choice of the second branch as proposed (by Mr Spaight) viz. by the State Legislatures would be impracticable, unless it was to be very numerous, or *the idea of proportion* among the States was to be disregarded. According to this *idea*, there must be 80 or 100 members to entitle Delaware to the choice of one of them.—Mr SPAIGHT withdrew his motion.

Mr WILSON opposed both a nomination by the State Legislatures, and an election by the first branch of the national Legislature, because the second branch of the latter, ought to be independent of both. He thought both branches of the National Legislature ought to

---

[1] In the transcript the words " Resolution 4th " are changed to " the fourth Resolution " and the phrase " the qualifications of members of the National Legislature " is italicized.

[2] In the transcript the words " Resolution 5," are changed to " the fifth Resolution " and the words of the resolution are italicized.

be chosen by the people, but was not prepared with a specific proposition. He suggested the mode of chusing the Senate of N. York to wit of uniting several election districts, for one branch, in chusing members for the other branch, as a good model.

Mʳ MADISON observed that such a mode would destroy the influence of the smaller States associated with larger ones in the same district; as the latter would chuse from within themselves, altho' better men might be found in the former. The election of Senators in Virgᵃ where large & small counties were often formed into one district for the purpose, had illustrated this consequence Local partiality, would often prefer a resident within the County or State, to a candidate of superior merit residing out of it. Less merit also in a resident would be more known throughout his own State.

Mʳ SHERMAN favored an election of one member by each of the State Legislatures.

Mʳ PINKNEY moved to strike out the " nomination by the State Legislatures." On this question.

* Massᵗˢ no. Conᵗ no. N. Y. no. N. J. no. Penᵃ no. Del divᵈ Vᵃ no. N. C. no. S. C. no. Georg no.¹

On the whole question for electing by the first branch out of nominations by the State Legislatures, Mass. ay. Conᵗ no. N. Y. no. N. Jersey. no. Penᵃ no. Del. no. Virgᵃ ay. N. C. no. S. C. ay. Gᵃ no.²

So the clause was disagreed to & a chasm left in this part of the plan.

³ The sixth Resolution stating the cases in which the national Legislature ought to legislate was next taken into discussion: On the question whether each branch shᵈ originate laws, there was an unanimous affirmative without debate. On the question for transferring all the Legislative powers of the existing Congˢ to this Assembly, there was also a silent affirmative nem. con.

---

* This question ¹ omitted in the printed Journal, & the votes applied to the succeeding one, instead of the votes as here stated [this note to be in the bottom margin] ¹

---

¹ In the transcript the vote reads: " * Massachusetts, Connecticut, New York, New Jersey, Pennsylvania, Virginia, North Carolina, South Carolina, Georgia, no—9; Delaware divided "; and Madison's direction concerning the footnote is omitted. The word " is " is inserted after the word " question."·

² In the transcript the vote reads: " Massachusetts, Virginia, South Carolina, aye—3; Connecticut New York, New Jersey, Pennsylvania, Delaware, North Carolina, Georgia, no—7."

³ In this paragraph the transcript italicizes the following phrases: " the cases in which the national Legislature ought to legislate," " whether each branch shᵈ originate laws," " for transferring all the Legislative powers of the existing Congˢ to this Assembly "; and the phrase " a silent affirmative nem. con." is changed to " an unanimous affirmative, without debate."

On the proposition for giving "Legislative power in all cases to which the State Legislatures were individually incompetent."

M: PINKNEY & M: RUTLEDGE objected to the vagueness of the term *incompetent,* and said they could not well decide how to vote until they should see an exact enumeration of the powers comprehended by this definition.

M: BUTLER repeated his fears that we were running into an extreme in taking away the powers of the States, and called on M: Randolp for the extent of his meaning.

M: RANDOLPH disclaimed any intention to give indefinite powers to the national Legislature, declaring that he was entirely opposed to such an inroad on the State jurisdictions, and that he did not think any considerations whatever could ever change his determination. His opinion was fixed on this point.

M: MADISON said that he had brought with him into the Convention a strong bias in favor of an enemeration and definition of the powers necessary to be exercised by the national Legislature; but had also brought doubts concerning its practicability. His wishes remained unaltered; but his doubts had become stronger. What his opinion might ultimately be he could not yet tell. But he should shrink from nothing which should be found essential to such a form of Gov: as would provide for the safety, liberty and happiness of the community. This being the end of all our deliberations, all the necessary means for attaining it must, however reluctantly, be submitted to.

On the question for giving powers, in cases to which the States are not competent, Mass⁺ˢ ay. Con: div⁴ [Sharman no Elseworth ay] N. Y. ay. N. J. ay. Pᵃ ay. Del. ay. Vᵃ ay. N. C. ay. S. Carolina ay. Georgᵃ ay.[1]

The other clauses[2] giving powers necessary to preserve harmony among the States to negative all State laws contravening in the opinion of the Nat. Leg. the articles of union, down to the last clause, (the words "or any treaties subsisting under the authority of the Union," being added after the words "contravening &c. the articles of the Union," on motion of D: FRANKLIN) were agreed to with: debate or dissent.

---

[1] In the transcript the vote reads: "Massachusetts, New York, New Jersey, Pennsylvania, Delaware, Virginia, North Carolina, South Carolina, Georgia, aye—9; Connecticut divided (Sherman, no, Ellsworth, aye)."

[2] The phrase, "giving powers necessary to preserve harmony among the States to negative all State laws contravening in the opinion of the Nat. Leg. the articles of union" is italicized in the transcript.

The last clause of Resolution 6.[1] authorizing an exertion of the force of the whole ag.ˢᵗ a delinquent State came next into consideration.

M.ʳ MADISON, observed that the more he reflected on the use of force, the more he doubted the practicability, the justice and the efficacy of it when applied to people collectively and not individually.— A union of the States containing such an ingredient seemed to provide for its own destruction. The use of force ag.ˢᵗ a State, would look more like a declaration of war, than an infliction of punishment, and would probably be considered by the party attacked as a dissolution of all previous compacts by which it might be bound. He hoped that such a system would be framed as might render this recourse[2] unnecessary, and moved that the clause be postponed. This motion was agreed to nem. con.

The Committee then rose & the House
Adjourned

FRIDAY JUNE 1ˢᵗ 1787.

William Houston from Georgia took his seat.

The Committee of the whole proceeded to Resolution 7.[3] " that a national Executive be instituted, to be chosen by the national Legislature—for the term of   years &c to be ineligible thereafter, to possess the executive powers of Congress &c."

M.ʳ PINKNEY was for a vigorous Executive but was afraid the Executive powers of the existing Congress might extend to peace & war &c., which would render the Executive a monarchy, of the worst kind, to wit an elective one.

M.ʳ WILSON moved that the Executive consist of a single person. M.ʳ C PINKNEY seconded the motion, so as to read " that a National Ex. to consist of a single person, be instituted.

A considerable pause ensuing and the Chairman asking if he should put the question, Doc.ʳ FRANKLIN observed that it was a point of great importance and wished that the gentlemen would deliver their sentiments on it before the question was put.

M.ʳ RUTLIDGE animadverted on the shyness of gentlemen on this and other subjects. He said it looked as if they supposed themselves

---

[1] The words "the sixth Resolution" are substituted in the transcript for " Resolution 6 " and the phrase " authorizing an exertion of the force of the whole ag.ˢᵗ a delinquent State " is italicized.

[2] The word " resource " is substituted in the transcript for " recourse."

[3] The words " the seventh Resolution " are substituted in the transcript for " Resolution 7 " and the words of the resolution are italicized.

precluded by having frankly disclosed their opinions from afterwards changing them, which he did not take to be at all the case. He said he was for vesting the Executive power in a single person, tho' he was not for giving him the power of war and peace. A single man would feel the greatest responsibility and administer the public affairs best.

M! SHERMAN said he considered the Executive magistracy as nothing more than an institution for carrying the will of the Legislature into effect, that the person or persons ought to be appointed by and accountable to the Legislature only, which was the depositary of the supreme will of the Society. As they were the best judges of the business which ought to be done by the Executive department, and consequently of the number necessary from time to time for doing it, he wished the number might not be fixed, but that the legislature should be at liberty to appoint one or more as experience might dictate.

M! WILSON preferred a single magistrate, as giving most energy dispatch and responsibility to the office. He did not consider the Prerogatives of the British Monarch as a proper guide in defining the Executive powers. Some of these prerogatives were of a Legislative nature. Among others that of war & peace &c. The only powers he conceived [1] strictly Executive were those of executing the laws, and appointing officers, not appertaining to and appointed by the Legislature.

M! GERRY favored the policy of annexing a Council to the Executive in order to give weight & inspire confidence.

M! RANDOLPH strenuously opposed a unity in the Executive magistracy. He regarded it as the fœtus of monarchy. We had he said no motive to be governed by the British Governm! as our prototype. He did not mean however to throw censure on that Excellent fabric. If we were in a situation to copy it he did not know that he should be opposed to it; but the fixt genius of the people of America required a different form of Government. He could not see why the great requisites for the Executive department, vigor, despatch & responsibility could not be found in three men, as well as in one man. The Executive ought to be independent. It ought therefore in order to support its independence to consist of more than one.

M! WILSON said that unity in the Executive instead of being the fetus of monarchy would be the best safeguard against tyranny. He repeated that he was not governed by the British Model which was

---

[1] The transcript here substitutes the word " considered " for " conceived."

inapplicable to the situation of this Country; the extent of which was so great, and the manners so republican, that nothing but a great confederated Republic would do for it.

Mᵣ Wilson's motion for a single magistrate was postponed by common consent, the Committee seeming unprepared for any decision on it; and the first part of the clause agreed to, viz—"that a National Executive be instituted."

Mᵣ MADISON thought it would be proper, before a choice shᵈ be made between a unity and a plurality in the Executive, to fix the extent of the Executive authority; that as certain powers were in their nature Executive, and must be given to that departmᵗ whether administered by one or more persons, a definition of their extent would assist the judgment in determining how far they might be safely entrusted to a single officer. He accordingly moved that so much of the clause before the Committee as related to the powers of the Executive shᵈ be struck out & that after the words " that a national Executive ought to be instituted " there be inserted the words following viz. " with power to carry into effect the national laws, to appoint to offices in cases not otherwise provided for, and to execute such other powers " not Legislative nor Judiciary in their nature," as may from time to time be delegated by the national Legislature." The words " not legislative nor judiciary in their nature " were added to the proposed amendment in consequence of a suggestion by Genᶫ Pinkney that improper powers might otherwise be delegated.

Mᵣ WILSON seconded this motion—

Mᵣ PINKNEY moved to amend the amendment by striking out the last member of it; viz: " and to execute such other powers not Legislative nor Judiciary in their nature as may from time to time be delegated." He said they were unnecessary, the object of them being included in the " power [1] to carry into effect the national laws."

Mᵣ RANDOLPH seconded the motion.

Mᵣ MADISON did not know that the words were absolutely necessary, or even the preceding words—" to appoint to offices &c. the whole being perhaps included in the first member of the proposition. He did not however see any inconveniency [2] in retaining them, and cases might happen in which they might serve to prevent doubts and misconstructions.

In consequence of the motion of Mᵣ Pinkney, the question on Mᵣ Madison's motion was divided; and the words objected to by

---

[1] The transcript uses the word " power " in the plural.
[2] The transcript changes the word " inconveniency " to " inconvenience."

Mr Pinkney struck out; by the votes of Connecticut, N. Y. N. J. Pen^a Del. N. C. & Geo.[1] agst Mass. Virg^a & S. Carolina [1] the preceding part of the motion being first agreed to; Connecticut divided, all the other States in the affirmative.

The next clause in Resolution 7,[2] relating to the mode of appointing, & the duration of, the Executive being under consideration,

Mr WILSON said he was almost unwilling to declare the mode which he wished to take place, being apprehensive that it might appear chimerical. He would say however at least that in theory he was for an election by the people. Experience, particularly in N. York & Mass^{ts}, shewed that an election of the first magistrate by the people at large, was both a convenient & successful mode. The objects of choice in such cases must be persons whose merits have general notoriety.

Mr SHERMAN was for the appointment by the Legislature, and for making him absolutely dependent on that body, as it was the will of that which was to be executed. An independence of the Executive on the supreme Legislature, was in his opinion the very essence of tyranny if there was any such thing.

Mr WILSON moves that the blank for the term of duration should be filled with three years, observing at the same time that he preferred this short period, on the supposition that a re-eligibilty would be provided for.

Mr PINKNEY moves for seven years.

Mr SHERMAN was for three years, and agst the doctrine of rotation as throwing out of office the men best qualifyed to execute its duties.

Mr MASON was for seven years at least, and for prohibiting a re-eligibility as the best expedient both for preventing the effect of a false complaisance on the side of the Legislature towards unfit characters; and a temptation on the side of the Executive to intrigue with the Legislature for a re-appointment.

Mr BEDFORD was strongly opposed to so long a term as seven years. He begged the committee to consider what the situation of the Country would be, in case the first magistrate should be saddled on it for such a period and it should be found on trial that he did not possess the qualifications ascribed to him, or should lose them after his appointment. An impeachment he said would be no cure for this evil, as an impeachment would reach misfeasance only, not

---

[1] In the transcript the figures "7" and "3" are inserted after the States Georgia and South Carolina, respectively.

[2] The words "the seventh Resolution" are substituted in the transcript for "Resolution 7."

incapacity. He was for a triennial election, and for an ineligibility after a period of nine years.

On the question for seven years,[1]

Mass.[ts] divid.[d] Con.[t] no. N. Y. ay. N. J. ay. Pen.[a] ay. Del. ay. Virg.[a] ay. N. C. no. S. C. no. Geor. no.[2] There being 5 ays, 4 noes, 1 div.[d], a question was asked whether a majority had voted in the affirmative? The President decided that it was an affirmative vote.

The *mode of appointing* the Executive was the next question.

M.[r] WILSON renewed his declarations in favor of an appointment by the people. He wished to derive not only both branches of the Legislature from the people, without the intervention of the State Legislatures but the Executive also; in order to make them as independent as possible of each other, as well as of the States;

Col. MASON favors the idea, but thinks it impracticable. He wishes however that M.[r] Wilson might have time to digest it into his own form.—the clause " to be chosen by the National Legislature "— was accordingly postponed.—

M.[r] RUTLIDGE suggests an election of the Executive by the second branch only of the national Legislature.

The Committee then rose and the House
Adjourned.

SATURDAY JUNE 2.[D] [3] IN COMMITTEE OF WHOLE.

* [Insert the words noted here] [4] * William Sam.[l] Johnson from Connecticut, Daniel of St. Thomas Jennifer, from Mary.[d] & John Lansing J.[r] from N. York, took their seats.

It was mov.[d] & 2.[ded] to postpone ye Resol: of M.[r] Randolph respecting the Executive, in order to take up the 2.[d] branch of the Legislature; which being negatived by Mas: Con: Del: Virg: N. C. S. C. Geo: [5] ag.[st] N. Y. Pen.[a] Mary.[d] [5] The mode of appoint.[g] ye Executive was resumed.

M.[r] WILSON made the following motion, to be substituted for the mode proposed by M.[r] Randolph's resolution, " that the Executive

---

[1] The transcript italicizes the phrase "for seven years."
[2] In the transcript the vote reads: "New York, New Jersey, Pennsylvania, Delaware, Virginia, aye—5; Connecticut, North Carolina, South Carolina, Georgia, no—4; Massachusetts, divided."
[3] The year "1787" is here inserted in the transcript.
[4] Madison's direction is omitted in the transcript.
[5] In the transcript the figures "7" and "3" are inserted after the States Georgia and Maryland, respectively.

Magistracy shall be elected in the following manner: That the States be divided into   districts: & that the persons qualified to vote in each district for members of the first branch of the national Legislature elect   members for their respective districts to be electors of the Executive magistracy, that the said Electors of the Executive magistracy meet at   and they or any of them so met shall proceed to elect by ballot, but not out of their own body   person   in whom the Executive authority of the national Government shall be vested.''

M: WILSON repeated his arguments in favor of an election without the intervention of the States. He supposed too that this mode would produce more confidence among the people in the first magistrate, than an election by the national Legislature.

M: GERRY, opposed the election by the national legislature. There would be a constant intrigue kept up for the appointment. The Legislature & the candidates w:d bargain & play into one another's hands, votes would be given by the former under promises or expectations from the latter, of recompensing them by services to members of the Legislature or to [1] their friends. He liked the principle of M: Wilson's motion, but fears it would alarm & give a handle to the State partisans, as tending to supersede altogether the State authorities. He thought the Community not yet ripe for stripping the States of their powers, even such as might not be requisite for local purposes. He was for waiting till people should feel more the necessity of it. He seemed to prefer the taking the suffrages of the States instead of Electors, or letting the Legislatures nominate, and the electors appoint. He was not clear that the people ought to act directly even in the choice of electors, being too little informed of personal characters in large districts, and liable to deceptions.

M: WILLIAMSON could see no advantage in the introduction of Electors chosen by the people who would stand in the same relation to them as the State Legislatures, whilst the expedient would be attended with great trouble and expence.

On the question for agreeing to M: Wilson's substitute, it was negatived: Mass:ts no. Con: no. N. Y. no.* P:a ay. Del. no. Mar:d ay. Virg:a no. N. C. no. S. C. no. Geo:a no.[2]

* N. Y. in the printed Journal—'divided.'

---

[1] The word " to " is omitted in the transcript.
[2] In the transcript the vote reads: " Pennsylvania, Maryland, aye—2; Massachusetts, Connecticut, New York,* Delaware, Virginia, North Carolina, South Carolina, Georgia, no—8."

On the question for electing the Executive by the national Legislature for the term of seven years, it was agreed to   Mass^{ts} ay.   Con^t ay.   N. Y. ay.   Pen^a no.   Del. ay.   Mary^d no.   V^a ay.   N. C. ay. S. C. ay.   Geo. ay.[1]

Doc^r FRANKLIN moved that what related to the compensation for the services of the Executive be postponed, in order to substitute— " whose necessary expences shall be defrayed, but who shall receive no salary, stipend fee or reward whatsoever for their services "—He said that being very sensible of the effect of age on his memory, he had been unwilling to trust to that for the observations which seemed to support his motion, and had reduced them to writing, that he might with the permission of the Committee read instead of speaking them.   Mr WILSON made an offer to read the paper, which was accepted—The following is a literal copy of the paper.

Sir.

It is with reluctance that I rise to express a disapprobation of any one article of the plan for which we are so much obliged to the honorable gentleman who laid it before us.   From its first reading I have borne a good will to it, and in general wished it success.   In this particular of salaries to the Executive branch I happen to differ; and as my opinion may appear new and chimerical, it is only from a persuasion that it is right, and from a sense of duty that I hazard it.   The Committee will judge of my reasons when they have heard them, and their judgment may possibly change mine.—I think I see inconveniences in the appointment of salaries; I see none in refusing them, but on the contrary, great advantages.

Sir, there are two passions which have a powerful influence on the affairs of men.   These are ambition and avarice; the love of power, and the love of money.   Separately each of these has great force in prompting men to action; but when united in view of the same object, they have in many minds the most violent effects.   Place before the eyes of such men, a post of *honour* that shall be at the same time a place of *profit,* and they will move heaven and earth to obtain it.   The vast number of such places it is that renders the British Government so tempestuous.   The struggles for them are the true sources of all those factions which are perpetually dividing the Nation, distracting its Councils, hurrying sometimes into fruitless &

---

[1] In the transcript the vote reads: " Massachusetts, Connecticut, New York, Delaware, Virginia, North Carolina, South Carolina, Georgia, aye—8; Pennsylvania, Maryland, no—2."

mischievous wars, and often compelling a submission to dishonorable terms of peace.

And of what kind are the men that will strive for this profitable pre-eminence, through all the bustle of cabal, the heat of contention, the infinite mutual abuse of parties, tearing to pieces the best of characters? It will not be the wise and moderate; the lovers of peace and good order, the men fittest for the trust. It will be the bold and the violent, the men of strong passions and indefatigable activity in their selfish pursuits. These will thrust themselves into your Government and be your rulers.—And these too will be mistaken in the expected happiness of their situation: For their vanquished competitors of the same spirit, and from the same motives will perpetually be endeavouring to distress their administration, thwart their measures, and render them odious to the people.

Besides these evils, Sir, tho' we may set out in the beginning with moderate salaries, we shall find that such will not be of long continuance. Reasons will never be wanting for proposed augmentations. And there will always be a party for giving more to the rulers, that the rulers may be able in return to give more to them.— Hence as all history informs us, there has been in every State & Kingdom a constant kind of warfare between the governing & governed: the one striving to obtain more for its support, and the other to pay less. And this has alone occasioned great convulsions, actual civil wars, ending either in dethroning of the Princes, or enslaving of the people. Generally indeed the ruling power carries its point, the revenues of princes constantly increasing, and we see that they are never satisfied, but always in want of more. The more the people are discontented with the oppression of taxes; the greater need the prince has of money to distribute among his partizans and pay the troops that are to suppress all resistance, and enable him to plunder at pleasure. There is scarce a king in a hundred who would not, if he could, follow the example of Pharoah, get first all the peoples money, then all their lands, and then make them and their children servants for ever. It will be said, that we don't propose to establish Kings. I know it. But there is a natural inclination in mankind to Kingly Government. It sometimes relieves them from Aristocratic domination. They had rather have one tyrant than five hundred. It gives more of the appearance of equality among Citizens, and that they like. I am apprehensive therefore, perhaps too apprehensive, that the Government of these States, may in future times, end in a Monarchy. But this Catastrophe I think may be long delayed, if in our proposed System we do not sow the seeds of contention, faction

& tumult, by making our posts of honor, places of profit. If we do, I fear that tho' we do employ at first a number, and not a single person, the number will in time be set aside, it will only nourish the fœtus of a King, as the honorable gentleman from Virginia very aptly expressed it, and a King will the sooner be set over us.

It may be imagined by some that this is an Utopian Idea, and that we can never find men to serve us in the Executive department, without paying them well for their services. I conceive this to be a mistake. Some existing facts present themselves to me, which incline me to a contrary opinion. The high Sheriff of a County in England is an honorable office, but it is not a profitable one. It is rather expensive and therefore not sought for. But yet, it is executed and well executed, and usually by some of the principal Gentlemen of the County. In France, the office of Counsellor or Member of their Judiciary Parliaments is more honorable. It is therefore purchased at a high price: There are indeed fees on the law proceedings, which are divided among them, but these fees do not amount to more than three per Cent on the sum paid for the place. Therefore as legal interest is there at five per C^t they in fact pay two per C^t for being allowed to do the Judiciary business of the Nation, which is at the same time entirely exempt from the burden of paying them any salaries for their services. I do not however mean to recommend this as an eligible mode for our Judiciary department. I only bring the instance to shew that the pleasure of doing good & serving their Country and the respect such conduct entitles them to, are sufficient motives with some minds to give up a great portion of their time to the public, without the mean inducement of pecuniary satisfaction.

Another instance is that of a respectable Society who have made the experiment, and practised it with success more than an [1] hundred years. I mean the Quakers. It is an established rule with them, that they are not to go to law; but in their controversies they must apply to their monthly, quarterly and yearly meetings. Committees of these sit with patience to hear the parties, and spend much time in composing their differences. In doing this, they are supported by a sense of duty, and the respect paid to usefulness. It is honorable to be so employed, but it was [2] never made profitable by salaries, fees, or perquisites. And indeed in all cases of public service the less the profit the greater the honor.

To bring the matter nearer home, have we not seen, the great and most important of our offices, that of General of our armies

---

[1] The word " one " is substituted in the transcript for " an."
[2] The word " is " is substituted in the transcript for " was."

executed for eight years together without the smallest salary, by a Patriot whom I will not now offend by any other praise; and this through fatigues and distresses in common with the other brave men his military friends & companions, and the constant anxieties peculiar to his station? And shall we doubt finding three or four men in all the U. States, with public spirit enough to bear sitting in peaceful Council for perhaps an equal term, merely to preside over our civil concerns, and see that our laws are duly executed. Sir, I have a better opinion of our Country. I think we shall never be without a sufficient number of wise and good men to undertake and execute well and faithfully the office in question.

Sir, The saving of the salaries that may at first be proposed is not an object with me. The subsequent mischiefs of proposing them are what I apprehend. And therefore it is, that I move the amendment. If it is not seconded or accepted I must be contented with the satisfaction of having delivered my opinion frankly and done my duty.

The motion was seconded by Col. HAMILTON with the view he said merely of bringing so respectable a proposition before the Committee, and which was besides enforced by arguments that had a certain degree of weight. No debate ensued, and the proposition was postponed for the consideration of the members. It was treated with great respect, but rather for the author of it, than from any apparent conviction of its expediency or practicability.

M: DICKENSON moved "that the Executive be made removeable by the National Legislature on the request of a majority of the Legislatures of individual States." It was necessary he said to place the power of removing somewhere. He did not like the plan of impeaching the Great officers of State. He did not know how provision could be made for removal of them in a better mode than that which he had proposed. He had no idea of abolishing the State Governments as some gentlemen seemed inclined to do. The happiness of this Country in his opinion required considerable powers to be left in the hands of the States.

M: BEDFORD seconded the motion.

M: SHERMAN contended that the National Legislature should have power to remove the Executive at pleasure.

M: MASON. Some mode of displacing an unfit magistrate is rendered indispensable by the fallibility of those who choose, as well as by the corruptibility of the man chosen. He opposed decidedly the making the Executive the mere creature of the Legislature as a violation of the fundamental principle of good Government.

M⁛ MADISON & M⁛ WILSON observed that it would leave an equality of agency in the small with the great States; that it would enable a minority of the people to prevent y.ᵉ removal of an officer who had rendered himself justly criminal in the eyes of a majority; that it would open a door for intrigues ag⁛ him in States where his administration tho' just might be unpopular, and might tempt him to pay court to particular States whose leading partizans he might fear, or wish to engage as his partizans. They both thought it bad policy to introduce such a mixture of the State authorities, where their agency could be otherwise supplied.

M⁛ DICKENSON considered the business as so important that no man ought to be silent or reserved. He went into a discourse of some length, the sum of which was, that the Legislative, Executive, & Judiciary departments ought to be made as independ⁛ as possible; but that such an Executive as some seemed to have in contemplation was not consistent with a republic: that a firm Executive could only exist in a limited monarchy. In the British Gov⁛ itself the weight of the Executive arises from the attachments which the Crown draws to itself, & not merely from the force of its prerogatives. In place of these attachments we must look out for something else. One source of stability is the double branch of the Legislature. The division of the Country into distinct States formed the other principal source of stability. This division ought therefore to be maintained, and considerable powers to be left with the States. This was the ground of his consolation for the future fate of his Country. Without this, and in case of a consolidation of the States into one great Republic, we might read its fate in the history of smaller ones. A limited Monarchy he considered as *one* of the best Governments in the world. It was not *certain* that the same blessings were derivable from any other form. It was certain that equal blessings had never yet been derived from any of the republican form. A limited Monarchy however was out of the question. The spirit of the times—the state of our affairs, forbade the experiment, if it were desireable. Was it possible moreover in the nature of things to introduce it even if these obstacles were less insuperable. A House of Nobles was essential to such a Gov⁛ could these be created by a breath, or by a stroke of the pen? No. They were the growth of ages, and could only arise under a complication of circumstances none of which existed in this Country. But though a form the most perfect *perhaps* in itself be unattainable, we must not despair. If antient republics have been found to flourish for a moment only & then vanish for ever, it only proves that they were badly constituted; and that we ought to seek for every remedy for their diseases. One of these remedies he conceived to be the accidental lucky division of this Country into distinct States; a division which some seemed desirous to abolish altogether. As to the point of representation in the national Legislature as it might affect States of different sizes, he said it must probably end in mutual concession. He hoped that each State would retain an equal voice at least in one branch of the National Legislature, and supposed the sums paid within each State would form a better ratio for the other branch than either the number of inhabitants or the quantum of property.

A motion being made to strike out "on request by a majority of the Legislatures of the individual States " and rejected, Connecticut, S. Carol: & Geo. being ay, the rest no: the question was taken—

On M⁚ Dickenson's motion for making ¹ Executive removeable by ¹ Nat⁚ Legislature at ¹ request of ² majority of State Legislatures ³ was also rejected—all the States being in the negative Except Delaware which gave an affirmative vote.

The Question for making yᵉ Executive ineligible after seven years,⁴ was next taken, and agreed to:

Mass⁚ᵗˢ ay. Con⁚ no. N. Y. ay. Pᵃ div⁴ Del. ay. Mary⁴ ay. Vᵃ ay. N. C. ay. S. C. ay. Geo. no: * ⁵

M⁚ Williamson 2ᵈᵉᵈ by M⁚ Davie moved to add to the last Clause, the words—" and to be removeable on impeachment & conviction of mal-practice or neglect of duty "—which was agreed to.

M⁚ Rutlidge & M⁚ C. Pinkney moved that the blank for the nᵒ of persons in the Executive be filled with the words " one person." He supposed the reasons to be so obvious & conclusive in favor of one that no member would oppose the motion.

M⁚ Randolph opposed it with great earnestness, declaring that he should not do justice to the Country which sent him if he were silently to suffer the establishm⁚ of a Unity in the Executive department. He felt an opposition to it which he believed he should con-

* In ⁶ printed Journal Geo. ay.

---

¹ The word " the " is here inserted in the transcript.
² The word " a " is here inserted in the transcript.
³ The word " which " is here inserted in the transcript.
⁴ The phrase " ineligible after seven years " is italicized in the transcript.
⁵ In the transcript the vote reads: " Massachusetts, New York, Delaware, Maryland, Virginia, North Carolina, South Carolina, aye—7; Connecticut, Georgia,* no—2; Pennsylvania, divided."
⁶ The word " the " is here inserted in the transcript.

tinue to feel as long as he lived. He urged 1.[1] that the permanent temper of the people was adverse to the very semblance of Monarchy. 2.[1] that a unity was unnecessary a plurality being equally competent to all the objects of the department. 3.[1] that the necessary confidence would never be reposed in a single Magistrate. 4.[1] that the appointments would generally be in favor of some inhabitant near the center of the Community, and consequently the remote parts would not be on an equal footing. He was in favor of three members of the Executive to be drawn from different portions of the Country.

M[r] BUTLER contended strongly for a single magistrate as most likely to answer the purpose of the remote parts. If one man should be appointed he would be responsible to the whole, and would be impartial to its interests. If three or more should be taken from as many districts, there would be a constant struggle for local advantages. In Military matters this would be particularly mischievous. He said his opinion on this point had been formed under the opportunity he had had of seeing the manner in which a plurality of military heads[2] distracted Holland when threatened with invasion by the imperial troops. One man was for directing the force to the defence of this part, another to that part of the Country, just as he happened to be swayed by prejudice or interest.

The motion was then postp[d] the Committee rose & the House Adj[d]

MONDAY JUNE 4.[3] IN COMMITTEE OF THE WHOLE.

The Question was resumed on motion of M[r] PINKNEY 2[ded] by [4] WILSON, " shall the blank for the number of the Executive be filled with a single person? "

M[r] WILSON was in favor of the motion. It had been opposed by the gentleman from Virg[a] [M[r] Randolph] but the arguments used had not convinced him. He observed that the objections of M[r] R. were levelled not so much ag[st] the measure itself, as ag[st] its unpopularity. If he could suppose that it would occasion a rejection of the plan of which it should form a part, though the part was[5] an

---

[1] The figures " 1," " 2," " 3 " and " 4 " are changed to " first," " secondly," " thirdly " and " fourthly."
[2] The transcript italicizes the phrase " plurality of military heads."
[3] The year " 1787 " is here inserted in the transcript.
[4] The transcript inserts the word " Mr." before " Wilson."
[5] The word " was " is changed to " were " in the transcript.

important one, yet he would give it up rather than lose the whole. On examination he could see no evidence of the alledged antipathy of the people. On the contrary he was persuaded that it does not exist. All know that a single magistrate is not a King. One fact has great weight with him. All the 13 States tho agreeing in scarce any other instance, agree in placing a single magistrate at the head of the Govern͗ The idea of three heads has taken place in none. The degree of power is indeed different; but there are no co-ordinate heads. In addition to his former reasons for preferring a unity, he would mention another. The *tranquility* not less than the vigor of the Gov͗ he thought would be favored by it. Among three equal members, he foresaw nothing but uncontrouled, continued, & violent animosities; which would not only interrupt the public administration; but diffuse their poison thro' the other branches of Gov͗, thro' the States, and at length thro' the people at large. If the members were to be unequal in power the principle of the [1] opposition to the unity was given up. If equal, the making them an odd number would not be a remedy. In Courts of Justice there are two sides only to a question. In the Legislative & Executive departm͗ questions have commonly many sides. Each member therefore might espouse a separate one & no two agree.

M͗ SHERMAN. This matter is of great importance and ought to be well considered before it is determined. M͗ Wilson he said had observed that in each State a single magistrate was placed at the head of the Gov͗ It was so he admitted, and properly so, and he wished the same policy to prevail in the federal Gov͗ But then it should be also remarked that in all the States there was a Council of advice, without which the first magistrate could not act. A council he thought necessary to make the establishment acceptable to the people. Even in G. B. the King has a Council; and though he appoints it himself, its advice has its weight with him, and attracts the Confidence of the people.

M͗ WILLIAMSON asks M͗ WILSON whether he means to annex a Council.

M͗ WILSON means to have no Council, which oftener serves to cover, than prevent malpractices.

M͗ GERRY was at a loss to discover the policy of three members for the Executive. It w͗ be extremely inconvenient in many instances, particularly in military matters, whether relating to the militia, an army, or a navy. It would be a general with three heads.

---

[1] The word " the " is omitted in the transcript.

On the question for a single Executive it was agreed to Mass⁺ˢ ay. Con⁺ ay. N. Y. no. Pen⁰ ay. Del. no. Mary⁴ no. Virg. ay. [M: R. & M: Blair no—Doc: M:C⁵ M: M. & Gen W. ay. Col. Mason being no, but not in house, M: Wythe ay but gone home]. N. C. ay. S. C. ay. Georg⁰ ay.[1]

First Clause of Proposition 8ᵗʰ.[2] relating *to a Council of Revision* taken into consideration.

M: GERRY doubts whether the Judiciary ought to form a part of it, as they will have a sufficient check ag⁵ᵗ encroachments on their own department by their exposition of the laws, which involved a power of deciding on their Constitutionality. In some States the Judges had actually set aside laws as being ag⁵ᵗ the Constitution. This was done too with general approbation. It was quite foreign from the nature of yᵉ office to make them judges of the policy of public measures. He moves to postpone the clause in order to propose '' that the National Executive shall have a right to negative any Legislative act which shall not be afterwards passed by   parts of each branch of the national Legislature.''

M: KING seconds the motion, observing that the Judges ought to be able to expound the law as it should come before them, free from the bias of having participated in its formation.

M: WILSON thinks neither the original proposition nor the amendment go far enough. If the Legislative Exetv & Judiciary ought to be distinct & independent. The Executive ought to have an absolute negative. Without such a self-defence the Legislature can at any moment sink it into non-existence. He was for varying the proposition in such a manner as to give the Executive & Judiciary jointly an absolute negative.

On the question to postpone in order to take M: Gerry's proposition into consideration it was agreed to, Mass⁵ ay. Con⁺ no. N. Y. ay. P⁰ ay. Del. no. Mary⁴ no. Virg⁰ no. N. C. ay. S. C. ay. G⁰ ay.[3]

M: GERRY's proposition being now before[4] Committee, M: WILSON & M: HAMILTON move that the last part of it [viz. '' wᶜʰ s: not be

---

[1] In the transcript the vote reads: '' Massachusetts, Connecticut, Pennsylvania, Virginia, (Mr. Randolph and Mr. Blair, no; Doctor McClurg, Mr. Madison, and General Washington, aye; Colonel Mason being no, but not in the House, Mr. Wythe, aye, but gone home), North Carolina, South Carolina, Georgia, aye—7; New York, Delaware, Maryland, no—3.''

[2] The phrase '' the eighth Resolution '' is substituted in the transcript for '' Proposition 8ᵗʰ ''

[3] In the transcript the vote reads: '' Massachusetts, New York, Pennsylvania, North Carolina, South Carolina, Georgia, aye—6; Connecticut, Delaware, Maryland, Virginia, no—4.''

[4] The word '' the '' is here inserted in the transcript.

afterw.^ds passed unless [1] by ___ parts of each branch of the National legislature] be struck out, so as to give the Executive an absolute negative on the laws. There was no danger they thought of such a power being too much exercised. It was mentioned by Col: HAMILTON that the King of G. B. had not exerted his negative since the Revolution.

Mr GERRY sees no necessity for so great a controul over the legislature as the best men in the Community would be comprised in the two branches of it.

Doc.^r FRANKLIN, said he was sorry to differ from his colleague for whom he had a very great respect, on any occasion, but he could not help it on this. He had had some experience of this check in the Executive on the Legislature, under the proprietary Government of Pen.^a The negative of the Governor was constantly made use of to extort money. No good law whatever could be passed without a private bargain with him. An increase of his salary, or some donation, was always made a condition; till at last it became the regular practice, to have orders in his favor on the Treasury, presented along with the bills to be signed, so that he might actually receive the former before he should sign the latter. When the Indians were scalping the western people, and notice of it arrived, the concurrence of the Governor in the means of self-defence could not be got, till it was agreed that his Estate should be exempted from taxation: so that the people were to fight for the security of his property, whilst he was to bear no share of the burden. This was a mischievous sort of check. If the Executive was to have a Council, such a power would be less objectionable. It was true, the King of G. B. had not, as was said, exerted his negative since the Revolution; but that matter was easily explained. The bribes and emoluments now given to the members of parliament rendered it unnecessary, every thing being done according to the will of the Ministers. He was afraid, if a negative should be given as proposed, that more power and money would be demanded, till at last eno' would be gotten [2] to influence & bribe the Legislature into a compleat subjection to the will of the Executive.

Mr SHERMAN was ag.^st enabling any one man to stop the will of the whole. No one man could be found so far above all the rest in wisdom. He thought we ought to avail ourselves of his wisdom in revising the laws, but not permit him to overule the decided and cool opinions of the Legislature.

---

[1] The word "unless" is crossed out in the transcript.
[2] In the transcript the syllable "ten" is stricken from the word "gotten."

M.ʳ MADISON supposed that if a proper proportion of each branch should be required to overrule the objections of the Executive, it would answer the same purpose as an absolute negative. It would rarely if ever happen that the Executive constituted as ours is proposed to be would, have firmness eno' to resist the legislature, unless backed by a certain part of the body itself. The King of G. B. with all his splendid attributes would not be able to withstand y.ᵉ unanimous and eager wishes of both houses of Parliament. To give such a prerogative would certainly be obnoxious to the temper of this Country; its present temper at least.

M.ʳ WILSON believed as others did that this power would seldom be used. The Legislature would know that such a power existed, and would refrain from such laws, as it would be sure to defeat. Its silent operation would therefore preserve harmony and prevent mischief. The case of Pen.ᵃ formerly was very different from its present case. The Executive was not then as now to be appointed by the people. It will not in this case as in the one cited be supported by the head of a Great Empire, actuated by a different & sometimes opposite interest. The salary too is now proposed to be fixed by the Constitution, or if D.ʳ F.'s idea should be adopted all salary whatever interdicted. The requiring a large proportion of each House to overrule the Executive check might do in peaceable times; but there might be tempestuous moments in which animosities may run high between the Executive and Legislative branches, and in which the former ought to be able to defend itself.

M.ʳ BUTLER had been in favor of a single Executive Magistrate; but could he have entertained an idea that a compleat negative on the laws was to be given him he certainly should have acted very differently. It had been observed that in all countries the Executive power is in a constant course of increase. This was certainly the case in G. B. Gentlemen seemed to think that we had nothing to apprehend from an abuse of the Executive power. But why might not a Cataline or a Cromwell arise in this Country as well as in others.

M.ʳ BEDFORD was opposed to every check on the Legislative,[1] even the Council of Revision first proposed. He thought it would be sufficient to mark out in the Constitution the boundaries to the Legislative Authority, which would give all the requisite security to the rights of the other departments. The Representatives of the people were the best Judges of what was for their interest, and ought to

---

[1] In the transcript the syllable "tive" is stricken from the word "Legislative" and "ture" is written above it.

be under no external controul whatever. The two branches would produce a sufficient controul within the Legislature itself.

   Col. MASON observed that a vote had already passed he found
[he was out at the time] for vesting the executive powers in a single
person. Among these powers was that of appointing to offices in
certain cases. The probable abuses of a negative had been well explained by Dr F. as proved by experience, the best of all tests.
Will not the same door be opened here. The Executive may refuse
its assent to necessary measures till new appointments shall be referred to him; and having by degrees engrossed all these into his
own hands, the American Executive, like the British, will by bribery
& influence, save himself the trouble & odium of exerting his negative afterwards. We are Mr Chairman going very far in this business. We are not indeed constituting a British Government, but a
more dangerous monarchy, an elective one. We are introducing a
new principle into our system, and not necessary as in the British
Govt where the Executive has greater rights to defend. Do gentlemen mean to pave the way to hereditary Monarchy? Do they flatter
themselves that the people will ever consent to such an innovation?
If they do I venture to tell them, they are mistaken. The people
never will consent. And do gentlemen consider the danger of delay,
and the still greater danger of a a rejection, not for a moment but
forever, of the plan which shall be proposed to them. Notwithstanding
the oppressions & injustice experienced among us from democracy;
the genius of the people is in favor of it, and the genius of the
people must be consulted. He could not but consider the federal
system as in effect dissolved by the appointment of this Convention
to devise a better one. And do gentlemen look forward to the dangerous interval between the extinction of an old, and the establishment
of a new Governmt and to the scenes of confusion which may ensue.
He hoped that nothing like a Monarchy would ever be attempted in
this Country. A hatred to its oppressions had carried the people
through the late Revolution. Will it not be eno' to enable the Executive to suspend offensive laws, till they shall be coolly revised, and
the objections to them overruled by a greater majority than was required in the first instance. He never could agree to give up all the
rights of the people to a single Magistrate. If more than one had
been fixed on, greater powers might have been entrusted to the
Executive. He hoped this attempt to give such powers would have
its weight hereafter as an argument for increasing the number of
the Executive.

   Doct FRANKLIN. A Gentleman from S. C. [Mr Butler] a day or

two ago called our attention to the case of the U. Netherlands. He wished the gentleman had been a little fuller, and had gone back to the original of that Gov.ᵗ The people being under great obligations to the Prince of Orange whose wisdom and bravery had saved them, chose him for the Stadtholder. He did very well. Inconveniences however were felt from his powers; which growing more & more oppressive, they were at length set aside. Still however there was a party for the P. of Orange, which descended to his son who excited insurrections, spilt a great deal of blood, murdered the de Witts, and got the powers revested in the Stadtholder. Afterwards another Prince had power to excite insurrections & to¹ make the Stadtholdership hereditary. And the present Stadth.ᵈᵉʳ is ready to wade thro a bloody civil war to the establishment of a monarchy. Col. Mason had mentioned the circumstance of appointing officers. He knew how that point would be managed. No new appointment would be suffered as heretofore in Pens.ᵃ unless it be referred to the Executive; so that all profitable offices will be at his disposal. The first man put at the helm will be a good one. No body knows what sort may come afterwards. The Executive will be always increasing here, as elsewhere, till it ends in a Monarchy

On the question for striking out so as to give ² Executive an absolute negative—Mass.ᵗˢ no. Con.ᵗ no. N. Y. no. P.ᵃ no. Dl. no. M.ᵈ no. V.ᵃ no. N. C. no. S. C. no. Georg.ᵃ no.³

M.ʳ BUTLER moved that the Resol.ⁿ be altered so as to read—"Resolved that the National Executive have a power to suspend any Legislative act for the term of   ."

Doct.ʳ FRANKLIN seconds the motion.

M.ʳ GERRY observed that a ⁴ power of suspending might do all the mischief dreaded from the negative of useful laws; without answering the salutary purpose of checking unjust or unwise ones.

On ² question "for giving this suspending power" all the States, to wit Mass.ᵗˢ Con.ᵗ N. Y. P.ᵃ Del. Mary.ᵈ Virg.ᵃ N. C. S. C. Georgia, were *No.*

On a question for enabling *two thirds* of each branch of the Legislature to overrule the revisionary ⁵ check: it passed in the affirma-

---

¹ The word "to" is omitted in the transcript.
² The word "the" is here inserted in the transcript.
³ In the transcript the vote reads "Massachusetts, Connecticut, New York, Pennsylvania, Delaware, Maryland, Virginia, North Carolina, South Carolina, Georgia, no—10."
⁴ The word "the" is substituted in the transcript for "a."
⁵ In the transcript the word "provisionary" was erroneously used in place of "revisionary."

tive sub silentio; and was inserted in the blank of M: Gerry's motion.

On the question on M: Gerry's motion which gave the Executive alone without the Judiciary the revisionary controul on the laws unless overruled by ⅔ of each branch; Mass⁵⁵ ay. Con⁵ no. N. Y. ay. P: ay. Del. ay. Mary⁴ no. V⁴ ay. N. C. ay. S. C. ay. Geo. ay.[1]

It was moved by M: WILSON 2ᵈᵉᵈ by M: MADISON—that the following amendment be made to the last resolution—after the words "National Ex." to add "& a convenient number of the National Judiciary."

An objection of order being taken by M: HAMILTON to the introduction of the last amendment at this time, notice was given by M: W. & M: M.—that the same wᵈ be moved tomorrow,—whereupon Wednesday (the day after)[2] was assigned to reconsider the amendment of M: Gerry.

It was then moved & 2ᵈᵉᵈ to proceed to the consideration of the 9ᵗʰ resolution submitted by M: Randolph—when on motion to agree to the first clause namely " Resolved that a National Judiciary be established "[3] It passed in the affirmative nem. con.

It was then moved & 2ᵈᵉᵈ to add these words to the first clause of the ninth resolution namely—" to consist of one supreme tribunal, and of one or more inferior tribunals," which passed in the affirmative—

The Comm⁵ then rose and the House
Adjourned.

TEUSDAY JUNE 5.   IN COMMITTEE OF THE WHOLE.

Governor Livingston from [4] New Jersey, took his seat.

The words, " one or more " were struck out before " inferior tribunals " as an amendment to the last clause of Resol⁵ 9ᵗʰ [5] The Clause—" that the National Judiciary be chosen by the National Legislature," being under consideration.

M: WILSON opposed the appointm⁵ of Judges by the National Legisl: Experience shewed the impropriety of such appointm⁵ˢ by numerous bodies. Intrigue, partiality, and concealment were the

---

[1] In the transcript this vote reads: " Massachusetts, New York, Pennsylvania, Delaware, Virginia, North Carolina, South Carolina, Georgia, aye—8; Connecticut, Maryland, no—2."

[2] The phrase " (the day after) " is crossed out in the transcript.

[3] The phrase "Resolved that a National Judiciary be established" is italicized in the transcript.

[4] The word "of" is substituted in the transcript for " from."

[5] The phrase "the ninth Resolution" is used in the transcript in place of " Resol⁵ 9ᵗʰ "

necessary consequences. A principal reason for unity in the Executive was that officers might be appointed by a single, responsible person.

M.ʳ RUTLIDGE was by no means disposed to grant so great a power to any single person. The people will think we are leaning too much towards Monarchy. He was against establishing any national tribunal except a single supreme one. The State tribunals are most proper to decide in all cases in the first instance.

Docʳ FRANKLIN observed that two modes of chusing the Judges had been mentioned, to wit, by the Legislature and by the Executive. He wished such other modes to be suggested as might occur to other gentlemen; it being a point of great moment. He would mention one which he had understood was practiced in Scotland. He then in a brief and entertaining manner related a Scotch mode, in which the nomination proceeded from the Lawyers, who always selected the ablest of the profession in order to get rid of him, and share his practice among themselves. It was here he said the interest of the electors to make the best choice, which should always be made the case if possible.

Mr. MADISON disliked the election of the Judges by the Legislature or any numerous body. Besides, the danger of intrigue and partiality, many of the members were not judges of the requisite qualifications. The Legislative talents which were very different from those of a Judge, commonly recommended men to the favor of Legislative Assemblies. It was known too that the accidental circumstances of presence and absence, of being a member or not a member, had a very undue influence on the appointment. On the other hand he was not satisfied with referring the appointment to the Executive. He rather inclined to give it to the Senatorial branch, as numerous eno' to be confided in—as not so numerous as to be governed by the motives of the other branch; and as being sufficiently stable and independent to follow their deliberate judgments. He hinted this only and moved that the *appointment by the Legislature* might be struck out, & a blank left to be hereafter filled on maturer reflection. M.ʳ WILSON seconds it. On the question for striking out. Massᵗˢ. ay. Conᵗ no. N. Y. ay. N. J. ay. Penᵃ. ay. Del. ay. M.ᵈ ay. V.ᵃ ay. N. C. ay. S. C. no. Geo. ay.[1]

M.ʳ WILSON gave notice that he should at a future day move for a reconsideration of that clause which respects " inferior tribunals."

---

[1] In the transcript the vote reads: " Massachusetts, New York, New Jersey, Pennsylvania, Delaware, Maryland, Virginia, North Carolina, South Carolina, no, Georgia, aye—9; Connecticut, South Carolina,—2."

M? PINKNEY gave notice that when the clause respecting the appointment of the Judiciary should again come before the Committee he should move to restore the " appointment by the national Legislature."

The following clauses of Resol: 9.[1] were agreed to viz " to hold their offices during good behaviour, and to receive punctually at stated times, a fixed compensation for their services, in which no increase or diminution shall be made so as to affect the persons actually in office at the time of such increase or diminution."

The remaining clause of Resolution 9.[2] was posponed.

Resolution 10[3] was agreed to—viz—that provision ought to be made for the admission of States lawfully arising within the limits of the U. States, whether from a voluntary junction of Government & territory, or otherwise, with the consent of a number of voices in the National Legislature less than the whole.

The 11. propos:[4] " *for guarantying to States Republican Gov.* & *territory* &c., being read, M? PATTERSON wished the point of representation could be decided before this clause should be considered, and moved to postpone it: which was not opposed, and agreed to: Connecticut & S. Carolina only voting ag.st it.

Propos. 12[5] " *for continuing Cong.; till a given day and for fulfilling their engagements,*" produced no debate.

On the question, Mass. ay. Con.t no. N. Y. ay. N. J.* ay. P.a ay. Del. no. M.d ay. V.a ay. N. C. ay. S. C. ay. G. ay.

Propos: 13.[6] " that *provision ought to be made for hereafter amending the system now to be established, without requiring the assent of the Nat.l Legislature,*" being taken up,

M? PINKNEY doubted the propriety or necessity of it.

M? GERRY favored it. The novelty & difficulty of the experiment requires periodical revision. The prospect of such a revision would also give intermediate stability to the Gov.t Nothing had yet happened in the States where this provision existed to prove its impropriety.—The proposition was postponed for further consideration:

---

* New Jersey omitted in the printed Journal.

---

[1] The transcript uses the phrase " the ninth Resolution " in place of " Resol: 9," and italicizes the resolution.

[2] The transcript here uses the phrase " the ninth Resolution."

[3] The phrase " The tenth Resolution " is here used in the transcript.

[4] In place of the words " The 11. propos: " the transcript reads: " The eleventh Resolution."

[5] The transcript changes " Propos. 12 " to " The twelfth Resolution."

[6] The transcript changes " Propos: 13 " to read as follows: " The thirteenth Resolution, to the effect."

the votes being, Mas: Con. N. Y. P? Del. Ma. N. C.—ay Virg? S. C.
Geo: no
   Propos. 14.[1] " *requiring oath from the State officers to support
National Gov*" was postponed after a short uninteresting conversa-
tion: the votes, Con. N. Jersey. M? Virg: S. C. Geo. ay N. Y. P?
Del. N. C. - - - no Massachusetts - - - divided.
   Propos. 15 [2] for " *recommending Conventions under appointment
of the people to ratify the new Constitution* " &c. being taken up.
   M? SHARMAN thought such a popular ratification unnecessary: the
articles of Confederation providing for changes and alterations with
the assent of Cong? and ratification of State Legislatures.
   M? MADISON thought this provision essential. The articles of
Confed? themselves were defective in this respect, resting in many
of the States on the Legislative sanction only. Hence in conflicts
between acts of the States, and of Cong? especially where the former
are of posterior date, and the decision is to be made by State tribunals, an uncertainty must necessaily prevail, or rather perhaps
a certain decision in favor of the State authority. He suggested
also that as far as the articles of Union were to be considered as
a Treaty only of a particular sort, among the Governments of Independent States, the doctrine might be set up that a breach of any
one article, by any of the parties, absolved the other parties from
the whole obligation. For these reasons as well as others he thought
it indispensable that the new Constitution should be ratified in the
most unexceptionable form, and by the supreme authority of the
people themselves.
   M? GERRY observed that in the Eastern States the Confed? had
been sanctioned by the people themselves. He seemed afraid of
referring the new system to them. The people in that quarter have
at this time the wildest ideas of Government in the world. They
were for abolishing the Senate in Mass[ts] and giving all the other
powers of Gov? to the other branch of the Legislature.
   M? KING supposed that the last article of y[e] Confed? rendered
the legislature competent to the ratification. The people of the
Southern States where the federal articles had been ratified by the
Legislatures only, had since *impliedly* given their sanction to it.
He thought notwithstanding that there might be policy in varying
the mode. A Convention being a single house, the adoption may
more easily be carried thro' it, than thro' the Legislatures where
there are several branches. The Legislatures also being to lose

---

[1] The transcript changes " Propos. 14 " to " The fourteenth Resolution."
[2] The transcript changes " Propos. 15 " to " The fifteenth Resolution."

power, will be most likely to raise objections. The people having already parted with the necessary powers it is immaterial to them, by which Government they are possessed, provided they be well employed.

M͞r WILSON took this occasion to lead the Committee by a train of observations to the idea of not suffering a disposition in the plurality of States to confederate anew on better principles, to be defeated by the inconsiderate or selfish opposition of a few States. He hoped the provision for ratifying would be put on such a footing as to admit of such a partial union, with a door open for the accession of the rest.*

M͞r PINKNEY hoped that in case the experiment should not unanimously take place, nine States might be authorized to unite under the same Govern͞t

The propos. 15.[2] was postponed nem. con͞t

M͞r PINKNEY & M͞r RUTLIDGE moved that tomorrow be assigned to reconsider that clause of Propos. 4:[3] which respects the election of the first branch of the National Legislature—which passed in [4] affirmative: Con: N. Y. P͞a Del: M͞d V͞a—ay—6 Mas. N. J. N. C. S. C. Geo. no. 5.

M͞r RUTLIDGE hav͞g obtained a rule for reconsideration of the clause for establishing *inferior* tribunals under the national authority, now moved that that part of the clause in propos. 9.[5] should be expunged: arguing that the State Tribunals might and ought to be left in all cases to decide in the first instance the right of appeal to the supreme national tribunal being sufficient to secure the national rights & uniformity of Judgm͞ts: that it was making an unnecessary encroachment on the jurisdiction of the States and creating unnecessary obstacles to their adoption of the new system.—M͞r SHERMAN 2͞ded the motion.

M͞r MADISON observed that unless inferior tribunals were dispersed throughout the Republic with *final* jurisdiction in *many* cases, appeals would be multiplied to a most oppressive degree; that besides, an appeal would not in many cases be a remedy. What was to be done after improper Verdicts in State tribunals obtained under

---

* The note in brackets to be transferred to bottom margin.[1]
[This hint was probably meant in terrorem to the smaller States of N. Jersey & Delaware. Nothing was said in reply to it.]

---

[1] Madison's direction is omitted in the transcript.
[2] The transcript changes " The propos. 15 " to " The fifteenth Resolution."
[3] The transcript changes " Propos. 4 " to " the fourth Resolution."
[4] The word " the " is here inserted in the transcript.
[5] The transcript changes " propos. 9 " to " the ninth Resolution."

the biassed directions of a dependent Judge, or the local prejudices
of an undirected jury? To remand the cause for a new trial would
answer no purpose. To order a new trial at the Supreme bar would
oblige the parties to bring up their witnesses, tho' ever so distant
from the seat of the Court. An effective Judiciary establishment
commensurate to the legislative authority, was essential. A Government without a proper Executive & Judiciary would be the mere
trunk of a body, without arms or legs to act or move.

M⦂ Wilson opposed the motion on like grounds. he said the
admiralty jurisdiction ought to be given wholly to the national Government, as it related to cases not within the jurisdiction of particular states, & to a scene in which controversies with foreigners
would be most likely to happen.

M⦂ Sherman was in favor of the motion. He dwelt chiefly on the
supposed expensiveness of having a new set of Courts, when the
existing State Courts would answer the same purpose.

M⦂ Dickinson contended strongly that if there was to be a National
Legislature, there ought to be a national Judiciary, and that the
former ought to have authority to institute the latter.

On the question for M⦂ Rutlidge's motion to strike out '' inferior
tribunals ''[1]

Mass⦂ divided. Con⦂ ay. N. Y. div⦂ N. J. ay. P⦂ no. Del. no.
M⦂ no. V⦂ no. N. C. ay. S. C. ay. Geo. ay.[2]

M⦂ Wilson & M⦂ Madison then moved, in pursuance of the idea
expressed above by M⦂ Dickinson, to add to Resol: 9.[3] the words
following '' that the National Legislature be empowered to institute
inferior tribunals.'' They observed that there was a distinction between establishing such tribunals absolutely, and giving a discretion
to the Legislature to establish or not establish them. They repeated
the necessity of some such provision.

M⦂ Butler. The people will not bear such innovations. The
States will revolt at such encroachments. Supposing such an establishment to be useful, we must not venture on it. We must follow
the example of Solon who gave the Athenians not the best Gov⦂ he
could devise; but the best they w⦂ receive.

M⦂ King remarked as to the comparative expence that the estab-

---

[1] The phrase " it passed in the affirmative " is here inserted in the transcript.
[2] In the transcript the vote reads: " Connecticut, New York, New Jersey,
North Carolina, South Carolina, Georgia, aye—5; Pennsylvania, Delaware,
Maryland, Virginia, no—4; Massachusetts, divided." New York which was
" divided " was erroneously placed among the " ayes " in copying, although the
number was correctly given as " 5."
[3] The transcript changes " Resol: 9 " to " the ninth Resolution."

lishment of inferior tribunals w^d cost infinitely less than the appeals that would be prevented by them.

On this question as moved by Mr W. & M^r M.

Mass. ay. C^t no. N. Y. div^d N. J.* ay. P^a ay. Del. ay. M^d ay. V^a ay. N. C. ay. S. C. no. Geo. ay.

The Committee then rose & the House adjourned to 11 OC tom^w [1]

WEDNESDAY JUNE 6TH IN COMMITTEE OF THE WHOLE.

Mr PINKNEY according to previous notice & rule obtained, moved " that the first branch of the national Legislature be elected by the State Legislatures, and not by the people." contending that the people were less fit Judges in such a case, and that the Legislatures would be less likely to promote the adoption of the new Government, if they were to be excluded from all share in it.

Mr RUTLIDGE 2^ded the motion.

Mr GERRY. Much depends on the mode of election. In England, the people will probably lose their liberty from the smallness of the proportion having a right of suffrage. Our danger arises from the opposite extreme: hence in Mass^ts the worst men get into the Legislature. Several members of that Body had lately been convicted of infamous crimes. Men of indigence, ignorance & baseness, spare no pains, however dirty to carry their point ag^st men who are superior to the artifices practised. He was not disposed to run into extremes. He was as much principled as ever ag^st aristocracy and monarchy. It was necessary on the one hand that the people should appoint one branch of the Gov^t in order to inspire them with the necessary confidence. But he wished the election on the other to be so modified as to secure more effectually a just preference of merit. His idea was that the people should nominate certain persons in certain districts, out of whom the State Legislatures sh^d make the appointment.

Mr WILSON. He wished for vigor in the Gov^t, but he wished that vigorous authority to flow immediately from the legitimate source of all authority. The Gov^t ought to possess not only 1st the *force*, but 2dly the *mind or sense* of the people at large. The Legislature ought to be the most exact transcript of the whole Society. Representation is made necessary only because it is impossible for the people to act collectively. The opposition was to be expected he said from the

---

* In the printed Journal N. Jersey—no.

[1] The transcript omits the phrase " to 11 OC tom^w "

Governments, not from the Citizens of the States. The latter had parted as was observed [by M: King] with all the necessary powers;[1] and it was immaterial to them, by whom they were exercised, if well exercised. The State officers were to be the losers of power. The people he supposed would be rather more attached to the national Gov: than to the State Gov:[s] as being more important in itself, and more flattering to their pride. There is no danger of improper elections if made by *large* districts. Bad elections proceed from the smallness of the districts which give an opportunity to bad men to intrigue themselves into office.

M: Sherman. If it were in view to abolish the State Gov:[s] the elections ought to be by the people. If the State Gov:[s] are to be continued, it is necessary in order to preserve harmony between the National & State Gov:[s] that the elections to the former sh:[d] be made by the latter. The right of participating in the National Gov: would be sufficiently secured to the people by their election of the State Legislatures. The objects of the Union, he thought were few. 1.[2] defence ag:[st] foreign danger. 2[2] ag:[st] internal disputes & a resort to force. 3.[2] Treaties with foreign nations. 4[2] regulating foreign commerce, & drawing revenue from it. These & perhaps a few lesser objects alone rendered a Confederation of the States necessary. All other matters civil & criminal would be much better in the hands of the States. The people are more happy in small than [3] large States. States may indeed be too small as Rhode Island, & thereby be too subject to faction. Some others were perhaps too large, the powers of Gov: not being able to pervade them. He was for giving the General Gov: power to legislate and execute within a defined province.

Col. Mason. Under the existing Confederacy, Cong:[s] represent the *States* [4] not the *people* of the States: their acts operate on the *States,* not on the individuals.[5] The case will be changed in the new plan of Gov: The people will be represented; they ought therefore to choose the Representatives. The requisites in actual representation are that the Rep:[s] should sympathize with their constituents; sh:[d] think as they think, & feel as they feel; and that for these purposes sh:[d] even be residents among them. Much he s:[d] had been alledged ag:[st] democratic elections. He admitted that much might be said; but

---

[1] The phrase " with all the necessary powers " is italicized in the transcript.
[2] The figures " 1," " 2," " 3 " and " 4 " are changed to " first," " secondly," etc. in the transcript.
[3] The word " in " is here inserted in the transcript.
[4] The word " and " is here inserted in the transcript.
[5] The transcript italicizes the word " individuals."

it was to be considered that no Gov.^t was free from imperfections & evils; and that improper elections in many instances, were inseparable from Republican Gov.^{ts} But compare these with the advantage of this Form in favor of the rights of the people, in favor of human nature. He was persuaded there was a better chance for proper elections by the people, if divided into large districts, than by the State Legislatures. Paper money had been issued by the latter when the former were against it. Was it to be supposed that the State Legislatures then w.^d not send to the Nat.^l legislature patrons of such projects, if the choice depended on them.

Mr MADISON considered an election of one branch at least of the Legislature by the people immediately, as a clear principle of free Gov.^t and that this mode under proper regulations had the additional advantage of securing better representatives, as well as of avoiding too great an agency of the State Governments in the General one.—He differed from the member from Connecticut [Mr Sharman] in thinking the objects mentioned to be all the principal ones that required a National Gov.^t Those were certainly important and necessary objects; but he combined with them the necessity of providing more effectually for the security of private rights, and the steady dispensation of Justice. Interferences with these were evils which had more perhaps than any thing else, produced this convention. Was it to be supposed that republican liberty could long exist under the abuses of it practised in some of the States. The gentleman [Mr Sharman] had admitted that in a very small State, faction & oppression w.^d prevail. It was to be inferred then that wherever these prevailed the State was too small. Had they not prevailed in the largest as well as the smallest tho' less than in the smallest; and were we not thence admonished to enlarge the sphere as far as the nature of the Gov.^t would admit. This was the only defence ag.st the inconveniencies of democracy consistent with the democratic form of Gov.^t All civilized Societies would be divided into different Sects, Factions, & interests, as they happened to consist of rich & poor, debtors & creditors, the landed, the manufacturing, the commercial interests, the inhabitants of this district or that district, the followers of this political leader or that political leader, the disciples of this religious Sect or that religious Sect. In all cases where a majority are united by a common interest or passion, the rights of the minority are in danger. What motives are to restrain them? A prudent regard to the maxim that honesty is the best policy is found by experience to be as little regarded by bodies of men as by individuals. Respect for character is always diminished in proportion to the number among whom the blame or praise is to be divided. Conscience, the only remaining tie, is known to be inadequate in individuals: In large numbers, little is to be expected from it. Besides, Religion itself may become a motive to persecution & oppression.—These observations are verified by the Histories of every Country antient & modern. In Greece & Rome the rich & poor, the creditors & debtors, as well as the patricians & plebeians alternately oppressed each other with equal unmercifulness. What a source of oppression was the relation between the parent cities of Rome, Athens & Carthage, & their respective provinces: the former possessing the power, & the latter being sufficiently distinguished to be separate objects of it? Why was America so justly apprehensive of Parliamentary injustice? Because G. Britain had a separate interest real or supposed, & if her authority had been admitted, could have pursued that interest at our expence. We have seen the mere distinction of colour made in the most enlightened period of time, a ground of the most oppressive dominion ever exercised by man over man. What has been the source of those unjust laws complained of among ourselves? Has it not been the real or supposed interest of the major number? Debtors have defrauded their creditors. The landed interest has borne hard on the mercantile interest. The Holders of one species of property have thrown a disproportion of taxes on the holders of another species. The lesson we are to draw from the whole is that where a majority are united by a common sentiment, and have an opportunity, the rights of the minor party become insecure. In a Republican Gov^t the Majority if united have always an opportunity. The only remedy is to enlarge the sphere, & thereby divide the community into so great a number of interests & parties, that in the 1st place a majority will not be likely at the same moment to have a common interest separate from that of the whole or of the minority; and in the 2^d place, that in case they sh^d have such an interest, they may not be [1] apt to unite in the pursuit of it. It was incumbent on us then to try this remedy, and with that view to frame a republican system on such a scale & in such a form as will controul all the evils wch have been experienced.

Mr DICKENSON considered it as [2] essential that one branch of the Legislature sh^d be drawn ·immediately from the people; and as expedient that the other sh^d be chosen by the Legislatures of the States. This combination of the State Gov^{ts} with the national Gov^t was as politic as it was unavoidable. In the formation of the

---

[1] The word " so " is here inserted in the transcript.
[2] The word " as " is omitted in the transcript.

Senate we ought to carry it through such a refining process as will assimilate it as near as may be to the House of Lords in England. He repeated his warm eulogiums on the British Constitution. He was for a strong National Gov! but for leaving the States a considerable agency in the System. The objection ag!t making the former dependent on the latter might be obviated by giving to the Senate an authority permanent & irrevocable for three, five or seven years. Being thus independent they will speak[1] & decide with becoming freedom.

M! READ. Too much attachment is betrayed to the State Govern!t We must look beyond their continuance. A national Gov! must soon of necessity swallow all of them[2] up. They will soon be reduced to the mere office of electing the National Senate. He was ag!t patching up the old federal System: he hoped the idea w? be dismissed. It would be like putting new cloth on an old garment. The confederation was founded on temporary principles. It cannot last: it cannot be amended. If we do not establish a good Gov! on new principles, we must either go to ruin, or have the work to do over again. The people at large are wrongly suspected of being averse to a Gen! Gov! The aversion lies among interested men who possess their confidence.

M! PIERCE was for an election by the people as to the 1!t branch & by the States as to the 2d branch; by which means the Citizens of the States w? be represented both *individually* & *collectively.*

General PINKNEY wished to have a good National Gov! & at the same time to leave a considerable share of power in the States. An election of either branch by the people scattered as they are in many States, particularly in S. Carolina was totally impracticable. He differed from gentlemen who thought that a choice by the people w? be a better guard ag!t bad measures, than by the Legislatures. A majority of the people in S. Carolina were notoriously for paper money as a legal tender; the Legislature had refused to make it a legal tender. The reason was that the latter had some sense of character and were restrained by that consideration. The State Legislatures also he said would be more jealous, & more ready to thwart the National Gov!, if excluded from a participation in it. The Idea of abolishing these Legislatures w? never go down.

M! WILSON, would not have spoken again, but for what had fallen from M! Read; namely, that the idea of preserving the State Gov!s ought to be abandoned. He saw no incompatibility between the

---

[1] The word " check " is substituted in the transcript for " speak."
[2] The words " them all " are substituted in the transcript for " all of them."

National & State Gov^{ts} provided the latter were restrained to certain local purposes; nor any probability of their being devoured by the former. In all confederated Systems antient & modern the reverse had happened; the Generality being destroyed gradually by the usurpations of the parts composing it.

On the question for electing the 1st branch by the State Legislatures as moved by Mr Pinkney: it was negatived:

Mass. no. C^t ay. N. Y. no. N. J. ay. P^a no. Del. no. M^d no. V^a no. N. C. no. S. C. ay. Geo. no.[1]

Mr WILSON moved to reconsider the vote excluding the Judiciary from a share in the revision of the laws, and to add after " National Executive " the words " with a convenient number of the national Judiciary "; remarking the expediency of reinforcing the Executive with the influence of that Department.

Mr MADISON 2^{ded} the motion. He observed that the great difficulty in rendering the Executive competent to its own defence arose from the nature of Republican Gov^t which could not give to an individual citizen that settled pre-eminence in the eyes of the rest, that weight of property, that personal interest agst betraying the national interest, which appertain to an hereditary magistrate. In a Republic personal merit alone could be the ground of political exaltation, but it would rarely happen that this merit would be so pre-eminent as to produce universal acquiescence. The Executive Magistrate would be envied & assailed by disappointed competitors: His firmness therefore w^d need support. He would not possess those great emoluments from his station, nor that permanent stake in the public interest which w^d place him out of the reach of foreign corruption: He would stand in need therefore of being controuled as well as supported. An association of the Judges in his revisionary function w^d both double the advantage and diminish the danger. It w^d also enable the Judiciary Department the better to defend itself agst Legislative encroachments. Two objections had been made 1st that the Judges ought not to be subject to the bias which a participation in the making of laws might give in the exposition of them. 2dly that the Judiciary Departm^t ought to be separate & distinct from the other great Departments. The 1st objection had some weight; but it was much diminished by reflecting that a small proportion of the laws coming in question before a Judge w^d be such wherein he had been consulted; that a small part of this proportion w^d be so am-

---

[1] In the transcript the vote reads " Connecticut, New Jersey, South Carolina, aye—3; Massachusetts, New York, Pennsylvania Delaware, Maryland, Virginia, North Carolina, Georgia, no—8."

biguous as to leave room for his prepossessions; and that but a few cases w^d probably arise in the life of a Judge under such ambiguous passages. How much good on the other hand w^d proceed from the perspicuity, the conciseness, and the systematic character wch the Code of laws w^d receive from the Judiciary talents. As to the 2^d objection, it either had no weight, or it applied with equal weight to the Executive & to the Judiciary revision of the laws. The maxim on which the objection was founded required a separation of the Executive as well as of [1] the Judiciary from the Legislature & from each other. There w^d in truth however be no improper mixture of these distinct powers in the present case. In England, whence the maxim itself had been drawn, the Executive had an absolute negative on the laws; and the supreme tribunal of Justice [the House of Lords] formed one of the other branches of the Legislature. In short whether the object of the revisionary power was to restrain the Legislature from encroaching on the other co-ordinate Departments, or on the rights of the people at large; or from passing laws unwise in their principle, or incorrect in their form, the utility of annexing the wisdom and weight of the Judiciary to the Executive seemed incontestable.

Mr Gerry thought the Executive, whilst standing alone w^d be more impartial than when he c^d be covered by the sanction & seduced by the sophistry of the Judges.

Mr King. If the Unity of the Executive was preferred for the sake of responsibility, the policy of it is as applicable to the revisionary as to the Executive power.

Mr Pinkney had been at first in favor of joining the heads of the principal departm^ts the Secretary at War, of foreign affairs &— in the council of revision. He had however relinquished the idea from a consideration that these could be called in [2] by the Executive Magistrate whenever he pleased to consult them. He was opposed to an [3] introduction of the Judges into the business.

Col. Mason was for giving all possible weight to the revisionary institution. The Executive power ought to be well secured ag^st Legislative usurpations on it. The purse & the sword ought never to get into the same hands whether Legislative or Executive.

Mr Dickenson. Secrecy, vigor & despatch are not the principal properties req^d in the Executive. Important as these are, that of responsibility is more so, which can only be preserved;

---

[1] The word "of" is omitted in the transcript.
[2] The word "on" is substituted in the transcript for "in."
[3] The word "the" is substituted in the transcript for "an."

by leaving it singly to discharge its functions. He thought too a junction of the Judiciary to it, involved an improper mixture of powers.

M: WILSON remarked, that the responsibility required belonged to his Executive duties. The revisionary duty was an extraneous one, calculated for collateral purposes.

M: WILLIAMSON, was for substituting a clause requiring ⅔ for every effective act of the Legislature, in place of the revisionary provision.

On the question for joining the Judges to the Executive in the revisionary business, Mass. no. Conᵗ ay. N. Y. ay. N. J. no. Pᵃ no. Del. no. Mᵈ no. Vᵃ ay. N. C. no. S. C. no. Geo. no.¹

M: PINKNEY gave notice that tomorrow he should move for the reconsideration of that clause in the sixth Resolution adopted by the Commᵉ which vests a negative in the National Legislature on the laws of the several States.

The Comᵉ rose & the House adjᵈ to 11 OC.²

THURSDAY JUNE 7ᵀᴴ 1787 ³—IN COMMITTEE OF THE WHOLE.

M: PINKNEY according to notice moved to reconsider the clause respecting the negative on State laws, which was agreed to and tomorrow for fixed ⁴ the purpose.

The Clause providing for yᵉ appointment of the 2ᵈ branch of the national Legislature, having lain blank since the last vote on the mode of electing it, to wit, by the 1ˢᵗ branch, M: DICKENSON now moved " that the members of the 2ᵈ branch ought to be chosen by the individual Legislatures."

M: SHARMAN seconded the motion; observing that the particular States would thus become interested in supporting the national Governmᵗ and that a due harmony between the two Governments would be maintained. He admitted that the two ought to have separate and distinct jurisdictions, but that they ought to have a mutual interest in supporting each other.

M: PINKNEY. If the small States should be allowed one Senator only, the number will be too great, there will be 80 at least.

---

¹ In the transcript the vote reads: "Connecticut, New York, Virginia, aye—3; Massachusetts, New Jersey, Pennsylvania, Delaware, Maryland, North Carolina, South Carolina, Georgia, no—8."
² The expression " to 11 OC " is omitted in the transcript.
³ The year " 1787 " is omitted in the transcript.
⁴ The words " for fixed " are corrected in the transcript to " fixed for."

M! DICKENSON had two reasons for his motion. 1.[1] because the sense of the States would be better collected through their Governments; than immediately from the people at large; 2.[1] because he wished the Senate to consist of the most distinguished characters, distinguished for their rank in life and their weight of property, and bearing as strong a likeness to the British House of Lords as possible; and he thought such characters more likely to be selected by the State Legislatures, than in any other mode. The greatness of the number was no objection with him. He hoped there would be 80 and twice 80. of them. If their number should be small, the popular branch could not be balanced by them. The legislature of a numerous people ought to be a numerous body.

M! WILLIAMSON, preferred a small number of Senators, but wished that each State should have at least one. He suggested 25 as a convenient number. The different modes of representation in the different branches, will serve as a mutual check.

M! BUTLER was anxious to know the ratio of representation before he gave any opinion.

M! WILSON. If we are to establish a national Government, that Government ought to flow from the people at large. If one branch of it should be chosen by the Legislatures, and the other by the people, the two branches will rest on different foundations, and dissensions will naturally arise between them. He wished the Senate to be elected by the people as well as the other branch, and the people might be divided into proper districts for the purpose &[2] moved to postpone the motion of M! Dickenson, in order to take up one of that import.

M! MORRIS 2^{ded} him.

M! READ proposed " that the Senate should be appointed by the Executive Magistrate out of a proper number of persons to be nominated by the individual legislatures." He said he thought it his duty, to speak his mind frankly. Gentlemen he hoped would not be alarmed at the idea. Nothing short of this approach towards a proper model of Government would answer the purpose, and he thought it best to come directly to the point at once.—His proposition was not seconded nor supported.

M! MADISON, if the motion [of Mr. Dickenson] should be agreed to, we must either depart from the doctrine of proportional representation; or admit into the Senate a very large number of mem-

---

[1] The figures " 1 " and " 2 " are changed to " First " and " secondly " in the transcript.

[2] The word " he " is here inserted in the transcript.

bers. The first is inadmissible, being evidently unjust. The second is inexpedient. The use of the Senate is to consist in its proceeding with more coolness, with more system, & with more wisdom, than the popular branch. Enlarge their number and you communicate to them the vices which they are meant to correct. He differed from M: D. who thought that the additional number would give additional weight to the body. On the contrary it appeared to him that their weight would be in an inverse ratio to their number.[1] The example of the Roman Tribunes was applicable. They lost their influence and power, in proportion as their number was augmented. The reason seemed to be obvious: They were appointed to take care of the popular interests & pretensions at Rome, because the people by reason of their numbers could not act in concert;[2] were liable to fall into factions among themselves, and to become a prey to their aristocratic adversaries. The more the representatives of the people therefore were multiplied, the more they partook of the infirmities of their constituents, the more liable they became to be divided among themselves either from their own indiscretions or the artifices of the opposite faction, and of course the less capable of fulfilling their trust. When the weight of a set of men depends merely on their personal characters; the greater the number the greater the weight. When it depends on the degree of political authority lodged in them the smaller the number the greater the weight. These considerations might perhaps be combined in the intended Senate; but the latter was the material one.

M: GERRY. 4 modes of appointing the Senate have been mentioned. 1.[3] by the 1st branch of the National Legislature. This would create a dependence contrary to the end proposed. 2.[3] by the National Executive. This is a stride towards monarchy that few will think of. 3.[3] by the people. The people have two great interests, the landed interest, and the commercial including the stockholders. To draw both branches from the people will leave no security to the latter interest; the people being chiefly composed of the landed interest, and erroneously supposing, that the other interests are adverse to it. 4 [3] by the Individual Legislatures. The elections being carried thro' this refinement, will be most likely to provide some check in favor of the commercial interest agst the landed; without which

---

[1] The transcript uses the word "number" in the plural.
[2] The word "and " is here inserted in the transcript.
[3] The figures " 1," " 2," " 3 " and " 4 " are changed to " First," " Secondly," etc., in the transcript.

oppression will take place, and no free Gov.ᵗ can last long where that is the case. He was therefore in favor of this last.

Mʳ DICKENSON.* The preservation of the States in a certain degree of agency is indispensable. It will produce that collision between the different authorities which should be wished for in order to check each other. To attempt to abolish the States altogether, would degrade the Councils of our Country, would be impracticable, would be ruinous. He compared the proposed National System to the Solar System, in which the States were the planets, and ought to be left to move freely in their proper orbits. The Gentleman from Pᵃ [Mʳ Wilson] wished he said to extinguish these planets. If the State Governments were excluded from all agency in the national one, and all power drawn from the people at large, the consequence would be that the national Gov.ᵗ would move in the same direction as the State Gov.ᵗˢ now do, and would run into all the same mischiefs. The reform would only unite the 13 small streams into one great current pursuing the same course without any opposition whatever. He adhered to the opinion that the Senate ought to be composed of a large number, and that their influence from family weight & other causes would be increased thereby. He did not admit that the Tribunes lost their weight in proportion as their n.ᵒ was augmented and gave a historical sketch of this institution. If the reasoning of [Mʳ Madison] was good it would prove that the number of the Senate ought to be reduced below ten, the highest n.ᵒ of the Tribunitial corps.

Mʳ WILSON. The subject it must be owned is surrounded with doubts and difficulties. But we must surmount them. The British Governm.ᵗ cannot be our model. We have no materials for a similar one. Our manners, our laws, the abolition of entails and of primogeniture, the whole genius of the people, are opposed to it. He did not see the danger of the States being devoured by the Natioⁿˡ Gov.ᵗ On the contrary, he wished to keep them from devouring the national Gov.ᵗ He was not however for extinguishing these planets as was supposed by Mʳ D.—neither did he on the other hand, believe that they would warm or enlighten the Sun. Within their proper orbits they must still be suffered to act for subordinate purposes for which their existence is made essential by the great extent of our Country. He could not comprehend in what manner the landed interest wᵈ be rendered less predominant in the Senate, by an election through the medium of the Legislatures than by the people themselves. If

---

* It will throw light on this discussion to remark that an election by the State Legislatures involved a surrender of the principle insisted on by the large States & dreaded by the small ones, namely that of a proportional representation in the Senate. Such a rule wᵈ make the body too numerous, as the smallest State must elect one member at least.

the Legislatures, as was now complained, sacrificed the commercial to the landed interest, what reason was there to expect such a choice from them as would defeat their own views. He was for an election by the people in large districts which w^d be most likely to obtain men of intelligence & uprightness; subdividing the districts only for the accomodation of voters.

Mr MADISON could as little comprehend in what manner family weight, as desired by Mr D. would be more certainly conveyed into the Senate through elections by the State Legislatures, than in some other modes. The true question was in what mode the best choice w^d be made? If an election by the people, or thro' any other channel than the State Legislatures promised as uncorrupt & impartial a preference of merit, there could surely be no necessity for an appointment by those Legislatures. Nor was it apparent that a more useful check would be derived thro' that channel than from the people thro' some other. The great evils complained of were that the State Legislatures run into schemes of paper money &c. whenever solicited by the people, & sometimes without even the sanction of the people. Their influence then, instead of checking a like propensity in the National Legislature, may be expected to promote it. Nothing can be more contradictory than to say that the Nat^l Legislature with^t a proper check, will follow the example of the State Legislatures, & in the same breath, that the State Legislatures are the only proper check.

Mr SHARMAN opposed elections by the people in districts, as not likely to produce such fit men as elections by the State Legislatures.

Mr GERRY insisted that the commercial & monied interest w^d be more secure in the hands of the State Legislatures, than of the people at large. The former have more sense of character, and will be restrained by that from injustice. The people are for paper money when the Legislatures are ag^st it. In Mass^ts the County Conventions had declared a wish for a *depreciating* paper that w^d sink itself. Besides, in some States there are two Branches in the Legislature, one of which is somewhat aristocratic. There w^d therefore be so far a better chance of refinement in the choice. There seemed, he thought to be three powerful objections ag^st elections by districts. 1.[1] it is impracticable; the people cannot be brought to one place for the purpose; and whether brought to the same place or not, numberless frauds w^d be unavoidable. 2.[1] small States forming part of the same district with a large one, or[2] large part of a large one, w^d have no chance of gaining an appointment for its citizens of merit. 3[1] a new

---

[1] The figures " 1," " 2 " and " 3 " are changed to " First," " Secondly " and " Thirdly " in the transcript.

[2] The word " a " is here inserted in the transcript.

source of discord w⁴ be opened between different parts of the same district.

M⁵ PINKNEY thought the 2ᵈ branch ought to be permanent & independent, & that the members of it w⁴ be rendered more so by receiving their appointment ¹ from the State Legislatures. This mode w⁴ avoid the rivalships & discontents incident to the election by districts. He was for dividing the States into three classes according to their respective sizes, & for allowing to the 1ˢᵗ class three members—to the 2ᵈ two, & to the 3ᵈ one.

On the question for postponing M⁵ Dickinson's motion referring the appointment of the Senate to the State Legislatures, in order to consider M⁵ Wilson's for referring it to the people

Mass. no. Con⁵ no. N. Y. no. N. J. no. P⁴ ay Del. no. M⁴ no. V⁴ no. N. C. no. S. C. no. Geo. no.²

Col. MASON. whatever power may be necessary for the Nat! Gov⁵ a certain portion must necessarily be left in ³ the States. It is impossible for one power to pervade the extreme parts of the U. S. so as to carry equal justice to them. The State Legislatures also ought to have some means of defending themselves ag⁵ᵗ encroachments of the Nat! Gov⁵ In every other department we have studiously endeavored to provide for its self-defence. Shall we leave the States alone unprovided with the means for this purpose? And what better means can we provide than the giving them some share in, or rather to make them a constituent part of, the Nat! Establishment. There is danger on both sides no doubt; but we have only seen the evils arising on the side of the State Gov⁵ˢ Those on the other side remain to be displayed. The example of Cong⁵ does not apply. Cong⁵ had no power to carry their acts into execution as the Nat! Gov⁵ will have.

On M⁵ DICKINSON's motion for an appointment of the Senate by the State-Legislatures.

Mass. ay. C⁵ ay. N. Y. ay. P⁴ ay Del. ay. M⁴ ay. V⁴ ay N. C. ay. S. C. ay. Geo. ay.⁴

M⁵ GERRY gave notice that he w⁴ tomorrow move for a reconsidera-

---

¹ The word "appointment" is used in the plural in the transcript.

² In the transcript the vote reads: "Pennsylvania, aye—1; Massachusetts, Connecticut, New York, New Jersey, Delaware, Maryland, Virginia, North Carolina, South Carolina, Georgia, no—10."

³ The word "with" is substituted in the transcript for "in."

⁴ In the transcript the vote reads: "Massachusetts, Connecticut, New York, Pennsylvania, Delaware, Maryland, Virginia, North Carolina, South Carolina, Georgia, aye—10."

tion of the mode of appointing the Nat! Executive in order to substitute an appointm! by the State Executives

The Committee rose & The House adj?

FRIDAY JUNE 8ᵀᴴ IN COMMITTEE OF THE WHOLE.

On a reconsideration of the clause giving the Nat! Legislature a negative on such laws of the States as might be contrary to the articles of Union, or Treaties with foreign nations,

M? PINKNEY moved ''that the National Legislature sh? have authority to negative all laws which they sh? judge to be improper.'' He urged that such a universality of the power was indispensably necessary to render it effectual; that the States must be kept in due subordination to the nation; that if the States were left to act of themselves in any case, it w? be impossible to defend the national prerogatives, however extensive they might be on paper; that the acts of Congress had been defeated by this means; nor had foreign treaties escaped repeated violations; that this universal negative was in fact the corner stone of an efficient national Gov!; that under the British Gov! the negative of the Crown had been found beneficial, and the *States* are more one nation now, than the *Colonies* were then.

M? MADISON seconded the motion. He could not but regard an indefinite power to negative legislative acts of the States as abso lutely necessary to a perfect system. Experience had evinced a con. stant tendency in the States to encroach on the federal authority; to violate national Treaties; to infringe the rights & interests of each other; to oppress the weaker party within their respective jurisdictions. A negative was the mildest expedient that could be devised for preventing these mischiefs. The existence of such a check would prevent attempts to commit them. Should no such precaution be engrafted, the only remedy w? lie [1] in an appeal to coercion. Was such a remedy eligible? was it practicable? Could the national resources, if exerted to the utmost enforce a national decree ag.ˢᵗ Mass.ᵗˢ abetted perhaps by several of her neighbours? It w? not be possible. A small proportion of the Community, in a compact situation, acting on the defensive, and at one of its extremities might at any time bid defiance to the National authority. Any Gov! for the U. States formed on the supposed practicability of using force ag.ˢᵗ the

---

[1] The word "be" is substituted in the transcript for "lie."

unconstitutional proceedings of the States, w^d prove as visionary & fallacious as the Gov^t of Cong^s. The negative w^d render the use of force unnecessary. The States c^d of themselves then [1] pass no operative act, any more than one branch of a Legislature where there are two branches, can proceed without the other. But in order to give the negative this efficacy, it must extend to all cases. A discrimination w^d only be a fresh source of contention between the two authorities. In a word, to recur to the illustrations borrowed from the planetary system. This prerogative of the General Gov^t is the great pervading principle that must controul the centrifugal tendency of the States; which, without it, will continually fly out of their proper orbits and destroy the order & harmony of the political System.

Mr WILLIAMSON was agst giving a power that might restrain the States from regulating their internal police.

Mr GERRY c^d not see the extent of such a power, and was agst every power that was not necessary. He thought a remonstrance agst unreasonable acts of the States w^d reclaim [2] them. If it sh^d not force might be resorted to. He had no objection to authorize a negative to paper money and similar measures. When the confederation was depending before Congress, Massachussetts was then for inserting the power of emitting paper money am^g the exclusive powers of Congress. He observed that the proposed negative w^d extend to the regulations of the Militia, a matter on which the existence of a [3] State might depend. The Nat^l Legislature with such a power may enslave the States. Such an idea as this will never be acceded to. It has never been suggested or conceived among the people. No speculative projector, and there are eno' of that character among us, in politics as well as in other things, has in any pamphlet or newspaper thrown out the idea. The States too have different interests and are ignorant of each other's interests. The negative therefore will be abused. New States too having separate views from the old States will never come into the Union. They may even be under some foreign influence; are they in such case to participate in the negative on the will of the other States?

Mr SHERMAN thought the cases in which the negative ought to be exercised, might be defined. He wished the point might not be decided till a trial at least sh^d be made for that purpose

Mr WILSON would not say what modifications of the proposed power might be practicable or expedient. But however novel it

---

[1] The word "then" is omitted in the transcript.
[2] The word "restrain" is substituted in the transcript for "reclaim."
[3] The word "the" is substituted in the transcript for "a."

might appear the principle of it when viewed with a close & steady eye, is right. There is no instance in which the laws say that the individual sh^d be bound in one case, & at liberty to judge whether he will obey or disobey in another. The cases are parallel. Abuses of the power over the individual person may happen as well as over the individual States. Federal liberty is to [1] States, what civil liberty, is to private individuals. And States are not more unwilling to purchase it, by the necessary concession of their political sovereignty, that [2] the savage is to purchase civil liberty by the surrender of his [3] personal sovereignty, which he enjoys in a State of nature. A definition of the cases in which the Negative should be exercised, is impracticable. A discretion must be left on one side or the other? will it not be most safely lodged on the side of the Nat! Gov!? Among the first sentiments expressed in the first Cong? one was that Virg? is no more, that Mas^{ts} is no [4], that P? is no more &c. We are now one nation of brethren. We must bury all local interests & distinctions. This language continued for some time. The tables at length began to turn. No sooner were the State Gov^{ts} formed than their jealousy & ambition began to display themselves. Each endeavoured to cut a slice from the common loaf, to add to its own morsel, till at length the confederation became frittered down to the impotent condition in which it now stands. Review the progress of the articles of Confederation thro' Congress & compare the first & last draught of it. To correct its vices is the business of this convention. One of its vices is the want of an effectual controul in the whole over its parts. What danger is there that the whole will unnecessarily sacrifice a part? But reverse the case, and leave the whole at the mercy of each part, and will not the general interest be continually sacrificed to local interests?

Mr Dickenson deemed it impossible to draw a line between the cases proper & improper for the exercise of the negative. We must take our choice of two things. We must either subject the States to the danger of being injured by the power of the Nat! Gov! or the latter to the danger of being injured by that of the States. He thought the danger greater from the States. To leave the power doubtful, would be opening another spring of discord, and he was for shutting as many of them as possible.

Mr Bedford. In answer to his colleague's question where w^d be

---

[1] The word "the" is here inserted in the transcript.
[2] The word "that" is changed to "than" in the transcript.
[3] The word "the" is substituted in the transcript for "his."
[4] The word "more" is here inserted in the transcript.

the danger to the States from this power, would refer him to the smallness of his own State which may be injured at pleasure without redress. It was meant he found to strip the small States of their equal right of suffrage. In this case Delaware would have about ⅟₉₀ for its share in the General Councils, whilst Pᵃ & Vᵃ would possess ⅓ of the whole. Is there no difference of interests, no rivalship of commerce, of manufactures? Will not these large States crush the small ones whenever they stand in the way of their ambitious or interested views. This shews the impossibility of adopting such a system as that on the table, or any other founded on a change in the principle of representation. And after all, if a State does not obey the law of the new System, must not force be resorted to as the only ultimate remedy, in this as in any other system. It seems as if Pᵃ & Vᵃ by the conduct of their deputies wished to provide a system in which they would have an enormous & monstrous influence. Besides, How can it be thought that the proposed negative can be exercised? are the laws of the States to be suspended in the most urgent cases until they can be sent seven or eight hundred miles, and undergo the deliberations [1] of a body who may be incapable of Judging of them? Is the National Legislature too to sit continually in order to revise the laws of the States?

Mʳ MADISON observed that the difficulties which had been started were worthy of attention and ought to be answered before the question was put. The case of laws of urgent necessity must be provided for by some emanation of the power from the Natˡ Govᵗ into each State so far as to give a temporary assent at least. This was the practice in Royal Colonies before the Revolution and would not have been inconvenient, if the supreme power of negativing had been faithful to the American interest, and had possessed the necessary information. He supposed that the negative might be very properly lodged in the senate alone, and that the more numerous & expensive branch therefore might not be obliged to sit constantly.—He asked Mʳ B. what would be the consequence to the small States of a dissolution of the Union wᶜʰ seemed likely to happen if no effectual substitute was made for the defective System existing, and he did not conceive any effectual system could be substituted on any other basis than that of a proportional suffrage? If the large States possessed the avarice & ambition with which they were charged, would the small ones in their neighbourhood, be more secure when all controul of a Genˡ Govᵗ was withdrawn.

---

[1] The transcript uses the word " deliberations " in the singular.

M̲ᴿ Butler was vehement ag̲ˢᵗ the Negative in the proposed extent, as cutting off all hope of equal justice to the distant States. The people there would not he was sure give it a hearing.

On the question for extending the negative power to all cases as propos̲ᵈ by [M̲ᴿ P. & M̲ᴿ M—] Mass. ay. Con̲ᵗ no. N. Y. no. N. J. no. P̲ᵃ ay. Del. div̲ᵈ M̲ᴿ Read & M̲ᴿ Dickenson ay. M̲ᴿ Bedford & M̲ᴿ Basset no. Mary̲ᵈ no. V̲ᵃ ay. M̲ᴿ R. M̲ᴿ Mason no. M̲ᴿ Blair, Doc̲ᴿ M̲ᶜC̲ᵍ M̲ᴿ M. ay. Gen̲ˡ W. not consulted. N. C. no. S. C. no. Geo. no.[1]

On motion of M̲ᴿ Gerry and M̲ᴿ King tomorrow was assigned for reconsidering the mode of appointing the National Executive: the reconsideration being voted for by all the States except Connecticut & N. Carolina.

M̲ᴿ Pinkney and M̲ᴿ Rutlidge moved to add to Resol̲ⁿ 4.[2] agreed to by the Com̲ᵉ the following, viz. " that the States be divided into three classes, the 1̲ˢᵗ class to have 3 members, the 2̲ᵈ two. & the 3̲ᵈ one member each; that an estimate be taken of the comparative importance of each State at fixed periods, so as to ascertain the number of members they may from time to time be entitled to" The Committee then rose and the House adjourned.

Saturday June 9̲ᵀᴴ M̲ᴿ Luther Martin from Maryland took his seat In committee of the whole.

M̲ᴿ Gerry, according to previous notice given by him, moved " that the National Executive should be elected by the Executives of the States whose proportion of votes should be the same with that allowed to the States in the election of the Senate." If the appointm̲ᵗ should be made by the Nat̲ˡ Legislature, it would lessen that independence of the Executive which ought to prevail, would give birth to intrigue and corruption between the Executive & Legislature previous to the election, and to partiality in the Executive afterwards to the friends who promoted him. Some other mode therefore appeared to him necessary. He proposed that of appointing by the State Executives as most analogous to the principle observed in elect-

---

[1] In the transcript the vote reads: " Massachusetts, Pennsylvania, Virginia, [Mr. Randolph and Mr. Mason, no; Mr. Blair, Doctor McClurg and Mr. Madison, aye; General Washington not consulted,] aye—3; Connecticut, New York, New Jersey, Maryland, North Carolina, South Carolina, Georgia, no—7; Delaware, divided, [Mr. Read and Mr. Dickinson, aye; Mr. Bedford and Mr. Basset, no)."

[2] The words " the fourth Resolution " are substituted in the transcript for " Resol̲ⁿ 4."

ing the other branches of the Nat! Gov!; the first branch being chosen by the *people* of the States, & the 2ᵈ by the Legislatures of the States; he did not see any objection agˢᵗ letting the Executive be appointed by the Executives of the States. He supposed the Executives would be most likely to select the fittest men, and that it would be their interest to support the man of their own choice.

Mʳ RANDOLPH, urged strongly the inexpediency of Mʳ Gerry's mode of appointing the Nat! Executive. The confidence of the people would not be secured by it to the Nat! magistrate. The small States would lose all chance of an appointmᵗ from within themselves. Bad appointments would be made; the Executives of the States being little conversant with characters not within their own small spheres. The State Executives too notwithstanding their constitutional independence, being in fact dependent on the State Legislatures will generally be guided by the views of the latter, and prefer either favorites within the States, or such as it may be expected will be most partial to the interests of the State. A Nat! Executive thus chosen will not be likely to defend with becoming vigilance & firmness the National rights agˢᵗ State encroachments. Vacancies also must happen. How can these be filled? He could not suppose either that the Executives would feel the interest in supporting the Nat! Executive which had been imagined. They will not cherish the great Oak which is to reduce them to paltry shrubs.

On the question for referring the appointment of the Nat! Executive to the State Executives as propᵈ by Mʳ Gerry Massᵗˢ no. Conᵗ no. N. Y. no. N. J. no. Pᵃ no. Del. divᵈ Mᵈ no. Vᵃ no. S. C. no. Geo. no.[1]

Mʳ PATTERSON moves that the Committee resume the clause relating to the rule of suffrage in the Nat! Legislature.

Mʳ BREARLY seconds him. He was sorry he said that any question on this point was brought into view. It had been much agitated in Congˢ at the time of forming the Confederation, and was then rightly settled by allowing to each sovereign State an equal vote. Otherwise the smaller States must have been destroyed instead of being saved. The substitution of a ratio, he admitted carried fairness on the face of it; but on a deeper examination was unfair and unjust. Judging of the disparity of the States by the quota of Congˢ Virgᵃ would have 16 votes, and Georgia but one. A like proportion to the others will make the whole number ninity. There

---

[1] In the transcript the vote reads: "Massachusetts, Connecticut, New York, New Jersey, Pennsylvania, Maryland, Virginia, South Carolina, Georgia, no; Delaware divided."

will be 3. large states, and 10 small ones. The large States by which
he meant Mass^{ts}. Pen^a. & Virg^a. will carry every thing before them.
It had been admitted, and was known to him from facts within N.
Jersey that where large & small counties were united into a district
for electing representatives for the district, the large counties always
carried their point, and Consequently that[1] the large States would
do so. Virg^a. with her sixteen votes will be a solid column indeed,
a formidable phalanx. While Georgie with her Solitary vote, and the
other little States will be obliged to throw themselves constantly into
the scale of some large one, in order to have any weight at all.
He had come to the convention with a view of being as useful as he
could in giving energy and stability to the federal Government.
When the proposition for destroying the equality of votes came forward, he was astonished, he was alarmed. Is it fair then it will be
asked that Georgia should have an equal vote with Virg^a? He would
not say it was. What remedy then? One only, that a map of the
U. S. be spread out, that all the existing boundaries be erased, and
that a new partition of the whole be made into 13 equal parts.

M^r. PATTERSON considered the proposition for a proportional representation as striking at the existence of the lesser States. He w^d.
premise however to an investigation of this question some remarks
on the nature structure and powers of the Convention. The Convention he said was formed in pursuance of an Act of Cong^s. that this
act was recited in several of the Commissions, particularly that of
Mass^{ts}. which he required to be read: that the amendment of the
confederacy was the object of all the laws and commissions on the
subject; that the articles of the Confederation were therefore the
proper basis of all the proceedings of the Convention.[2] We ought
to keep within its limits, or we should be charged by our Constituents
with usurpation, that the people of America were sharpsighted and
not to be deceived. But the Commissions under which we acted were
not only the measure of our power, they denoted also the sentiments
of the States on the subject of our deliberation. The idea of a
national Gov^t. as contradistinguished from a federal one, never entered
into the mind of any of them, and to the public mind we must accomodate ourselves. We have no power to go beyond the federal
scheme, and if we had the people are not ripe for any other. We
must follow the people; the people will not follow us.—The *proposition* could not be maintained whether considered in reference to
us as a nation, or as a confederacy. A confederacy supposes sov-

---

[1] The word "that" is omitted in the transcript.
[2] The word "that" is here inserted in the transcript.

ereignty in the members composing it & sovereignty supposes equality. If we are to be considered as a nation, all State distinctions must be abolished, the whole must be thrown into hotchpot, and when an equal division is made, then there may be fairly an equality of representation. He held up Virg.ᵃ Mass.ᵗˢ & P.ᵃ as the three large States, and the other ten as small ones; repeating the calculations of Mr. Brearly as to the disparity of votes which wᵈ take place, and affirming that the small States would never agree to it. He said there was no more reason that a great individual State contributing much, should have more votes than a small one contributing little, than that a rich individual citizen should have more votes than an indigent one. If the rateable property of A was to that of B as 40 to 1, ought A for that reason to have 40 times as many votes as B. Such a principle would never be admitted, and if it were admitted would put B entirely at the mercy of A. As A. has more to be protected than B so he ought to contribute more for the common protection. The same may be said of a large State wᶜʰ has more to be protected than a small one. Give the large States an influence in proportion to their magnitude, and what will be the consequence? Their ambition will be proportionally increased, and the small States will have every thing to fear. It was once proposed by Galloway & some others that America should be represented in the British Parlᵗ and then be bound by its laws. America could not have been entitled to more than ⅓ of the n.ᵒ of [1] Representatives which would fall to the share of G. B. Would American rights & interests have been safe under an authority thus constituted? It has been said that if a Natᶫ Govᵗ is to be formed so as to operate on the people and not on the States, the representatives ought to be drawn from the people. But why so? May not a Legislature filled by the State Legislatures operate on the people who chuse the State Legislatures? or may not a practicable coercion be found. He admitted that there was none such in the existing System.—He was attached strongly to the plan of the existing confederacy, in which the people chuse their Legislative representatives; and the Legislatures their federal representatives. No other amendments were wanting than to mark the orbits of the States with due precision, and provide for the use of coercion, which was the great point. He alluded to the hint thrown out heretofore by Mr. Wilson of the necessity to which the large States might be reduced of confederating among themselves, by a refusal of the others to concur. Let them unite if they please, but let them re-

---

[1] The words " n.ᵒ of " are omitted in the transcript.

member that they have no authority to compel the others to unite. N. Jersey will never confederate on the plan before the Committee. She would be swallowed up. He had rather submit to a monarch, to a despot, than to such a fate. He would not only oppose the plan here but on his return home do every thing in his power to defeat it there.

Mr. Wilson. hoped if the Confederacy should be dissolved, that a *majority,* that a *minority* of the States would unite for their safety. He entered elaborately into the defence of a proportional representation, stating for his first position that as all authority was derived from the people, equal numbers of people ought to have an equal no. of representatives, and different numbers of people different numbers of representatives. This principle had been improperly violated in the Confederation, owing to the urgent circumstances of the time. As to the case of A. & B, stated by Mr. Patterson, he observed that in districts as large as the States, the number of people was the best measure of their comparative wealth. Whether therefore wealth or numbers were[1] to form the ratio it would be the same. Mr. P. admitted persons, not property to be the measure of suffrage. Are not the Citizens of Pena. equal to those of N. Jersey? does it require 150 of the former to balance 50 of the latter? Representatives of different districts ought clearly to hold the same proportion to each other, as their respective Constituents hold to each other. If the small States will not confederate on this plan, Pena. & he presumed some other States, would not confederate on any other. We have been told that each State being sovereign, all are equal. So each man is naturally a sovereign over himself, and all men are therefore naturally equal. Can he retain this equality when he becomes a member of Civil Government? He can not. As little can a Sovereign State, when it becomes a member of a federal Governt. If N. J. will not part with her Sovereignty it is in vain to talk of Govt. A new partition of the States is desireable, but evidently & totally impracticable.

Mr. Williamson, illustrated the cases by a comparison of the different States, to Counties of different sizes within the same State; observing that proportional representation was admitted to be just in the latter case, and could not therefore be fairly contested in the former.

The Question being about to be put Mr. Patterson hoped that as

---

[1] The word "was" is substituted in the transcript for "were."

so much depended on it, it might be thought best to postpone the decision till tomorrow, which was done nem. con.

The Com.ᵉ rose & the House adjourned.

MONDAY. JUNE 11.ᵀᴴ Mᴿ ABRAHAM BALDWIN FROM GEOᴿGIA TOOK HIS SEAT. IN COMMITTEE OF THE WHOLE.

The clause concerning the rule of suffrage in the natˡ Legislature postponed on Saturday was resumed.

Mʳ SHARMAN proposed that the proportion of suffrage in the 1ˢᵗ branch should be according to the respective numbers of free inhabitants; and that in the second branch or Senate, each State should have one vote and no more. He said as the States would remain possessed of certain individual rights, each State ought to be able to protect itself: otherwise a few large States will rule the rest. The House of Lords in England he observed had certain particular rights under the Constitution, and hence they have an equal vote with the House of Commons that they may be able to defend their rights.

Mʳ RUTLIDGE proposed that the proportion of suffrage in the 1ˢᵗ branch should be according to the quotas of contribution. The justice of this rule he said could not be contested. Mʳ BUTLER urged the same idea: adding that money was power; and that the States ought to have weight in the Gov.ᵗ in proportion to their wealth.

Mʳ KING & Mʳ WILSON,* in order to bring the question to a point moved " that the right of suffrage in the first branch of the national Legislature ought not to be according[1] the rule established in the articles of Confederation, but according to some equitable ratio of representation." The clause so far as it related to suffrage in the first branch was postponed in order to consider this motion.

Mʳ DICKENSON contended for the *actual* contributions of the States as the rule of their representation & suffrage in the first branch. By thus connecting the interest[2] of the States with their duty, the latter would be sure to be performed.

Mʳ KING remarked that it was uncertain what mode might be used in levying a national revenue; but that it was probable, imposts would be one source of it. If the *actual* contributions were to be the rule the non-importing States, as Con.ᵗ & N. Jersey, wᵈ be in a

* In the printed Journal Mr. Rutlidge is named as the seconder of the motion.

---

[1] The word "to" is here inserted in the transcript.
[2] The transcript uses the word "interest" in the plural.

bad situation indeed. It might so happen that they w^d have no representation. This situation of particular States had been always one powerful argument in favor of the 5 Per C^t impost.

The question being ab^t to be put Doc^r FRANKLIN s^d he had thrown his ideas of the matter on a paper wch Mr Wilson read to the Committee in the words following—

Mr CHAIRMAN

It has given me great pleasure to observe that till this point, the proportion of representation, came before us, our debates were carried on with great coolness & temper. If any thing of a contrary kind, has on this occasion appeared, I hope it will not be repeated; for we are sent here to *consult*, not to *contend*, with each other; and declarations of a fixed opinion, and of determined resolution, never to change it, neither enlighten nor convince us. Positiveness and warmth on one side, naturally beget their like on the other; and tend to create and augment discord & division in a great concern, wherein harmony & Union are extremely necessary to give weight to our Councils, and render them effectual in promoting & securing the common good.

I must own that I was originally of opinion it would be better if every member of Congress, or our national Council, were to consider himself rather as a representative of the whole, than as an Agent for the interests of a particular State; in which case the proportion of members for each State would be of less consequence, & it would not be very material whether they voted by States or individually. But as I find this is not to be expected, I now think the number of Representatives should bear some proportion to the number of the Represented; and that the decisions sh^d be by the majority of members, not by the majority of [1] States. This is objected to from an apprehension that the greater States would then swallow up the smaller. I do not at present clearly see what advantage the greater States could propose to themselves by swallowing [2] the smaller, and therefore do not apprehend they would attempt it. I recollect that in the beginning of this Century, when the Union was proposed of the two Kingdoms, England & Scotland, the Scotch Patriots were full of fears, that unless they had an equal number of Representatives in Parliament, they should be ruined by the superiority of the English. They finally agreed however that the different proportions of importance in the Union, of the two Nations should

---

[1] The word "the" is here inserted in the transcript.
[2] The word "up" is here inserted in the transcript.

be attended to, whereby they were to have only forty members in the House of Commons, and only sixteen in the House of Lords; A very great inferiority of numbers! And yet to this day I do not recollect that any thing has been done in the Parliament of Great Britain to the prejudice of Scotland; and whoever looks over the lists of public officers, Civil & military of that nation will find I believe that the North Britons enjoy at least their full proportion of emolument.

But, Sir, in the present mode of voting by States, it is equally in the power of the lesser States to swallow up the greater; and this is mathematically demonstrable.   Suppose for example, that 7 smaller States had each 3 members in the House, and the 6 larger to have one with another 6 members; and that upon a question, two members of each smaller State should be in the affirmative and one in the Negative; they will [1] make

> Affirmatives .... 14 ...... Negatives   7
> And that all the larger States
>   should be unanimously in
>   the Negative, they would
>   make .... Negatives   36
>   ———
>   In all   43

It is then apparent that the 14 carry the question against the 43. and the minority overpowers the majority, contrary to the common practice of Assemblies in all Countries and Ages.

The greater States Sir are naturally as unwilling to have their property left in the disposition of the smaller, as the smaller are to have theirs in the disposition of the greater.   An honorable gentleman has, to avoid this difficulty, hinted a proposition of equalizing the States.   It appears to me an equitable one, and I should, for my own part, not be against such a measure, if it might be found practicable.   Formerly, indeed, when almost every province had a different Constitution, some with greater others with fewer privileges, it was of importance to the borderers when their boundaries were contested, whether by running the division lines, they were placed on one side or the other.   At present when such differences are done away, it is less material.   The Interest of a State is made up of the interests of its individual members.   If they are not injured, the State is not injured.   Small States are more easily well & hap-

---

[1] The word " will " is changed to " would " in the transcript.

pily governed than large ones. If therefore in such an equal division, it should be found necessary to diminish Pennsylvania, I should not be averse to the giving a part of it to N. Jersey, and another to Delaware. But as there would probably be considerable difficulties in adjusting such a division; and however equally made at first, it would be continually varying by the augmentation of inhabitants in some States, and their [1] fixed proportion in others; and thence frequent occasion for new divisions, I beg leave to propose for the consideration of the Committee another mode, which appears to me, to be as equitable, more easily carried into practice, and more permanent in its nature.

Let the weakest State say what proportion of money or force it is able and willing to furnish for the general purposes of the Union.

Let all the others oblige themselves to furnish each an equal proportion.

The whole of these joint supplies to be absolutely in the disposition of Congress.

The Congress in this case to be composed of an equal number of Delegates from each State.

And their decisions to be by the Majority of individual members voting.

If these joint and equal supplies should on particular occasions not be sufficient, Let Congress make requisitions on the richer and more powerful States for farther aids, to be voluntarily afforded, leaving to each State the right of considering the necessity and utility of the aid desired, and of giving more or less as it should be found proper.

This mode is not new, it was formerly practised with success by the British Government with respect to Ireland and the Colonies. We sometimes gave even more than they expected, or thought just to accept; and in the last war carried on while we were united, they gave us back in 5 years a million Sterling. We should probably have continued such voluntary contributions, whenever the occasions appeared to require them for the common good of the Empire. It was not till they chose to force us, and to deprive us of the merit and pleasure of voluntary contributions that we refused & resisted. Those [2] contributions however were to be disposed of at the pleasure of a Government in which we had no representative. I am therefore

---

[1] The word " more " is in the Franklin manuscript.
[2] The word " These " is substituted in the transcript for " Those."

persuaded, that they will not be refused to one in which the Representation shall be equal

My learned Colleague [M: Wilson] has already mentioned that the present method of voting by States, was submitted to originally by Congress, under a conviction of its impropriety, inequality, and injustice. This appears in the words of their Resolution. It is of Sep: 6. 1774. The words are

"Resolved that in determining questions in this Cong: each Colony or province shall have one vote: The Cong: not being possessed of or at present able to procure materials for ascertaining the importance of each Colony."

On the question for agreeing to M: Kings and M: Wilsons motion it passed in the affirmative

Massᵗˢ. ay. C: ay. N. Y. no. N. J. no. P: ay. Del. no. M: div:. V: ay. N. C. ay. S. C. ay. Geo. ay.[1]

It was then moved by M: RUTLIDGE 2ᵈᵉᵈ by M: BUTLER to add to the words " equitable ratio of representation " at the end of the motion just agreed to, the words " according to the quotas of contribution." On motion of M: WILSON seconded by M: C. PINCKNEY, this was postponed; in order to add, after, after the words "equitable ratio of representation " the words following " in proportion to the whole number of white & other free Citizens & inhabitants of every age sex & condition including those bound to servitude for a term of years and three fifths of all other persons not comprehended in the foregoing description, except Indians not paying taxes, in each State," this being the rule in the Act of Congress agreed to by eleven States, for apportioning quotas of revenue on the States, and requiring a Census only every 5-7, or 10 years.

M: GERRY thought property not the rule of representation. Why then sh: the blacks, who were property in the South, be in the rule of representation more than the Cattle & horses of the North.

On the question,—Mass: Con: N. Y. Pen: Mary: Virg: N. C. S. C. & Geo: were in the affirmative:[2] N. J. & Del: in the negative.[2]

M: SHARMAN moved that a question be taken whether each State shall have one vote in the 2: branch. Every thing he said depended on this. The smaller States would never agree to the plan on any

---

[1] In the transcript the vote reads: "Massachusetts, Connecticut, Pennsylvania, Virginia, North Carolina, South Carolina, Georgia, aye—7; New York, New Jersey, Delaware, no—3; Maryland divided."

[2] In place of the phrase "were in the affirmative" the transcript substitutes "aye—9; " and instead of "in the negative" the expression "no—2 " is used.

other principle than an equality of suffrage in this branch. Mr ELSWORTH seconded the motion. On the question for allowing each State one vote in the 2^d branch.

Mass^{ts} no. Con^t ay. N. Y. ay. N. J. ay. P^a no. Del. ay. M^d ay. V^a no. N. C. no. S. C. no. Geo. no.[1]

Mr WILSON & Mr HAMILTON moved that the right of suffrage in the 2^d branch ought to be according to the same rule as in the 1st branch. On this question for making the ratio of representation the same in the 2^d as in the 1st branch it passed in the affirmative:

Mass^{ts} ay. Con^t no. N. Y. no. N. J. no. P^a ay. Del. no. M^d no. V^a ay. N. C. ay. S. C. ay. Geo. ay.[2]

Resol: 11,[3] for guarantying Republican Gov^t & territory to each State being considered: the words " or partition " were, on motion of Mr MADISON, added, after the words " voluntary junction: "

Mas. N. Y. P. V^a \N. C. S. C. G. ay [4] Con: N. J. Del. M^d no.[4]

Mr READ disliked the idea of guarantying territory. It abetted the idea of distinct States wch would be a perpetual source of discord. There can be no cure for this evil but in doing away States altogether and uniting them all into one great Society.

Alterations having been made in the Resolution, making it read "that a republican Constitution & its existing laws ought to be guaranteed to each State by the U. States " the whole was agreed to nem. con.

Resolution 13,[5] for amending the national Constitution hereafter without consent of [6] Nat^l Legislature being considered, several members did not see the necessity of the Resolution at all, nor the propriety of making the consent of the Nat^l Legisl. unnecessary.

Col. MASON urged the necessity of such a provision. The plan now to be formed will certainly be defective, as the Confederation has been found on trial to be. Amendments therefore will be necessary, and it will be better to provide for them, in an easy, regular and Constitutional way than to trust to chance and violence. It

---

[1] In the transcript the vote reads: "Connecticut, New York, New Jersey, Delaware, Maryland, aye—5; Massachusetts, Pennsylvania, Virginia, North Carolina, South Carolina, Georgia, no—6."

[2] In the transcript the vote reads: "Massachusetts, Pennsylvania, Virginia, North Carolina, South Carolina, Georgia, aye; Connecticut, New York, New Jersey, Delaware, Maryland, no."

[3] The words "The eleventh Resolution" are substituted in the transcript for "Resol: 11."

[4] The figures "7" and "4" are inserted in the transcript after "ay" and "no," respectively.

[5] The words "The thirteenth Resolution" are substituted in the transcript for "Resolution 13."

[6] The word "the" is here inserted in the transcript.

would be improper to require the consent of the Nat! Legislature, because they may abuse their power, and refuse their consent [1] on that very account. The opportunity for such an abuse, may be the fault of the Constitution calling for amendm!

M.ʳ RANDOLPH enforced these arguments.

The words, "without requiring the consent of the Nat! Legislature" were postponed. The other provision in the clause passed nem. con.

Resolution 14,[2] requiring oaths from the members of the State Gov!ˢ to observe the Nat! Constitution & laws, being considered.

M.ʳ SHARMAN opposed it as unnecessarily intruding into the State jurisdictions.

M.ʳ RANDOLPH considered it as [3] necessary to prevent that competition between the National Constitution & laws & those of the particular States, which had already been felt. The officers of the States are already under oath to the States. To preserve a due impartiality they ought to be equally bound to the Nat! Gov! The Nat! authority needs every support we can give it. The Executive & Judiciary of the States, notwithstanding their nominal independence on the State Legislatures are in fact, so dependent on them, that unless they be brought under some tie to the Nat! System, they will always lean too much to the State systems, whenever a contest arises between the two.

M.ʳ GERRY did not like the clause. He thought there was as much reason for requiring an oath of fidelity to the States, from Nat! officers, as vice. versa.

M.ʳ LUTHER MARTIN moved to strike out the words requiring such an oath from the State officers, viz "within the several States" observing that if the new oath should be contrary to that already taken by them it would be improper; if coincident the oaths already taken will be sufficient.

On the question for striking out as proposed by M.ʳ L. Martin

Mass!ˢ no. Con! ay. N. Y. no. N. J. ay. P.ª no. Del. ay. M.ᵈ ay. V.ª no. N. C. no. S. C. no. Geo. no.[4]

Question on [5] whole Resolution as proposed by M.ʳ Randolph;

---

[1] The word "assent" is substituted in the transcript for "consent."

[2] The words "The fourteenth Resolution" are substituted in the transcript for "Resolution 14."

[3] The word "as" is crossed out in the transcript.

[4] In the transcript the vote reads: "Connecticut, New Jersey, Delaware, Maryland, aye—4; Massachusetts, New York, Pennsylvania, Virginia, North Carolina, South Carolina, Georgia, no—7."

[5] The word "the" is here inserted in the transcript.

Mass^{ts} ay. Con^t no. N. Y. no. N. J. no. P^a ay. Del. no. M^d no. V^a ay. N. C. ay. S. C. ay. Geo. ay.[1]

[2] Com^e rose & [2] House adj^d

TEUSDAY JUNE 12TH IN COMMITTEE OF [2] WHOLE

The Question [3] taken on Resolution 15,[4] to wit, referring the new system to the people of the [5] States for ratification it passed in the affirmative: Mass^{ts} ay. Con^t no. N. Y. no. N. J. no. P^a * ay. Del. div^d M^d div^d V^a ay. N. C. ay. S. C. ay. Geo. ay.[6]

Mr SHARMAN & Mr ELSEWORTH moved to fill the blank left in the 4th Resolution for the periods of electing the members of the first branch with the words, " every year." Mr SHARMAN observing that he did it in order to bring on some question.

Mr RUTLIDGE proposed " every two years."

Mr JENNIFER prop^d " every three years," observing that the too great frequency of elections rendered the people indifferent to them, and made the best men unwilling to engage in so precarious a service.

Mr MADISON seconded the motion for three years. Instability is one of the great vices of our republics, to be remedied. Three years will be necessary, in a Government so extensive, for members to form any knowledge of the various interests of the States to which they do not belong, and of which they can know but little from the situation and affairs of their own. One year will be almost consumed in preparing for and travelling to & from the seat of national business.

Mr GERRY. The people of New England will never give up the point of annual elections, they know of the transition made in England from triennial to septennial elections, and will consider such an innovation here as the prelude to a like usurpation. He considered annual elections as the only defence of the people agst tyranny. He was as much agst a triennial House as agst a hereditary Executive.

* Pennsylvania omitted in the printed Journal. The vote is there entered as of June 11th.

---

[1] In the transcript the vote reads: "Massachusetts, Pennsylvania, Virginia, North Carolina, South Carolina, Georgia, aye—6; Connecticut, New York, New Jersey, Delaware, Maryland, no—5."

[2] The word "the" is here inserted in the transcript.

[3] The word "was" is here inserted in the transcript.

[4] The words "the fifteenth Resolution" are substituted in the transcript for "Resolution 15."

[5] The word "United" is here inserted in the transcript.

[6] In the transcript the vote reads: "Massachusetts, Pennsylvania,* Virginia, North Carolina, South Carolina, Georgia, aye—6; Connecticut, New York, New Jersey, no—3; Delaware, Maryland, divided."

M: MADISON, observed that if the opinions of the people were to be our guide, it w⁴ be difficult to say what course we ought to take. No member of the Convention could say what the opinions of his Constituents were at this time; much less could he say what they would think if possessed of the information & lights possessed by the members here; & still less what would be their way of thinking 6 or 12 months hence. We ought to consider what was right & necessary in itself for the attainment of a proper Governm: A plan adjusted to this idea will recommend itself—The respectability of this convention will give weight to their recommendation of it. Experience will be constantly urging the adoption of it, and all the most enlightened & respectable citizens will be its advocates. Should we fall short of the necessary & proper point, this influential class of Citizens will be turned against the plan, and little support in opposition to them can be gained to it from the unreflecting multitude.

M: GERRY repeated his opinion that it was necessary to consider what the people would approve. This had been the policy of all Legislators. If the reasoning of M: Madison were just, and we supposed a limited Monarchy the best form in itself, we ought to recommend it, tho' the genius of the people was decidedly adverse to it, and having no hereditary distinctions among us, we were destitute of the essential materials for such an innovation.

On the question for [1] triennial election of the 1ˢᵗ branch

Mass. no. [M: King ay.] M: Ghorum wavering. Con: no. N. Y. ay. N. J. ay. P: ay. Del. ay. M⁴ ay. V: ay. N. C. no. S. C. no. Geo. ay.[2]

The words requiring members of yᵉ 1ˢᵗ branch to be of the age of   years were struck out Maryland alone, no. The words " *liberal compensation for members* " being consid⁴ M: MADISON moves to insert the words, " *& fixt.* " He observed that it would be improper to leave the members of the Nat: legislature to be provided for by the State Legisl: because it would create an improper dependence; and to leave them to regulate their own wages, was an indecent thing, and might in time prove a dangerous one. He thought wheat or some other article of which the average price throughout a reasonable period preceding might be settled in some convenient mode, would form a proper standard.

Col. MASON seconded the motion; adding that it would be im-

---

[1] The word " the " is here inserted in the transcript.
[2] In the transcript the vote reads: " New York, New Jersey, Pennsylvania, Delaware, Maryland, Virginia, Georgia, aye—7; Massachusetts [Mr. King, aye, Mr. Gorham, wavering] Connecticut, North Carolina, South Carolina, no—4."

proper for other reasons to leave the wages to be regulated by the States. 1.¹ the different States would make different provision for their representatives, and an inequality would be felt among them, whereas he thought they ought to be in all respects equal. 2.¹ the parsimony of the States might reduce the provision so low that as had already happened in choosing delegates to Congress, the question would be not who were most fit to be chosen, but who were most willing to serve.

On the question for inserting the words "and fixt."

Mass⁺ˢ no. Con⁺ no. N. Y. ay. N. J. ay. P⁺ ay. Del. ay. M⁴ ay. V⁺ ay. N. C. ay. S. C. no. Geo. ay.²

Doct⁺ FRANKLYN said he approved of the amendment just made for rendering the salaries as fixed as possible; but disliked the word " *liberal*." he would prefer the word moderate if it was necessary to substitute any other. He remarked the tendency of abuses in every case, to grow of themselves when once begun, and related very pleasantly the progression in ecclesiastical benefices, from the first departure from the gratuitous provision for the Apostles, to the establishment of the papal system. The word " liberal " was struck out nem. con.

On the motion of M⁺ PIERCE, that the wages should be paid out of the National Treasury, Mass⁺ˢ ay. C⁺ no. N. Y. no. N. J. ay. P⁺ ay. Del. ay. M⁴ ay. V⁺ ay. N. C. ay. S. C. no. G. ay.³

Question on the clause relating to term of service & compensation of⁴ 1ˢᵗ branch

Mass⁺ˢ ay. C⁺ no. N. Y no. N. J. ay. P⁺ ay. Del. ay. M⁴ ay. V⁺ ay. N. C. ay. S. C. no. Geo. ay.⁵

On a question for striking out the " *ineligibility* of members of ⁴ Nat⁺ Legis: to *State offices*."

Mass⁺ˢ div⁴ Con⁺ ay. N. Y. ay. N. J. no. P⁺ no. Del. no. M⁴ div⁴ V⁺ no. N. C. ay. S. C. ay. Geo. no ⁶

---

¹ The figures "1" and "2" are changed to "First" and "Secondly" in the transcript.

² In the transcript the vote reads: New York, New Jersey, Pennsylvania, Delaware, Maryland, Virginia, North Carolina, Georgia, aye—8; Massachusetts, Connecticut, South Carolina, no—3."

³ In the transcript the vote reads: "Massachusetts, New Jersey, Pennsylvania, Delaware, Maryland, Virginia, North Carolina, Georgia, aye—8; Connecticut, New York, South Carolina, no—3."

⁴ The word "the" is here inserted in the transcript.

⁵ In the transcript the vote reads: "Massachusetts, New Jersey, Pennsylvania, Delaware, Maryland, Virginia, North Carolina, Georgia, aye—8; Connecticut, New York, South Carolina, no—3."

⁶ In the transcript the vote reads: "Connecticut, New York, North Carolina, South Carolina, aye—4; New Jersey, Pennsylvania, Delaware, Virginia, Georgia, no—5; Massachusetts, Maryland, divided."

On the question for agreeing to the clause as amended.
Mass^{ts} ay. Con^t no. N. Y. ay. N. J. ay. P^a ay. Del. ay M^d ay. V^a ay. N. C. ay. S. C. ay. Geo. ay.[1]

On a question for making Members of [2] Nat^l legislature *ineligible* to any office under the Nat^l Gov^t for the term of 3 years after ceasing to be members.

Mass^{ts} no. Con^t no. N. Y. no. N. J. no. P^a no. Del. no. M^d ay V^a no. N C. no. S. C. no. Geo. no.[3]

On the question for such ineligibility for one year

Mass^{ts} ay. C^t ay. N. Y. no. N. J. ay. P^a ay. Del. ay. M^d div^d V^a ay. N. C. ay. S. C. ay. Geo. no.[4]

On [2] question moved by Mr PINCKNEY for striking out "incapable of re-election into [2] 1st branch of [2] Nat^l Legisl. for   years, and subject to recall" ag^d to nem. con.

On [2] question for striking out from Resol: 5 [5] the words requiring members of the senatorial branch to be of the age of   years at least

Mass^{ts} no. Con^t ay. N. Y. no. N. J. ay. P^a ay. Del. no. M^d no. V^a no. N. C. div^d S. C. no. Geo. div^d [6]

On the question for filling the blank with 30 years as the qualification; it was agreed to.

Mass^{ts} ay. Con^t no. N. Y. ay N. J. no. P^a ay Del. no M^d ay V^a ay N. C. ay S. C. ay Geo. no [7]

Mr SPAIGHT moved to fill the blank for the duration of the appointm^{ts} to the 2^d branch of the National Legislature with the words "7 years.

Mr SHERMAN, thought 7 years too long. He grounded his opposition he said on the principle that if they did their duty well, they would be reelected. And if they acted amiss, an earlier opportunity

---

[1] In the transcript the vote reads: "Massachusetts, New York, New Jersey, Pennsylvania, Delaware, Maryland, Virginia, North Carolina, South Carolina, Georgia, aye—10; Connecticut, no—1."

[2] The word "the" is here inserted in the transcript.

[3] In the transcript the vote reads: "Maryland, aye—1; Massachusetts, Connecticut, New York, New Jersey, Pennsylvania, Delaware, Virginia, North Carolina, South Carolina, Georgia, no—10."

[4] In the transcript the vote reads: "Massachusetts, Connecticut, New Jersey, Pennsylvania, Delaware, Virginia, North Carolina, South Carolina, aye—8; New York, Georgia, no—2; Maryland, divided."

[5] The words "the fifth Resolution" are substituted in the transcript for "Resol: 5."

[6] In the transcript the vote reads: "Connecticut, New Jersey, Pennsylvania, aye—3; Massachusetts, New York, Delaware, Maryland, Virginia, South Carolina, no—6; North Carolina, Georgia, divided."

[7] In the transcript the vote reads: "Massachusetts, New York, Pennsylvania, Maryland, Virginia, North Carolina, South Carolina, aye—7; Connecticut, New Jersey, Delaware, Georgia, no—4."

should be allowed for getting rid of them. He preferred 5 years which w^d be between the terms of [1] 1st branch & of the executive

Mr PIERCE proposed 3 years. 7 years would raise an alarm. Great mischiefs had [2] arisen in England from their septennial act which was reprobated by most of their patriotic Statesmen.

Mr RANDOLPH was for the term of 7 years. The democratic licentiousness of the State Legislatures proved the necessity of a firm Senate. The object of this 2^d branch is to controul the democratic branch of the Nat^l Legislature. If it be not a firm body, the other branch being more numerous, and coming immediately from the people, will overwhelm it. The Senate of Maryland constituted on like principles had been scarcely able to stem the popular torrent. No mischief can be apprehended, as the concurrence of the other branch, and in some measure, of the Executive, will in all cases be necessary. A firmness & independence may be the more necessary also in this branch, as it ought to guard the Constitution agst encroachments of the Executive who will be apt to form combinations with the demagogues of the popular branch.

Mr MADISON, considered 7 years as a term by no means too long. What we wished was to give to the Gov^t that stability which was every where called for, and which the Enemies of the Republican form alledged to be inconsistent with its nature. He was not afraid of giving too much stability by the term of Seven years. His fear was that the popular branch would still be too great an overmatch for it. It was to be much lamented that we had so little direct experience to guide us. The Constitution of Maryland was the only one that bore any analogy to this part of the plan. In no instance had the Senate of Mary^d created just suspicions of danger from it. In some instances perhaps it may have erred by yielding to the H. of Delegates. In every instance of their opposition to the measures of the H. of D. they had had with them the suffrages of the most enlightened and impartial people of the other States as well as of their own. In the States where the Senates were chosen in the same manner as the other branches, of the Legislature, and held their seats for 4 years, the institution was found to be no check whatever agst the instabilities of the other branches. He conceived it to be of great importance that a stable & firm Gov^t organized in the republican form should be held out to the people. If this be not done, and the people be left to judge of this species of Gov^t by ye operations of the defective systems under which they now live, it is much to be feared

---

[1] The word " the " is here inserted in the transcript.
[2] The word " have " is substituted in the transcript for " had."

the time is not distant when, in universal disgust, they will renounce the blessing which they have purchased at so dear a rate, and be ready for any change that may be proposed to them.

On the question for " seven years " as the term for the 2ᵈ branch Mass.ᵗˢ divided (Mʳ King, Mʳ Ghorum ay—Mʳ Gerry, Mʳ Strong, no) Conᵗ no. N. Y. divᵈ N. J. ay. Pᵃ ay Del. ay. Mᵈ ay. Vᵃ ay. N. C. ay. S. C. ay. Geo. ay.¹

Mʳ BUTLER & Mʳ RUTLIDGE proposed that the members of the 2ᵈ branch should be entitled to no salary or compensation for their services On the question,* Mass.ᵗˢ divᵈ Conᵗ ay. N. Y. no. N. J. no. P. no. Del. ay. Mᵈ no. Vᵃ no. N. C. no. S. C. ay. Geo. no.³

It was then moved & agreed that the clauses respecting the stipends & ineligibility of the 2ᵈ branch be the same as, of the 1ˢᵗ branch: Con: disagreeing to the ineligibility.

It was moved & 2ᵈᵉᵈ to alter Resol: 9.⁴ so as to read " that the jurisdiction of the supreme tribunal shall be to hear & determine in the dernier resort, all piracies, felonies &c."

It was moved & 2ᵈᵉᵈ to strike out " all piracies & felonies on the high seas," which was agreed to.

It was moved & agreed to strike out " all captures from an enemy."

It was moved & agreed to strike out " other States " and insert " two distinct States of the Union "

It was moved & agreed to postpone the consideration of Resolution 9,⁴ relating to the Judiciary:

The Comᵉ then rose & the House adjourned

WEDNESDAY JUNE 13. IN COMMITTEE OF THE WHOLE

Resol: 9 ⁴ being resumed

The latter parts of the clause relating to the jurisdiction of the

* [It is probable yᵉ votes here turned chiefly on the idea that if the salaries were not here provided for, the members would be paid by their respective States]
This note for the bottom margin.²

---

¹ In the transcript the vote reads: "New Jersey, Pennsylvania, Delaware, Maryland, Virginia, North Carolina, South Carolina, Georgia, aye—8; Connecticut, no—1; Massachusetts [Mr. Gorham and Mr. King, aye; Mr. Gerry and Mr. Strong, no] New York, divided."

² Madison's direction is omitted in the transcript.

³ In the transcript the vote reads: " Connecticut, Delaware, South Carolina, aye—3; New York, New Jersey, Pennsylvania, Maryland, Virginia, North Carolina, Georgia, no—7; Massachusetts, divided."

⁴ The words "the ninth Resolution" are substituted in the transcript for " Resol: 9."

Nati! tribunals, was struck out nem. con in order to leave full room for their organization.

M: RANDOLPH & M: MADISON, then moved the following resolution respecting a National Judiciary, viz "that the jurisdiction of the National Judiciary shall extend to cases, which respect the collection of the national revenue, impeachments of any national officers, and questions which involve the national peace and harmony " which was agreed to.

M: PINKNEY & M: SHERMAN moved to insert after the words " one supreme tribunal " the words " the Judges of which to be appointed by the national Legislature."

M: MADISON, objected to an app: by the whole Legislature. Many of them were [1] incompetent Judges of the requisite qualifications. They were too much influenced by their partialities. The candidate who was present, who had displayed a talent for business in the legislative field, who had perhaps assisted ignorant members in business of their own, or of their Constituents, or used other winning means, would without any of the essential qualifications for an expositor of the laws prevail over a competitor not having these recommendations, but possessed of every necessary accomplishment. He proposed that the appointment should be made by the Senate, which as a less numerous & more select body, would be more competent judges, and which was sufficiently numerous to justify such a confidence in them.

M: SHARMAN & M: PINKNEY withdrew their motion, and the app: by the Senate was ag⁴ to nem. con.

M: GERRY. moved to restrain the Senatorial branch from originating money bills. The other branch was more immediately the representatives of the people, and it was a maxim that the people ought to hold the purse-strings. If the Senate should be allowed to originate such bills, they w⁴ repeat the experiment, till chance should furnish a sett of representatives in the other branch who will fall into their snares.

M: BUTLER saw no reason for such a discrimination. We were always following the British Constitution when the reason of it did not apply. There was no analogy between the H. of Lords and the body proposed to be established. If the Senate should be degraded by any such discriminations, the best men would be apt to decline serving in it in favor of the other branch. And it will lead the latter into the practice of tacking other clauses to money bills.

M: MADISON observed that the Commentators on the Brit: Const:

---

[1] The word "are" is substituted in the transcript for "were."

had not yet agreed on the reason of the restriction on the H. of L. in money bills. Certain it was there could be no similar reason in the case before us. The Senate would be the representatives of the people as well as the 1ˢᵗ branch. If they sᵈ have any dangerous influence over it, they would easily prevail on some member of the latter to originate the bill they wished to be passed. As the Senate would be generally a more capable sett of men, it wᵈ be wrong to disable them from any preparation of the business, especially of that which was most important, and in our republics, worse prepared than any other. The Gentleman in pursuance of his principle ought to carry the restraint to the *amendment*, as well as the originating of money bills, since, an addition of a given sum wᵈ be equivalent to a distinct proposition of it.

Mʳ KING differed from Mʳ GERRY, and concurred in the objections to the proposition.

Mʳ READ favored the proposition, but would not extend the restraint to the case of amendments.

Mʳ PINKNEY thinks the question premature. If the Senate shᵈ be formed on the *same* proportional representation as it stands at present, they sᵈ have equal power, otherwise if a different principle sᵈ be introduced.

Mʳ SHERMAN. As both branches must concur, there can be no danger whichever way the Senate[1] be formed. We establish two branches in order to get more wisdom, which is particularly needed in the finance business—The Senate bear their share of the taxes, and are also the representatives of the people. What a man does by another, he does by himself is a maxim. In Conⁿᵗ both branches can originate in all cases, and it has been found safe & convenient. Whatever might have been the reason of the rule as to The H. of Lords, it is clear that no good arises from it now even there.

Genˡ PINKNEY. This distinction prevails in S. C. & has been a source of pernicious disputes between yᵉ 2 branches. The Constitution is now evaded, by informal schedules of amendments handed from yᵉ Senate to the other House.

Mʳ WILLIAMSON wishes for a question chiefly to prevent re-discussion. The restriction will have one advantage, it will oblige some member in[2] lower branch to move, & people can then mark him.

On the question for excepting money bills as propᵈ by Mʳ Gerry,

---

[1] The word "may" is here inserted in the transcript.
[2] The word "the" is here inserted in the transcript.

SESSION OF WEDNESDAY, JUNE 13, 1787   99

Mass. no. Con! no. N. Y. ay. N. J. no. Del. ay. M⁴ no. Vᵃ ay.
N. C. no. S. C. no. Geo. no.¹

² Committee rose & M⁺ GHORUM made report, which was postponed till tomorrow, to give an opportunity for other plans to be proposed. The report was in the words following:

REPORT OF THE COMMITTEE OF WHOLE ON M⁺ RANDOLPH'S PROPOSITIONS ³

1. Res⁴ that it is the opinion of this Committee that a National Governm! ought to be established, consisting of a supreme Legislative, Executive & Judiciary.

  2. Resol⁴ that the National Legislature ought to consist of two branches.

  3. Res⁴ that the members of the first branch of the National Legislature ought to be elected by the people of the several States for the term of three years, to receive fixed Stipends by which they may be compensated for the devotion of their time to ² public service, to be paid out of the National Treasury: to be ineligible to any office established by a particular State, or under the authority of the U. States, (except those peculiarly belonging to the functions of the first branch), during the term of service, and under the national Government for the space of one year after its expiration.

  4. Res⁴ that the members of the second branch of the Nat! Legislature ought to be chosen by the individual Legislatures, to be of the age of 30 years at least, to hold their offices for a term sufficient to ensure their independency,⁴ namely, seven years, to receive fixed stipends by which they may be compensated for the devotion of their time to ² public service to be paid out of the National Treasury; to be ineligible to any office established by a particular State, or under the authority of the U. States, (except those peculiarly belonging to the functions of the second branch) during the term of service, and under the Nat! Gov! for the space of one year after its expiration.

  5. Res⁴ that each branch ought to possess the right of originating Acts

  6. Res⁴ that the Nat! Legislature ought to be empowered to enjoy the Legislative rights vested in Congˢ by the Confederation, and moreover to legislate in all cases to which the separate States are incompetent; or in which the harmony of the U. S. may be interrupted by the exercise of individual legislation; to negative all laws passed by the several States contravening in the opinion of the National Legislature the articles of Union, or any treaties subsisting under the authority of the Union.

---

¹ In the transcript the vote reads: " New York, Delaware, Virginia, aye—3; Massachusetts, Connecticut, New Jersey, Maryland, North Carolina, South Carolina, Georgia no—7."
² The word " the " is here inserted in the transcript.
³ This heading is omitted in the transcript.
⁴ The word " independency " is changed to " independence " in the transcript.

7. Res^d that the rights of suffrage in the 1st branch of the National Legislature, ought not to be according to the rule established in the articles of confederation but according to some equitable ratio of representation, namely, in proportion to the whole number of white & other free citizens & inhabitants, of every age sex and condition, including those bound to servitude for a term of years, & three fifths of all other persons, not comprehended in the foregoing description, except Indians not paying taxes in each State:

8. Resolved that the right of suffrage in the 2^d branch of the National Legislature ought to be according to the rule established for the first.

9. Resolved that a National Executive be instituted to consist of a single person, to be chosen by the Nat^l Legislature for the term of seven years, with power to carry into execution the national laws, to appoint to offices in cases not otherwise provided for—to be ineligible a second time, & to be removeable on impeachment and conviction of malpractices or neglect of duty—to receive a fixed stipend by which he may be compensated for the devotion of his time to [1] public service to be paid out of the national Treasury.

10. Resol^d that the Nat^l Executive shall have a right to negative any Legislative Act, which shall not be afterwards passed unless [2] by two thirds of each branch of the National Legislature.

11. Resol^d that a Nat^l Judiciary be established, to consist of one supreme tribunal, the Judges of which to [3] be appointed by the 2^d branch of the Nat^l Legislature, to hold their offices during good behaviour, & to receive punctually at stated times a fixed compensation for their services, in which no increase or diminution shall be made, so as to affect the persons actually in office at the time of such increase or diminution.

12. Resol^d that the Nat^l Legislature be empowered to appoint inferior Tribunals.

13. Res^d that the jurisdiction of the Nat^l Judiciary shall extend to all cases which respect the collection of the Nat^l revenue, impeachments of any Nat^l Officers, and questions which involve the national peace & harmony.

14. Res^d that provision ought to be made for the admission of States lawfully arising within the limits of the U. States, whether from a voluntary junction of Government & territory or otherwise, with the consent of a number of voices in the Nat^l Legislature less than the whole.

15. Res^d that provision ought to be made for the continuance of Congress and their authorities and privileges untill a given day after the reform of the articles of Union shall be adopted and for the completion of all their engagements.

16. Res^d that a Republican Constitution & its existing laws ought to be guaranteed to each State by the U. States.

---

[1] The word " the " is here inserted in the transcript.
[2] The word " unless " is omitted in the transcript.
[3] The word " shall " is substituted in the transcript for " to."

17. Res.d that provision ought to be made for the amendment of the Articles of Union whensoever it shall seem necessary.

18. Res.d that the Legislative, Executive & Judiciary powers within the several States ought to be bound by oath to support the articles of Union.

19. Res.d that the amendments which shall be offered to the confederation by the Convention ought at a proper time or times after the approbation of Cong.s to be submitted to an Assembly or Assemblies recommended by the several Legislatures to be expressly chosen by the people to consider and decide thereon.

THURSDAY JUNE 14. IN CONVENTION [1]

M.r PATTERSON, observed to the Convention that it was the wish of several deputations, particularly that of N. Jersey, that further time might be allowed them to contemplate the plan reported from the Committee of the Whole, and to digest one purely federal, and contradistinguished from the reported plan. He said they hoped to have such an one ready by tomorrow to be laid before the Convention: And the Convention adjourned that leisure might be given for the purpose.

FRIDAY JUNE 15.TH 1787. [2]

[3] M.r PATTERSON, laid before the Convention the plan which he said several of the deputations wished to be substituted in place of that proposed by M.r Randolph. After some little discussion of the most proper mode of giving it a fair deliberation it was agreed that it should be referred to a Committee of the whole, and that in order to place the two plans in due comparison, the other should be recommitted. At the earnest desire [4] of M.r Lansing & some other gentlemen, it was also agreed that the Convention should not go into Committee of the whole on the subject till tomorrow, by which delay the friends of the plan proposed by M.r Patterson w.d be better prepared to explain & support it, and all would have an opportu.y of taking copies.*

[* this plan had been concerted among the deputations or members thereof, from Cont. N. Y. N. J. Del. and perhaps M.r Martin from Mary.d who made with

---

[1] The words " In Convention " are crossed out in the transcript.
[2] The year " 1787 " is omitted in the transcript.
[3] The words " In Convention " are here inserted in the transcript.
[4] The word " request " is substituted in the transcript for " desire."

The propositions from N. Jersey moved by M<u>r</u> Patterson were in the words following.

1. Res<u>d</u> that the articles of Confederation ought to be so revised, corrected & enlarged, as to render the federal Constitution adequate to the exigencies of Government, & the preservation of the Union.

2. Res<u>d</u> that in addition to the powers vested in the U. States in Congress, by the present existing articles of Confederation, they be authorized to pass acts for raising a revenue, by levying a duty or duties on all goods or merchandizes of foreign growth or manufacture, imported into any part of the U. States, by Stamps on paper, vellum or parchment, and by a postage on all letters or packages passing through the general post-office, to be applied to such federal purposes as they shall deem proper & expedient; to make rules & regulations for the collection thereof; and the same from time to time, to alter & amend in such manner as they shall think proper: to pass Acts for the regulation of trade & commerce as well with foreign nations as with each other: provided that all punishments, fines, forfeitures & penalties to be incurred for contravening such acts rules and regulations shall be adjudged by the Common law Judiciaries of the State in which any offence contrary to the true intent & meaning of such Acts rules & regulations shall have been committed or perpetrated, with liberty of commencing in the first instance all suits & prosecutions for that purpose in the superior common law Judiciary in such State, subject nevertheless, for the correction of all errors, both in law & fact in rendering Judgment, to an appeal to the Judiciary of the U. States.

3. Res<u>d</u> that whenever requisitions shall be necessary, instead of the rule for making requisitions mentioned in the articles of Confederation, the United States in Cong<u>s</u> be authorized to make such requisitions in proportion to the whole number of white & other free citizens & inhabitants of every age sex and condition including those bound to servitude for a term of years & three fifths of all other

them a common cause [1] on different principles. Cont & N. Y. were ag<u>st</u> a departure from the principle of the Confederation, wishing rather to add a few new powers to Cong<u>s</u> than to substitute, a National Gov<u>t</u> The States of N. J. & Del. were opposed to a National Gov<u>t</u> because its patrons considered a proportional representation of the States as the basis of it. The eagourness displayed by the members opposed to a Nat<u>l</u> Gov<u>t</u> from these different motives began now to produce serious anxiety for the result of the Convention. M<u>r</u> Dickenson said to M<u>r</u> Madison—You see the consequence of pushing things too far. Some of the members from the small States wish for two branches in the General Legislature, and are friends to a good National Government; but we would sooner submit to a foreign power, than submit to be deprived of an equality of suffrage,[2] in both branches of the legislature, and thereby be thrown under the domination of the large States.]
        * The note in brackets for the margin.[3]

---

[1] The word "though" is here inserted in the transcript.
[2] The phrase "of an equality of suffrage" is transposed so that the transcript reads "deprived, in both branches of the legislature of an equality of suffrage, and thereby" . . .
[3] Madison's direction is omitted in the transcript.

persons not comprehended in the foregoing description, except Indians not paying taxes; that if such requisitions be not complied with, in the time specified therein, to direct the collection thereof in the non complying States & for that purpose to devise and pass acts directing & authorizing the same; provided that none of the powers hereby vested in the U. States in Cong? shall be exercised without the consent of at least   States, and in that proportion if the number of Confederated States should hereafter be increased or diminished.

4. Res? that the U. States in Cong? be authorized to elect a federal Executive to consist of   persons, to continue in office for the term of   years, to receive punctually at stated times a fixed compensation for their services, in which no increase or diminution shall be made so as to affect the persons composing the Executive at the time of such increase or diminution, to be paid out of the federal treasury; to be incapable of holding any other office or appointment during their time of service and for   years thereafter; to be ineligible a second time, & removeable by Cong? on application by a majority of the Executives of the several States; that the Executives [1] besides their general authority to execute the federal acts ought to appoint all federal officers not otherwise provided for, & to direct all military operations; provided that none of the persons composing the federal Executive shall on any occasion take command of any troops, so as personally to conduct any [2] enterprise as General or in other capacity.

5. Res? that a federal Judiciary be established to consist of a supreme Tribunal the Judges of which to be appointed by the Executive, & to hold their offices during good behaviour, to receive punctually at stated times a fixed compensation for their services in which no increase or diminution shall be made, so as to affect the persons actually in office at the time of such increase or diminution; that the Judiciary so established shall have authority to hear & determine in the first instance on all impeachments of federal officers, & by way of appeal in the dernier resort in all cases touching the rights of Ambassadors, in all cases of captures from an enemy, in all cases of piracies & felonies on the high Seas, in all cases in which foreigners may be interested, in the construction of any treaty or treaties, or which may arise on any of the Acts for [3] regulation of trade, or the collection of the federal Revenue: that none of the Judiciary shall during the time they remain in office be capable of receiving or holding any other office or appointment during their time [4] of service, or for   thereafter.

6. Res? that all Acts of the U. States in Cong? made by virtue & in pursuance of the powers hereby & by the articles of Confederation vested in them, and all Treaties made & ratified under the authority of the U. States shall be the supreme law of the respective

---

[1] The transcript uses the word "Executives" in the singular.
[2] The word "military" is here inserted in the transcript.
[3] The word "the" is here inserted in the transcript.
[4] The word "term" is substituted in the transcript for "time."

States so far forth as those Acts or Treaties shall relate to the said States or their Citizens, and that the Judiciary of the several States shall be bound thereby in their decisions, any thing in the respective laws of the Individual States to the contrary notwithstanding; and that if any State, or any body of men in any State shall oppose or prevent y.ᵉ carrying into execution such acts or treaties, the federal Executive shall be authorized to call forth y.ᵉ power of the Confederated States, or so much thereof as may be necessary to enforce and compel an obedience to such Acts, or an observance of such Treaties.

7. Res.ᵈ that provision be made for the admission of new States into the Union.

8. Res.ᵈ ¹ the rule for naturalization ought to be the same in every State.

9. Res.ᵈ that a Citizen of one State committing an offence in another State of the Union, shall be deemed guilty of the same offence as if it had been committed by a Citizen of the State in which the offence was committed.*

Adjourned.

SATURDAY JUNE 16.   IN COMMITTEE OF THE WHOLE ON ² RESOLUTIONS PROPOS.ᴰ BY M.ᴿ P. & M.ᴿ R

M.ʳ LANSING called for the reading of the 1.ˢᵗ resolution of each plan, which he considered as involving principles directly in contrast; that of M.ʳ Patterson says he sustains the sovereignty of the respective States, that of M.ʳ Randolph distroys it: the latter requires a negative on all the laws of the particular States; the former, only certain general powers for the general good.   The plan of M.ʳ R. in short absorbs all power except what may be exercised in the little local matters of the States which are not objects worthy of the supreme cognizance.   He grounded his preference of M.ʳ P.'s plan, chiefly on two objections ag.ˢᵗ ³ that of M.ʳ R.   1.⁴ want of power in the Convention to discuss & propose it.   2 ⁴ the improbability of its being

* This copy of M.ʳ Patterson's propositions varies in a few clauses from that in the printed Journal furnished from the papers of M.ʳ Brearley a Colleague of M.ʳ Patterson.   A confidence is felt, notwithstanding, in its accuracy.   That the copy in the Journal is not entirely correct is shewn by the ensuing speech of M.ʳ Wilson [June 16] in which he refers to the mode of removing the Executive by impeachment & conviction as a feature in the Virg.ᵃ plan forming one of its contrasts to that of M.ʳ Patterson, which proposed a removal on the application of a majority of the Executives of the States.   In the copy printed in the Journal, the two modes are combined in the same clause; whether through inadvertence, or as a contemplated amendment does not appear.

¹ The word "that" is here inserted in the transcript.
² The word "the" is here inserted in the transcript.
³ The word "to" is substituted in the transcript for "ag.ˢᵗ"
⁴ The figures "1" and "2" are changed to "first" and "secondly" in the transcript.

adopted. 1. He was decidedly of opinion that the power of the Convention was restrained to amendments of a federal nature, and having for their basis the Confederacy in being. The Act of Congress The tenor of the Acts of the States, the Commissions produced by the several deputations all proved this. And this limitation of the power to an amendment of the Confederacy, marked the opinion of the States, that it was unnecessary & improper to go farther. He was sure that this was the case with his State. N. York would never have concurred in sending deputies to the convention, if she had supposed the deliberations were to turn on a consolidation of the States, and a National Government.

2. was it probable that the States would adopt & ratify a scheme, which they had never authorized us to propose? and which so far exceeded what they regarded as sufficient? We see by their several Acts particularly in relation to the plan of revenue proposed by Cong. in 1783, not authorized by the Articles of Confederation, what were the ideas they then entertained. Can so great a change be supposed to have already taken place. To rely on any change which is hereafter to take place in the sentiments of the people would be trusting to too great an uncertainty. We know only what their present sentiments are. And it is in vain to propose what will not accord with these. The States will never feel a sufficient confidence in a general Government to give it a negative on their laws. The Scheme is itself totally novel. There is no parallel to it to be found. The authority of Congress is familiar to the people, and an augmentation of the powers of Congress will be readily approved by them.

M: PATTERSON, said as he had on a former occasion given his sentiments on the plan proposed by M: R. he would now avoiding repetition as much as possible give his reasons in favor of that proposed by himself. He preferred it because it accorded 1.[1] with the powers of the Convention, 2[1] with the sentiments of the people. If the confederacy was radically wrong, let us return to our States, and obtain larger powers, not assume them of ourselves. I came here not to speak my own sentiments, but the sentiments of those who sent me. Our object is not such a Governm! as may be best in itself, but such a one as our Constituents have authorized us to prepare, and as they will approve. If we argue the matter on the supposition that no Confederacy at present exists, it can not be denied that all the

---

[1] The figures " 1 " and " 2 " are changed to " first " and " secondly " in the transcript.

States stand on the footing of equal sovereignty. All therefore must concur before any can be bound. If a proportional representation be right, why do we not vote so here? If we argue on the fact that a federal compact actually exists, and consult the articles of it we still find an equal Sovereignty to be the basis of it. He reads the 5th art: of [1] Confederation giving each State a vote—& the 13th declaring that no alteration shall be made without unanimous consent. This is the nature of all treaties. What is unanimously done, must be unanimously undone. It was observed [by M[r] Wilson] that the larger States gave up the point, not because it was right, but because the circumstances of the moment urged the concession. Be it so. Are they for that reason at liberty to take it back. Can the donor resume his gift without the consent of the donee. This doctrine may be convenient, but it is a doctrine that will sacrifice the lesser States. The large States acceded readily to the confederacy. It was the small ones that came in reluctantly and slowly. N. Jersey & Maryland were the two last, the former objecting to the want of power in Congress over trade: both of them to the want of power to appropriate the vacant territory to the benefit of the whole.—If the sovereignty of the States is to be maintained, the Representatives must be drawn immediately from the States, not from the people: and we have no power to vary the idea of equal sovereignty. The only expedient that will cure the difficulty, is that of throwing the States into Hotchpot. To say that this is impracticable, will not make it so. Let it be tried, and we shall see whether the Citizens of Mass[ts] Pen[a] & V[a] accede to it. It will be objected that Coercion will be impracticable. But will it be more so in one plan than the other? Its efficacy will depend on the quantum of power collected, not on its being drawn from the States, or from the individuals; and according to his plan it may be exerted on individuals as well as according [2] that of M[r] R. A distinct executive & Judiciary also were equally provided by his plan. It is urged that two branches in the Legislature are necessary. Why? for the purpose of a check. But the reason of [3] the precaution is not applicable to this case. Within a particular State, where party heats prevail, such a check may be necessary. In such a body as Congress it is less necessary, and besides, the delegations of the different States are checks on each other. Do the people at large complain of Cong[s]? No, what they wish is that Cong[s] may have more power. If the power now proposed be not eno',

---

[1] The word "the" is here inserted in the transcript.
[2] The word "to" is here inserted in the transcript.
[3] The word "for" is substituted in the transcript for "of."

the people hereafter will make additions to it. With proper powers Cong? will act with more energy & wisdom than the proposed Nat! Legislature; being fewer in number, and more secreted & refined by the mode of election. The plan of M? R. will also be enormously expensive. Allowing Georgia & Del. two representatives each in the popular branch the aggregate number of that branch will be 180. Add to it half as many for the other branch and you have 270. members coming once at least a year from the most distant as well as the most central parts of the republic. In the present deranged state of our finances can so expensive a system be seriously thought of? By enlarging the powers of Cong? the greatest part of this expence will be saved, and all purposes will be answered. At least a trial ought to be made.

M? WILSON entered into a contrast of the principal points of the two plans so far he said as there had been time to examine the one last proposed. These points were 1. in the Virg? plan there are *2* & in some degree 3 branches in the Legislature: in the plan from N. J. there is to be a *single* legislature only—2. Representation of the people at large is the basis of the [1] one:—the State Legislatures, the pillars of the other—3. proportional representation prevails in one; —equality of suffrage in the other—4. A single Executive Magistrate is at the head of the one:—a plurality is held out in the other.—5. in the one the [2] majority of the people of the U. S. must prevail:—in the other a minority may prevail. 6. the Nat! Legislature is to make laws in all cases to which the separate States are incompetent &-:— in place of this Cong? are to have additional power in a few cases only—7. A negative on the laws of the States:—in place of this coertion to be substituted—8. The Executive to be removeable on impeachment & conviction;—in one plan: in the other to be remove-able at the instance of [3] majority of the Executives of the States— 9. Revision of the laws provided for in one:—no such check in the other—10. inferior national tribunals in one:—none such in the other. 11. In y? one jurisdiction of Nat! tribunals to extend &c—; an appellate jurisdiction only allowed in the other. 12. Here the juris-diction is to extend to all cases affecting the Nation! peace & har-mony: there, a few cases only are marked out. 13. finally y? ratifica-tion is in this to be by the people themselves:—in that by the legis-lative authorities according to the 13 art: of [4] Confederation.

---

[1] The word "the" is omitted in the transcript.
[2] The word "a" is substituted in the transcript for "the."
[3] The word "a" is here inserted in the transcript.
[4] The word "the" is here inserted in the transcript.

With regard to the *power of the Convention,* he conceived himself authorized to *conclude nothing,* but to be at liberty to *propose any thing.* In this particular he felt himself perfectly indifferent to the two plans.

With *regard to the sentiments of the people,* he conceived it difficult to know precisely what they are. Those of the particular circle in which one moved, were commonly mistaken for the general voice. He could not persuade himself that the State Gov^ts. & Sovereignties were so much the idols of the people, nor a Nat! Gov^t so obnoxious to them, as some supposed. Why s^d a Nat! Gov^t be unpopular? Has it less dignity? will each Citizen enjoy under it less liberty or protection? Will a Citizen of *Delaware* be degraded by becoming a Citizen of the *United States?* [1] Where do the people look at present for relief from the evils of which they complain? Is it from an internal reform of their Gov^ts.? no, Sir. It is from the Nat! Councils that relief is expected. For these reasons he did not fear, that the people would not follow us into a national Gov^t and it will be a further recommendation of Mr R.'s plan that it is to be submitted to *them,* and not to the *Legislatures,* for ratification.

proceeding now to the 1st point on which he had contrasted the two plans, he observed that anxious as he was for some augmentation of the federal powers, it would be with extreme reluctance indeed that he could ever consent to give powers to Cong^s he had two reasons either of wch was sufficient. 1.[2] Cong^s as a Legislative body does not stand on the people. 2.[2] it is a *single* body. 1. He would not repeat the remarks he had formerly made on the principles of Representation. he would only say that an inequality in it, has ever been a poison contaminating every branch of Gov^t In G. Britain where this poison has had a full operation, the security of private rights is owing entirely to the purity of Her tribunals of Justice, the Judges of which are neither appointed nor paid, by a venal Parliament. The political liberty of that Nation, owing to the inequality of representation is at the mercy of its rulers. He means not to insinuate that there is any parallel between the situation of that Country & ours at present. But it is a lesson we ought not to disregard, that the smallest bodies in G. B. are notoriously the most corrupt. Every other source of influence must also be stronger in small than [3] large bodies of men. When Lord Chesterfield had told us that one of the Dutch provinces

---

[1] The transcript does not italicize the word " States."
[2] The figures " 1 " and " 2 " are changed to " first " and " secondly " in the transcript.
[3] The word " in " is here inserted in the transcript.

had been seduced into the views of France, he need not have added, that it was not Holland, but one of the *smallest* of them. There are facts among ourselves which are known to all. Passing over others, he [1] will only remark that the *Impost*, so anxiously wished for by the public was defeated not by any of the *larger* States in the Union. 2. *Congress is a single Legislature.* Despotism comes on Mankind in different Shapes, sometimes in an Executive, sometimes in a Military, one. Is there no danger of a Legislative despotism? Theory & practice both proclaim it. If the Legislative authority be not restrained, there can be neither liberty nor stability; and it can only be restrained by dividing it within itself, into distinct and independent branches. In a single House there is no check, but the inadequate one, of the virtue & good sense of those who compose it.

On another great point, the contrast was equally favorable to the plan reported by the Committee of the whole. It vested the Executive powers in a single Magistrate. The plan of N. Jersey, vested them in a plurality. In order to controul the Legislative authority, you must divide it. In order to controul the Executive you must unite it. One man will be more responsible than three. Three will contend among themselves till one becomes the master of his colleagues. In the triumvirates of Rome first Cæsar, then Augustus, are witnesses of this truth. The Kings of Sparta, & the Consuls of Rome prove also the factious consequences of dividing the Executive Magistracy. Having already taken up so much time he wᵈ not he sᵈ proceed to any of the otʰer points. Those on which he had dwelt, are sufficient of themselves: and on a decision of them, the fate of the others will depend.

Mʳ PINKNEY, the whole comes to this, as he conceived. Give N. Jersey an equal vote, and she will dismiss her scruples, and concur in the Natⁱ system. He thought the Convention authorized to go any length in recommending, which they found necessary to remedy the evils which produced this Convention.

Mʳ ELSEWORTH proposed as a more distinctive form of collecting the mind of the Committee on the subject, " that the Legislative power of the U. S. should remain in Congˢ" This was not seconded, though it seemed better calculated for the purpose than the 1ˢᵗ proposition of Mʳ Patterson in place of which Mʳ E. wished to substitute it.

Mʳ RANDOLPH, was not scrupulous on the point of power. When the salvation of the Republic was at stake, it would be treason to

---

[1] The word " we " is substituted in the transcript for " he."

our trust, not to propose what we found necessary. He painted in strong colours, the imbecility of the existing Confederacy, & the danger of delaying a substantial reform. In answer to the objection drawn from the sense of our Constituents as denoted by their acts relating to the Convention and the objects of their deliberation, he observed that as each State acted separately in the case, it would have been indecent for it to have charged the existing Constitution with all the vices which it might have perceived in it. The first State that set on foot this experiment would not have been justified in going so far, ignorant as it was of the opinion of others, and sensible as it must have been of the uncertainty of a successful issue to the experiment. There are certainly seasons [1] of a peculiar nature where the ordinary cautions must be dispensed with; and this is certainly one of them. He w^d not as far as depended on him leave any thing that seemed necessary, undone. The present moment is favorable, and is probably the last that will offer.

The true question is whether we shall adhere to the federal plan, or introduce the national plan. The insufficiency of the former has been fully displayed by the trial already made. There are but two modes, by which the end of a Genl Gov^t can be attained: the 1st is [2] by coercion as proposed by Mr P.s plan 2.[3] by real legislation as prop^d by the other plan. Coercion he pronounced to be *impracticable, expensive, cruel to individuals.* It tended also to habituate the instruments of it to shed the blood & riot in the spoils of their fellow Citizens, and consequently trained them up for the service of ambition. We must resort therefore to a National [4] *Legislation over individuals,* for which Cong^s are unfit. To vest such power in them, would be blending the Legislative with the Executive, contrary to the rec^d maxim on this subject: If the Union of these powers heretofore in Cong^s has been safe, it has been owing to the general impotency of that body. Cong^s are moreover not elected by the people, but by the Legislatures who retain even a power of recall. They have therefore no will of their own, they are a mere diplomatic body, and are always obsequious to the views of the States, who are always encroaching on the authority of the U. States. A provision for harmony among the States, as in trade, naturalization &c.—for crushing rebellion whenever it may rear its crest—and for certain other general

---

[1] The words "certainly seasons" are transposed to read "seasons certainly" in the transcript; but the word "seasons" was erroneously printed "reasons," which error has been followed in other editions of Madison's notes.
[2] The word "is" is omitted in the transcript.
[3] The figure "2" is changed to "the second" in the transcript.
[4] The transcript italicizes the word "National."

benefits, must be made. The powers for these purposes, can never be given to a body, inadequate as Congress are in point of representation, elected in the mode in which they are, and possessing no more confidence than they do: for notwithstanding what has been said to the contrary, his own experience satisfied him that a rooted distrust of Congress pretty generally prevailed. A Nat! Gov! alone, properly constituted, will answer the purpose; and he begged it to be considered that the present is the last moment for establishing one. After this select experiment, the people will yield to despair.

The Committee rose & the House adjourned.

MONDAY JUNE 18. IN COMMITTEE OF THE WHOLE ON THE PROPOSITIONS OF M? PATTERSON & M? RANDOLPH

On motion of M? DICKINSON to postpone the 1st Resolution in M? Patterson's plan, in order to take up the following viz—" that the Articles of Confederation ought to be revised and amended, so as to render the Government of the U. S. adequate to the exigences, the preservation and the prosperity of the Union " the postponement was agreed to by 10 States, Pen: divided.

M? HAMILTON, had been hitherto silent on the business before the Convention, partly from respect to others whose superior abilities age & experience rendered him unwilling to bring forward ideas dissimilar to theirs, and partly from his delicate situation with respect to his own State, to whose sentiments as expressed by his Colleagues, he could by no means accede. The crisis however which now marked our affairs, was too serious to permit any scruples whatever to prevail over the duty imposed on every man to contribute his efforts for the public safety & happiness. He was obliged therefore to declare himself unfriendly to both plans. He was particularly opposed to that from N. Jersey, being fully convinced, that no amendment of the Confederation, leaving the States in possession of their Sovereignty could possibly answer the purpose. On the other hand he confessed he was much discouraged by the amazing extent of Country in expecting the desired blessings from any general sovereignty that could be substituted.—As to the powers of the Convention, he thought the doubts started on that subject had arisen from distinctions & reasonings too subtle. A *federal* Gov! he conceived to mean an association of independent Communities into one. Different Confederacies have different powers, and exercise them in different ways. In some instances the powers are exercised over collective bodies; in others over individuals, as in the German Diet—& among ourselves in cases of piracy. Great latitude therefore must be given to the signification of the term. The plan last proposed departs itself from the *federal* idea, as understood by some, since it is to operate eventually on individuals. He agreed moreover with the Honble gentleman from V.ª [M.ʳ R.] that we owed it to our Country, to do on this emergency whatever we should deem essential to its happiness. The States sent us here to provide for the exigences of the Union. To rely on & propose any plan not adequate to these exigences, merely because it was not[1] clearly within our powers, would be to sacrifice the means to the end. It may be said that the *States* can not *ratify* a plan not within the purview of the article of[2] Confederation providing for alterations & amendments. But may not the States themselves in which no constitutional authority equal to this purpose exists in the Legislatures, have had ·in view a reference to the people at large. In the Senate of N. York, a proviso was moved, that no act of the Convention should be binding untill it should be referred to the people & ratified; and the motion was lost by a single voice only, the reason assigned ag.ˢᵗ it being, that it might possibly be found an inconvenient shackle.

The great question is what provision shall we make for the happiness of our Country? He would first make a comparative examination of the two plans—prove that there were essential defects in both—and point out such changes as might render a *national one*, efficacious.—The great & essential principles necessary for the support of Government are 1. an active & constant interest in supporting it. This principle does not exist in the States in favor of the federal Gov.ᵗ They have evidently in a high degree, the esprit de corps. They constantly pursue internal interests adverse to those of the whole. They have their particular debts—their particular plans of finance &c. All these when opposed to, invariably prevail over the requisitions & plans of Congress. 2. The love of power. Men love power. The same remarks are applicable to this principle. The States have constantly shewn a disposition rather to regain the powers delegated by them than to part with more, or to give effect to what they had parted with. The ambition of their demagogues is known to hate the controul of the Gen.ˡ Government. It may be remarked too

---

[1] The word "not" is blotted in the notes but is retained because it is in the transcript.
[2] The word "the" is here inserted in the transcript.

that the Citizens have not that anxiety to prevent a dissolution of the Gen! Gov! as of the particular Gov!? A dissolution of the latter would be fatal; of the former would still leave the purposes of Gov! attainable to a considerable degree. Consider what such a State as Virg? will be in a few years, a few compared with the life of nations. How strongly will it feel its importance & self-sufficiency? 3. An habitual attachment of the people. The whole force of this tie is on the side of the State Gov! Its sovereignty is immediately before the eyes of the people: its protection is immediately enjoyed by them. From its hand distributive justice, and all those acts which familiarize & endear [1] Gov! to a people, are dispensed to them. 4. *Force* by which may be understood a *coertion of laws* or *coertion of arms.* Cong? have not the former except in few cases. In particular States, this coercion is nearly sufficient; tho' he held it in most cases, not entirely so. A certain portion of military force is absolutely necessary in large communities. Mass. is now feeling this necessity & making provision for it. But how can this force be exerted on the States collectively. It is impossible. It amounts to a war between the parties. Foreign powers also will not be idle spectators. They will interpose, the confusion will increase, and a dissolution of the Union ensue. 5. *influence.* he did not mean corruption, but a dispensation of those regular honors & emoluments, which produce an attachment to the Gov! Almost all the weight of these is on the side of the States; and must continue so as long as the States continue to exist. All the passions then we see, of avarice, ambition, interest, which govern most individuals, and all public bodies, fall into the current of the States, and do not flow in the stream of the Gen! Gov! The former therefore will generally be an overmatch for the Gen! Gov! and render any confederacy, in its very nature precarious. Theory is in this case fully confirmed by experience. The Amphyctionic Council had it would seem ample powers for general purposes. It had in particular the power of fining and using force ag.st delinquent members. What was the consequence. Their decrees were mere signals of war. The Phocian war is a striking example of it. Philip at length taking advantage of their disunion, and insinuating himself into their Councils, made himself master of their fortunes. The German Confederacy affords another lesson. The authority of Charlemagne seemed to be as great as could be necessary. The great feudal chiefs however, exercising their local sovereignties, soon felt the spirit & found the means of, encroachments, which reduced

---

[1] The word " a " is here inserted in the transcript.

the imperial authority to a nominal sovereignty. The Diet has succeeded, which tho' aided by a Prince at its head, of great authority
independently of his imperial attributes, is a striking illustration of
the weakness of Confederated Governments. Other examples instruct
us in the same truth. The Swiss cantons have scarce any Union at
all, and have been more than once at war with one another—How
then are all these evils to be avoided? only by such a compleat sovereignty in the general Governm! as will turn all the strong principles
& passions above mentioned on its side. Does the scheme of N. Jersey
produce this effect? does it afford any substantial remedy whatever?
On the contrary it labors under great defects, and the defect of some
of its provisions will destroy the efficacy of others. It gives a direct
revenue to Cong? but this will not be sufficient. The balance can
only be supplied by requisitions: which experience proves can not be
relied on. If States are to deliberate on the mode, they will also
deliberate on the object of the supplies, and will grant or not grant
as they approve or disapprove of it. The delinquency of one will
invite and countenance it in others. Quotas too must in the nature
of things be so unequal as to produce the same evil. To what
standard will you resort? Land is a fallacious one. Compare
Holland with Russia: France or Eng? with other countries of Europe.
Pen? with N. Carol? will the relative pecuniary abilities in those
instances, correspond with the relative value of land. Take numbers
of inhabitants for the rule and make like comparison of different
countries, and you will find it to be equally unjust. The different
degrees of industry and improvement in different Countries render the
first object a precarious measure of wealth. Much depends too on
situation. Con! N. Jersey & N. Carolina, not being commercial States
& contributing to the wealth of the commercial ones, can never bear
quotas assessed by the ordinary rules of proportion. They will & must
fail in their duty, their example will be followed, and the Union itself
be dissolved. Whence then is the national revenue to be drawn?
from Commerce? even from exports which notwithstanding the common opinion are fit objects of moderate taxation, from excise, &c &c.
These tho' not equal, are less unequal than quotas. Another destructive ingredient in the plan, is that equality of suffrage which is so
much desired by the small States. It is not in human nature that V?
& the large States should consent to it, or if they did that they sh?
long abide by it. It shocks too much the ¹ ideas of Justice, and every
human feeling. Bad principles in a Gov! tho slow are sure in their

---

¹ The word "all" is substituted in the transcript for "the."

operation, and will gradually destroy it. A doubt has been raised whether Cong. at present have a right to keep Ships or troops in time of peace. He leans to the negative. M. P. plan provides no remedy.—If the powers proposed were adequate, the organization of Cong. is such that they could never be properly & effectually exercised. The members of Cong. being chosen by the States & subject to recall, represent all the local prejudices. Should the powers be found effectual, they will from time to time be heaped on them, till a tyrannic sway shall be established. The general power whatever be its form if it preserves itself, must swallow up the State powers. Otherwise it will be swallowed up by them. It is ag.st all the principles of a good Government to vest the requisite powers in such a body as Cong. Two Sovereignties can not co-exist within the same limits. Giving powers to Cong. must eventuate in a bad Gov.t or in no Gov.t The plan of N. Jersey therefore will not do. What then is to be done? Here he was embarrassed. The extent of the Country to be governed, discouraged him. The expence of a general Gov.t was also formidable; unless there were such a diminution of expence on the side of the State Gov.ts as the case would admit. If they were extinguished, he was persuaded that great œconomy might be obtained by substituting a general Gov.t He did not mean however to shock the public opinion by proposing such a measure. On the other hand he saw no *other* necessity for declining it. They are not necessary for any of the great purposes of commerce, revenue, or agriculture. Subordinate authorities he was aware would be necessary. There must be district tribunals: corporations for local purposes. But cui bono, the vast & expensive apparatus now appertaining to the States. The only difficulty of a serious nature which occurred to him, was that of drawing representatives from the extremes to the center of the Community. What inducements can be offered that will suffice? The moderate wages for the 1.st branch would [1] only be a bait to little demagogues. Three dollars or thereabouts he supposed would be the utmost. The Senate he feared from a similar cause, would be filled by certain undertakers who wish for particular offices under the Gov.t This view of the subject almost led him to despair that a Republican Gov.t could be established over so great an extent. He was sensible at the same time that it would be unwise to propose one of any other form. In his private opinion he had no scruple in declaring, supported as he was by the opinions of so many of the wise & good, that the British Gov.t was the best in the world: and that he

---

[1] The word "could" is substituted in the transcript for "would."

doubted much whether any thing short of it would do in America. He hoped Gentlemen of different opinions would bear with him in this, and begged them to recollect the change of opinion on this subject which had taken place and was still going on. It was once thought that the power of Cong⁵ was amply sufficient to secure the end of their institution. The error was now seen by every one. The members most tenacious of republicanism, he observed, were as loud as any in declaiming ag⁵ᵗ the vices of democracy. This progress of the public mind led him to anticipate the time, when others as well as himself would join in the praise bestowed by M⁵ Neckar on the British Constitution, namely, that it is the only Gov⁵ in the world " which unites public strength with individual security."—In every community where industry is encouraged, there will be a division of it into the few & the many. Hence separate interests will arise. There will be debtors & creditors &c. Give all power to the many, they will oppress the few. Give all power to the few, they will oppress the many. Both therefore ought to have ¹ power, that each may defend itself ag⁵ᵗ the other. To the want of this check we owe our paper money, instalment laws &c. To the proper adjustment of it the British owe the excellence of their Constitution. Their house of Lords is a most noble institution. Having nothing to hope for by a change, and a sufficient interest by means of their property, in being faithful to the national interest, they form a permanent barrier ag⁵ᵗ every pernicious innovation, whether attempted on the part of the Crown or of the Commons. No temporary Senate will have firmness eno' to answer the purpose. The Senate [of Maryland] which seems to be so much appealed to, has not yet been sufficiently tried. Had the people been unanimous & eager, in the late appeal to them on the subject of a paper emission they would would have yielded to the torrent. Their acquiescing in such an appeal is a proof of it.—Gentlemen differ in their opinions concerning the necessary checks, from the different estimates they form of the human passions. They suppose seven years a sufficient period to give the senate an adequate firmness, from not duly considering the amazing violence & turbulence of the democratic spirit. When a great object of Gov⁵ is pursued, which seizes the popular passions, they spread like wild fire, and become irresistable. He appealed to the gentlemen from the N. England States whether experience had not there verified the remark.—As to the Executive, it seemed to be admitted that no good one could be established on Republican principles. Was not this giving up the merits of the ques-

---

¹ The word " the " is here inserted in the transcript.

tion: for can there be a good Gov.? without a good Executive. The English model was the only good one on this subject. The Hereditary interest of the King was so interwoven with that of the Nation, and his personal emoluments so great, that he was placed above the danger of being corrupted from abroad—and at the same time was both sufficiently independent and sufficiently controuled, to answer the purpose of the institution at home. one of the weak sides of Republics was their being liable to foreign influence & corruption. Men of little character, acquiring great power become easily the tools of intermedling Neibours. Sweeden was a striking instance. The French & English had each their parties during the late Revolution which was effected by the predominant influence of the former.—What is the inference from all these observations? That we ought to go as far in order to attain stability and permanency, as republican principles will admit. Let one branch of the Legislature hold their places for life or at least during good behaviour. Let the Executive also be for life. He appealed to the feelings of the members present whether a term of seven years, would induce the sacrifices of private affairs which an acceptance of public trust would require, so so as to ensure the services of the best Citizens. On this plan we should have in the Senate a permanent will, a weighty interest, which would answer essential purposes. But is this a Republican Gov.?, it will be asked? Yes if all the Magistrates are appointed, and vacancies are filled, by the people, or a process of election originating with the people. He was sensible that an Executive constituted as he proposed would have in fact but little of the power and independence that might be necessary. On the other plan of appointing him for 7 years, he thought the Executive ought to have but little power. He would be ambitious, with the means of making creatures; and as the object of his ambition w.^d be to *prolong* his power, it is probable that in case of a [1] war, he would avail himself of the emergence,[2] to evade or refuse a degradation from his place. An Executive for life has not this motive for forgetting his fidelity, and will therefore be a safer depository of power. It will be objected probably, that such an Executive will be an *elective Monarch,* and will give birth to the tumults which characterize that form of Gov.? He w.^d reply that *Monarch* is an indefinite term. It marks not either the degree or duration of power. If this Executive Magistrate w.^d be a monarch for life —the other prop.^d by the Report from the Comtte of the whole, w.^d

---

[1] The word " a " is omitted in the transcript.
[2] The word " emergence " is changed to " emergency " in the transcript.

be a monarch for seven years. The circumstance of being elective was also applicable to both. It had been observed by judicious writers that elective monarchies w^d be the best if they could be guarded agst the *tumults* excited by the ambition and intrigues of competitors. He was not sure that tumults were an inseparable evil. He rather thought this character of Elective Monarchies had been taken rather from particular cases than from general principles. The election of Roman Emperors was made by the *Army*. In *Poland* the election is made by great rival *princes* with independent power, and ample means, of raising commotions. In the German Empire, the appointment is made by the Electors & Princes, who have equal motives & means, for exciting cabals & parties. Might not such a mode of election be devised among ourselves as will defend the community agst these effects in any dangerous degree? Having made these observations he would read to the Committee a sketch of a plan which he sh^d prefer to either of those under consideration. He was aware that it went beyond the ideas of most members. But will such a plan be adopted out of doors? In return he would ask will the people adopt the other plan? At present they will adopt neither. But he sees the Union dissolving or already dissolved—he sees evils operating in the States which must soon cure the people of their fondness for democracies—he sees that a great progress has been already made & is still going on in the public mind. He thinks therefore that the people will in time be unshackled from their prejudices; and whenever that happens, they will themselves not be satisfied at stopping where the plan of Mr R. w^d place them, but be ready to go as far at least as he proposes. He did not mean to offer the paper he had sketched as a proposition to the Committee. It was meant only to give a more correct view of his ideas, and to suggest the amendments which he should probably propose to the plan of Mr R. in the proper stages of its future discussion. He read [1] his sketch in the words following: towit

I. " The Supreme Legislative power of the United States of America to be vested in two different bodies of men; the one to be called the Assembly, the other the Senate who together shall form the Legislature of the United States with power to pass all laws whatsoever subject to the Negative hereafter mentioned.

II. The Assembly to consist of persons elected by the people to serve for three years.

III. The Senate to consist of persons elected to serve during good behaviour; their election to be made by electors chosen for that pur-

---

[1] The word " reads " is substituted in the transcript for " read."

pose by the people: in order to this the States to be divided into election districts. On the death, removal or resignation of any Senator his place to be filled out of the district from which he came.

IV. The supreme Executive authority of the United States to be vested in a Governour to be elected to serve during good behaviour— the election to be made by Electors chosen by the people in the Election Districts aforesaid—The authorities & functions of the Executive to be as follows: to have a negative on all laws about to be passed, and the execution of all laws passed; to have the direction of war when authorized or begun; to have with the advice and approbation of the Senate the power of making all treaties; to have the sole appointment of the heads or chief officers of the departments of Finance, War and Foreign Affairs; to have the nomination of all other officers (Ambassadors to foreign Nations included) subject to the approbation or rejection of the Senate; to have the power of pardoning all offences except Treason; which he shall not pardon without the approbation of the Senate.

V. On the death resignation or removal of the Governour his authorities to be exercised by the President of the Senate till a Successor be appointed.

VI. The Senate to have the sole power of declaring war, the power of advising and approving all Treaties, the power of approving or rejecting all appointments of officers except the heads or chiefs of the departments of Finance War and foreign affairs.

VII. The supreme Judicial authority to be vested in   Judges to hold their offices during good behaviour with adequate and permanent salaries. This Court to have original jurisdiction in all causes of capture, and an appellative jurisdiction in all causes in which the revenues of the general Government or the Citizens of foreign Nations are concerned.

VIII. The Legislature of the United States to have power to institute Courts in each State for the determination of all matters of general concern.

IX. The Governour Senators and all officers of the United States to be liable to impeachment for mal- and corrupt conduct; and upon conviction to be removed from office, & disqualified for holding any place of trust or profit—All impeachments to be tried by a Court to consist of the Chief   or Judge of the superior Court of Law of each State, provided such Judge shall hold his place during good behavior, and have a permanent salary.

X. All laws of the particular States contrary to the Constitution or laws of the United States to be utterly void; and the better to prevent such laws being passed, the Governour or president of each State shall be appointed by the General Government and shall have a negative upon the laws about to be passed in the State of which he is [1] Governour or President.

XI. No State to have any forces land or Naval; and the Militia of all the States to be under the sole and exclusive direction of the

---

[1] The word " the " is here inserted in the transcript.

United States, the officers of which to be appointed and commissioned by them.

On these several articles he entered into explanatory observations [1] corresponding with the principles of his introductory reasoning.[2]

[3] Committee rose & the House Adjourned.

TEUSDAY JUNE 19.TH IN COMMITTEE OF [3] WHOLE ON THE PROPOSITIONS OF M.R PATTERSON

The substitute offered yesterday by M.r Dickenson being rejected by a vote now taken on it; Con. N. Y. N. J. Del. ay.[4] Mas. P.a V. N. C. S. C. Geo. no.[5] May.d divided. M.r Patterson's plan was again at large before the Committee.

M.r MADISON. Much stress had [6] been laid by some gentlemen on the want of power in the Convention to propose any other than a *federal* plan. To what had been answered by others, he would only add, that neither of the characteristics attached to a *federal* plan would support this objection. One characteristic, was that in a *federal* Government, the power was exercised not on the people individually; [7] but on the people *collectively,* on the *States.* Yet in some instances as in piracies, captures &c. the existing Confederacy, and in many instances, the amendments to it proposed by M.r Patterson, must operate immediately on individuals. The other characteristic was, that a *federal* Gov.t derived its appointments not immediately from the people, but from the States which they respectively composed. Here too were facts on the other side. In two of the States, Connec.t and Rh. Island, the delegates to Cong.s were chosen, not by the Legisla-

---

[1] In the transcript the following footnote was inserted with reference mark after " observations ":

"The speech introducing the plan, as above taken down & written out was seen by Mr. Hamilton, who approved its correctness, with one or two verbal changes, which were made as he suggested. The explanatory observations which did not immediately follow, were to have been furnished by Mr. H. who did not find leisure at the time to write them out, and they were not obtained.

" Judge Yates, in his notes, appears to have consolidated the explanatory with the introductory observations of Mr. Hamilton (under date of June 19th, a typographical error). It was in the former, Mr. Madison observed, that Mr. Hamilton, in speaking of popular governments, however modified, made the remark attributed to him by Judge Yates, that they were ' but pork still with a little change of sauce.' "

[2] For the text of Hamilton's Plan handed to Madison about the close of the Convention, but not actually submitted to that body, see Appendix to Debates, V, pp. 608-618.

[3] The word " The " is here inserted in the transcript.

[4] The figure " 4 " is here inserted in the transcript.

[5] The figure " 6 " is here inserted in the transcript.

[6] The word " has " is substituted in the transcript for " had."

[7] The transcript italicizes the word " individually."

tures, but by the people at large; and the plan of M! P. intended no change in this particular.

It had been alledged [by Mʳ Patterson], that the Confederation having been formed by unanimous consent, could be dissolved by unanimous Consent only. Does this doctrine result from the nature of compacts? does it arise from any particular stipulation in the articles of Confederation? If we consider the federal union as analogous to the fundamental compact by which individuals compose one Society, and which must in its theoretic origin at least, have been the unanimous act of the component members, it can not be said that no dissolution of the compact can be effected without unanimous consent. A breach of the fundamental principles of the compact by a part of the Society would certainly absolve the other part from their obligations to it. If the breach of *any* article by *any* of the parties, does not set the others at liberty, it is because, the contrary is *implied* in the compact itself, and particularly by that law of it, which gives an indifinite authority to the majority to bind the whole in all cases. This latter circumstance shews that we are not to consider the federal Union as analogous to the social compact of individuals: for if it were so, a Majority would have a right to bind the rest, and even to form a new Constitution for the whole, which the Gentⁿ from N. Jersey would be among the last to admit. If we consider the federal Union as analogous not to the social compacts among individual men: but to the conventions among individual States. What is the doctrine resulting from these conventions? Clearly, according to the Expositors of the law of Nations, that a breach of any one article, by any one party, leaves all the other parties at liberty, to consider the whole convention as dissolved, unless they choose rather to compel the delinquent party to repair the breach. In some treaties indeed it is expressly stipulated that a violation of particular articles shall not have this consequence, and even that particular articles shall remain in force during war, which in general is [1] understood to dissolve all subsisting Treaties. But are there any exceptions of this sort to the Articles of confederation? So far from it that there is not even an express stipulation that force shall be used to compell an offending member of the Union to discharge its duty. He observed that the violations of the federal articles had been numerous & notorious. Among the most notorious was an act of N. Jersey herself; by which she *expressly refused* to comply with a constitutional requisition of Congˢ and yielded no farther to the expostulations of

---

[1] The words " in general is " are transposed to read " is in general " in the transcript.

their deputies, than barely to rescind her vote of refusal without passing any positive act of compliance. He did not wish to draw any rigid inferences from these observations. He thought it proper however that the true nature of the existing confederacy should be investigated, and he was not anxious to strengthen the foundations on which it now stands.

Proceeding to the consideration of M.ʳ Patterson's plan, he stated the object of a proper plan to be twofold. 1.[1] to preserve the Union. 2.[1] to provide a Governm.ᵗ that will remedy the evils felt by the States both in their united and individual capacities. Examine M.ʳ P.s plan, & say whether it promises satisfaction in these respects.

1. Will it prevent those violations of the law of nations & of Treaties which if not prevented must involve us in the calamities of foreign wars? The tendency of the States to these violations has been manifested in sundry instances. The files of Cong.ˢ contain complaints already, from almost every nation with which treaties have been formed. Hitherto indulgence has been shewn to us. This can not be the permanent disposition of foreign nations. A rupture with other powers is among the greatest of national calamities. It ought therefore to be effectually provided that no part of a nation shall have it in its power to bring them on the whole. The existing Confederacy does not sufficiently provide against this evil. The proposed amendment to it does not supply the omission. It leaves the will of the States as uncontrouled as ever.

2. Will it prevent encroachments on the federal authority? A tendency to such encroachments has been sufficiently exemplified, among ourselves, as well[2] in every other confederated republic antient and Modern. By the federal articles, transactions with the Indians appertain to Cong.ˢ Yet in several instances, the States have entered into treaties & wars with them. In like manner no two or more States can form among themselves any treaties &c. without the consent of Cong.ˢ Yet Virg.ᵃ & Mary.ᵈ in one instance—Pen.ᵃ & N. Jersey in another, have entered into compacts, without previous application or subsequent apology. No State again can of right raise troops in time of peace without the like consent. Of all cases of the league, this seems to require the most scrupulous observance. Has not Mass.ᵗˢ, notwithstanding, the most powerful member of the Union, already raised a body of troops? Is she not now augmenting them, without having even deigned to apprise Cong.ˢ of Her intention? In

---

[1] The figures "1" and "2" are changed to "first" and "secondly" in the transcript.

[2] The word "as" is here inserted in the transcript.

fine—Have we not seen the public land dealt out to Con! to bribe her acquiescence in the decree constitutionally awarded ag.ˢᵗ her claim on the territory of Pen.ᵃ? for no other possible motive can account for the policy of Cong.ˢ in that measure?—If we recur to the examples of other confederacies, we shall find in all of them the same tendency of the parts to encroach on the authority of the whole. He then reviewed the Amphyctionic & Achæan confederacies among the antients, and the Helvetic, Germanic & Belgic among the moderns, tracing their analogy to the U. States—in the constitution and extent of their federal authorities—in the tendency of the particular members to usurp on these authorities; and to bring confusion & ruin on the whole.—He observed that the plan of Mr. Pat-son besides omitting a controul over the States as a general defence of the federal pre-rogatives was particularly defective in two of its provisions. 1.[1] Its ratification was not to be by the people at large, but by the *legislatures*. It could not therefore render the Acts of Cong.ˢ in pursuance of theiɾ powers, even legally *paramount* to the Acts of the States. 2.[2] It gave to the federal Tribunal an appellate jurisdiction only—even in the criminal cases enumerated, The necessity of any such provision supposed a danger of undue acquittals [3] in the State tribunals. Of what avail c.ᵈ [4] an appellate tribunal be, after an acquittal? Besides in most if not all of the States, the Executives have by their respective *Constitutions* the right of pard.ˢ How could this be taken from them by a *legislative* [5] ratification only?

3. Will it prevent trespasses of the States on each other? Of these enough has been already seen. He instanced Acts of Virg.ᵃ & Maryland which give [6] a preference to their own Citizens in cases where the Citizens of other States are entitled to equality of privileges by the Articles of Confederation. He considered the emissions of paper money & other kindred measures as also aggressions. The States relatively to one an other being each of them either Debtor or Creditor; The creditor States must suffer unjustly from every emission by the debtor States. We have seen retaliating acts on this subject which threatened danger not to the harmony only, but the tranquility of the Union. The plan of M.ʳ Paterson, not giving even a negative on the acts of the States, left .them as much at liberty as ever to execute their unrighteous projects ag.ˢᵗ each other.

---

[1] The figure " 1 " is changed to " In the first place " in the transcript.
[2] The figure " 2 " is changed to " and in the second place " in the transcript.
[3] The transcript uses the word " acquittals " in the singular.
[4] The word " would " is substituted in the transcript for " c.ᵈ "
[5] The word " *legislative* " is not italicized in the transcript.
[6] The word " gave " is substituted in the transcript for " give."

4. Will it secure the internal tranquility of the States themselves? The insurrections in Mass^{ts} admonished all the States of the danger to which they were exposed. Yet the plan of Mr P. contained no provisions for supplying the defect of the Confederation on this point. According to the Republican theory indeed, Right & power being both vested in the majority, are held to be synonimous. According to fact & experience, a minority may in an appeal to force be an overmatch for the majority. 1.[1] If the minority happen to include all such as possess the skill & habits of military life, with such as possess the great pecuniary resources, one third may conquer the remaining two thirds. 2.[2] one third of those who participate in the choice of rulers may be rendered a majority by the accession of those whose poverty disqualifies them from a suffrage, & who for obvious reasons may [3] be more ready to join the standard of sedition than that of the [4] established Government. 3.[5] where slavery exists, the Republican Theory becomes still more fallacious.

5. Will it secure a good internal legislation & administration to the particular States? In developing the evils which vitiate the political system of the U. S. it is proper to take into view those which prevail within the States individually as well as those which affect them collectively: Since the former indirectly affect the whole; and there is great reason to believe that the pressure of them had a full share in the motives which produced the present Convention. Under this head he enumerated and animadverted on 1.[6] the multiplicity of the laws passed by the several States. 2.[6] the mutability of their laws. 3.[6] the injustice of them. 4.[7] the impotence of them: observing that Mr Patterson's plan contained no remedy for this dreadful class of evils, and could not therefore be received as an adequate provision for the exigences of the Community.

6. Will it secure the Union agst the influence of foreign powers over its members. He pretended not to say that any such influence had yet been tried: but it was naturally to be expected that occasions would produce it. As lessons which claimed particular attention, he cited the intrigues practised among the Amphyctionic Confederates first by the Kings of Persia, and afterwards fatally by Philip of Macedon: among the Achæans, first by Macedon & afterwards no less

---

[1] The figure " 1 " is changed to " in the first place " in the transcript.
[2] The figure " 2 " is changed to " in the second place" in the transcript.
[3] The word " must " is substituted in the transcript for " may."
[4] The word " the " is omitted in the transcript.
[5] The figure " 3 " is changed to " and in the third place."
[6] The figures " 1," " 2 " and " 3 " are changed to " first," " secondly " and " thirdly " in the transcript.
[7] The figure " 4 " is changed to " and fourthly " in the transcript.

fatally by Rome: among the Swiss by Austria, France & the lesser neighbouring powers: among the members of the Germanic Body by France, England, Spain & Russia—: and in the Belgic Republic, by all the great neighbouring powers. The plan of M.ʳ Patterson, not giving to the general Councils any negative on the will of the particular States, left the door open for the like pernicious machinations among ourselves.

7. He begged the smaller States which were most attached to M.ʳ Pattersons plan to consider the situation in which it would leave them. In the first place they would continue to bear the whole expence of maintaining their Delegates in Congress. It ought not to be said that if they were willing to bear this burden, no others had a right to complain. As far as it led the small States to forbear keeping up a representation, by which the public business was delayed, it was evidently a matter of common concern. An examination of the minutes of Congress would satisfy every one that the public business had been frequently delayed by this cause; and that the States most frequently unrepresented in Cong.ˢ were not the larger States. He reminded the convention of another consequence of leaving on a small State the burden of maintaining a Representation in Cong.ˢ During a considerable period of the War, one of the Representatives of Delaware, in whom alone before the signing of the Confederation the entire vote of that State and after that event one half of its vote, frequently resided, was a Citizen & Resident of Pen.ᵃ and held an office in his own State incompatible with an appointment from it to Cong.ˢ During another period, the same State was represented by three delegates two of whom were citizens of Penn.ᵃ and the third a Citizen of New Jersey. These expedients must have been intended to avoid the burden of supporting delegates from their own State. But whatever might have been y.ᵉ cause, was not in effect the vote of one State doubled, and the influence of another increased by it? In the 2.ᵈ place The coercion, on which the efficacy of the plan depends, can never be exerted but on themselves. The larger States will be impregnable, the smaller only can feel the vengeance of it. He illustrated the position by the history of the Amphyctionic Confederates: and the ban of the German Empire. It was the cobweb w.ᶜʰ could entangle the weak, but would be the sport of the strong.

8. He begged them to consider the situation in which they would remain in case their pertinacious adherence to an inadmissible plan, should prevent the adoption of any plan. The contemplation of such an event was painful; but it would be prudent to submit to the task of examining it at a distance, that the means of escaping it might be

·the more readily embraced. Let the Union of the States be dissolved, and one of two consequences must happen. Either the States must remain individually independent & sovereign; or two or more Confederacies must be formed among them. In the first event would the small States be more secure agst the ambition & power of their larger neighbours, than they would be under a general Government pervading with equal energy every part of the Empire, and having an equal interest in protecting every part agst every other part? In the second, can the smaller expect that their larger neighbours would confederate with them on the principle of the present confederacy, which gives to each member, an equal suffrage; or that they would exact less severe concessions from the smaller States, than are proposed in the scheme of Mr Randolph?

The great difficulty lies in the affair of Representation; and if this could be adjusted, all others would be surmountable. It was admitted by both the gentlemen from N. Jersey, [Mr Brearly and Mr Patterson] that it would not be *just to allow Virg^a* which was 16 times as large as Delaware an equal vote only. Their language was that it would not be *safe for Delaware* to allow Virg^a 16 times as many votes. The expedient proposed by them was that all the States should be thrown into one mass and a new partition be made into 13 equal parts. Would such a scheme be practicable? The dissimilarities existing in the rules of property, as well as in the manners, habits and prejudices of the [1] different States, amounted to a prohibition of the attempt. It had been found impossible for the power of one of the most absolute princes in Europe [K. of France] directed by the wisdom of one of the most enlightened and patriotic Ministers [Mr Neckar] that any age has produced to equalize in some points only the different usages & regulations of the different provinces. But admitting a general amalgamation and repartition of the States to be practicable, and the danger apprehended by the smaller States from a proportional representation to be real; would not a particular and voluntary coalition of these with their neighbours, be less inconvenient to the whole community, and equally effectual for their own safety. If N. Jersey or Delaware conceived that an advantage would accrue to them from an equalization of the States, in which case they would necessaryly form a junction with their neighbours, why might not this end be attained by leaving them at liberty by the Constitution to form such a junction whenever they pleased? And why should they wish to obtrude a like arrangement

---

[1] The word " the " is crossed out in the transcript.

on all the States, when it was, to say the least, extremely difficult, would be obnoxious to many of the States, and when neither the inconveniency,[1] nor the benefit of the expedient to themselves, would be lessened, by confining it to themselves.—The prospect of many new States to the Westward was another consideration of importance. If they should come into the Union at all, they would come when they contained but few inhabitants. If they sh⁀ be entitled to vote according to their proportions of inhabitants, all would be right & safe. Let them have an equal vote, and a more objectionable minority than ever might give law to the whole.

On a question for postponing generally the 1ˢᵗ proposition of Mʳ Patterson's plan, it was agreed to: N. Y. & N J. only being no—

On the question moved by Mʳ King whether the Committee should rise & Mʳ Randolphs propositions be re-reported without alteration, which was in fact a question whether Mʳ R's should be adhered to as preferable to those of Mʳ Patterson:

Massᵗˢ ay. Conᵗ ay. N. Y. no. N. J. no. Pᵃ ay. Del. no. Mᵈ divᵈ Vᵃ ay. N. C. ay. S. C. ay. Geo. ay.[2]

Insert here from Printed Journal p. 13 [3] copy of the Resolⁿˢ of Mʳ R. as altered in the Comᵉ and reported to the House [4]

[State of the resolutions submitted to the consideration of the House by the honorable Mr. Randolph, as altered, amended, and agreed to, in a Committee of the whole House.

1.	Resolved	that it is the opinion of this Committee that a national government ought to be established consisting of a Supreme Legislative, Judiciary, and Executive.
2.	Resolved.	that the national Legislature ought to consist of Two Branches.
3	Resolved	that the members of the first branch of the national Legislature ought to be elected by the People of the several States for the term of Three years. to receive fixed stipends, by which they may be compensated for the devotion of their time to public service to be paid out of the National-Treasury. to be ineligible to any Office established by a particular State or under the authority of the United-States (except those peculiarly belonging to the functions of the first branch) during the term of service, and under the national government for the space of one year after it's expiration.

---

[1] The word "inconveniency" is changed to "inconvenience" in the transcript.

[2] In the transcript the vote reads: "Massachusetts, Connecticut, Pennsylvania, Virginia, North Carolina, South Carolina, Georgia, aye—7; New York, New Jersey, Delaware, no—3; Maryland divided."

[3] Found at page 134 instead of page 13, and here printed from the original manuscript deposited in the Department of State by President Washington.

[4] Madison's direction concerning Mr. Randolph's Resolutions and the Resolutions themselves are omitted in the transcript.

4 Resolved. that the members of the second Branch of the national Legislature ought to be chosen by the individual Legislatures. to be of the age of thirty years at least. to hold their offices for a term sufficient to ensure their independency, namely seven years. to receive fixed stipends, by which they may be compensated for the devotion of their time to public service—to be paid out of the National Treasury to be ineligible to any office established by a particular State, or under the authority of the United States (except those peculiarly belonging to the functions of the second branch) during the term of service, and under the national government, for the space of one year after it's expiration.

5. Resolved that each branch ought to possess the right of originating acts.

6. Resolved. that the national Legislature ought to be empowered to enjoy the legislative rights vested in Congress by the confederation—and moreover to legislate in all cases to which the separate States are incompetent: or in which the harmony of the United States may be interrupted by the exercise of individual legislation. to negative all laws passed by the several States contravening, in the opinion of the national Legislature, the articles of union, or any treaties subsisting under the authority of the union.

7. Resolved. that the right of suffrage in the first branch of the national Legislature ought not to be according to the rule established in the articles of confederation: but according to some equitable ratio of representation—namely, in proportion to the whole number of white and other free citizens and inhabitants of every age, sex, and condition including those bound to servitude for a term of years, and three fifths of all other persons not comprehended in the foregoing description, except Indians, not paying taxes in each State.

8 Resolved. that the right of suffrage in the second branch of the national Legislature ought to be according to the rule established for the first.

9 Resolved. that a national Executive be instituted to consist of a single person. to be chosen by the National Legislature. for the term of seven years. with power to carry into execution the national Laws, to appoint to Offices in cases not otherwise provided for to be ineligible a second time, and to be removable on impeachment and conviction of mal practice or neglect of duty. to receive a fixed stipend, by which he may be compensated for the devotion of his time to public service to be paid out of the national Treasury.

10 Resolved. that the national executive shall have a right to negative any legislative act: which shall not be afterwards passed unless by two third parts of each branch of the national Legislature.

11 Resolved. that a national Judiciary be established to consist of One Supreme Tribunal. The Judges of which to be appointed by the second Branch of the National Legislature. to hold their offices during good behaviour to receive, punctually, at stated times, a fixed compensation for their services: in which no encrease or diminution shall be made so as to affect the persons actually in office at the time of such encrease or diminution

12 Resolved. That the national Legislature be empowered to appoint inferior Tribunals.

13 Resolved. that the jurisdiction of the national Judiciary shall extend to cases which respect the collection of the national revenue: impeachments of any national officers: and questions which involve the national peace and harmony.

14. Resolved. that provision ought to be made for the admission of States, lawfully arising within the limits of the United States,

		whether from a voluntary junction of government and terri-tory, or otherwise, with the consent of a number of voices in the national Legislature less than the whole.
15.	Resolved.	that provision ought to be made for the continuance of Congress and their authorities until a given day after the reform of the articles of Union shall be adopted; and for the completion of all their engagements.
16.	Resolved	that a republican constitution, and its existing laws, ought to be guaranteed to each State by the United States.
17.	Resolved.	that provision ought to be made for the amendment of the articles of Union, whensoever it shall seem necessary.
18	Resolved.	that the Legislative, Executive, and Judiciary powers within the several States ought to be bound by oath to support the articles of Union.
19	Resolved.	that the amendments which shall be offered to the confederation by the Convention, ought at a proper time or times, after the approbation of Congress to be submitted to an assembly or assemblies of representatives, recommended by the several Legislatures, to be expressly chosen by the People to consider and decide thereon.

(Of [1] M⁰ Randolph's plan as reported from the Committee) [2]. the 1. propos: " that a Nat! Gov⁰ ought to be established consisting &c." being taken up in the House.[3]

M⁰ WILSON observed that by a Nat! Gov⁰ he did not mean one that would swallow up the State Gov⁰ˢ as seemed to be wished by some gentlemen. He was tenacious of the idea of preserving the latter. He thought, contrary to the opinion of [Col. Hamilton] that they might not only subsist but subsist on friendly terms with the former. They were absolutely necessary for certain purposes which the former could not reach. All large Governments must be sub-divided into lesser jurisdictions. As Examples he mentioned Persia, Rome, and particularly the divisions & subdivisions of England by Alfred.

Col. HAMILTON coincided with the proposition as it stood in the Report. He had not been understood yesterday. By an abolition of the States, he meant that no boundary could be drawn between the National & State Legislatures; that the former must therefore have indefinite authority. If it were limited at all, the rivalship of the States would gradually subvert it. Even as Corporations the extent of some of them as V⁰ Mass⁰ˢ &c. would be formidable. As *States*, he thought they ought to be abolished. But he admitted the necessity of leaving in them, subordinate jurisdictions. The examples of Persia & the Roman Empire, cited by [M⁰ Wilson] were he thought in favor of his doctrine: the great powers delegated to the Satraps & pro-

---

[1] The word " of " is omitted in the transcript.
[2] The words " June 13 being before the house " are here inserted in the transcript.
[3] The words " in the House " are omitted in the transcript.

consuls, having frequently produced revolts, and schemes of independence.

M: KING, wished as every thing depended on this proposition, that no objections might be improperly indulged agst the phraseology of it. He conceived that the import of the terms " States " " Sovereignty " " *national* " " federal," had been often used & applied in the discussions inaccurately & delusively. The States were not " Sovereigns " in the sense contended for by some. They did not possess the peculiar features of sovereignty, they could not make war, nor peace, nor alliances nor treaties. Considering them as political Beings, they were dumb, for they could not speak to any foreign Sovereign whatever. They were deaf, for they could not hear any propositions from such Sovereign. They had not even the organs or faculties of defence or offence, for they could not of themselves raise troops, or equip vessels, for war. On the other side, if the Union of the States comprizes the idea of a confederation, it comprizes that also of consolidation. A Union of the States is a Union of the men composing them, from whence a *national* character results to the whole. Cong: can act alone without the States—they can act & their acts will be binding agst the Instructions of the States. If they declare war: war is de jure declared—captures made in pursuance of it are lawful—No acts of the States can vary the situation, or prevent the judicial consequences. If the States therefore retained some portion of their sovereignty, they had certainly divested themselves of essential portions of it. If they formed a confederacy in some respects—they formed a Nation in others—The Convention could clearly deliberate on & propose any alterations that Cong: could have done under ye federal articles, and could not Cong: propose by virtue of the last article, a change in any article whatever: and as well that relating to the equality of suffrage, as any other. He made these remarks to obviate some scruples which had been expressed. He doubted much the practicability of annihilating the States; but thought that much of their power ought to be taken from them.

M: MARTIN, said he considered that the separation from G. B. placed the 13 States in a state of Nature towards each other; that they would have remained in that state till this time, but for the confederation; that they entered into the confederation on the footing of equality; that they met now to to amend it on the same footing; and that he could never accede to a plan that would introduce an inequality and lay 10 States at the mercy of V^a Mass^{ts} and Penn^a.

M: WILSON, could not admit the doctrine that when the Colonies became independent of G. Britain, they became independent also of each other. He read the declaration of Independence, observing thereon that the *United Colonies* were declared to be free & independent States; and inferring that they were independent, not *individually* but *Unitedly* and that they were confederated as they were independent, States.

Col. Hamilton, assented to the doctrine of Mr Wilson. He denied the doctrine that the States were thrown into a State of Nature He was not yet prepared to admit the doctrine that the Confederacy, could be dissolved by partial infractions of it. He admitted that the States met now on an equal footing but could see no inference from that against concerting a change of the system in this particular. He took this occasion of observing for the purpose of appeasing the fears of the small States, that two circumstances would render them secure under a National Gov^{t} in which they might lose the equality of rank they now held: one was the local situation of the 3 largest States Virg^{a} Mas^{ts} & P^{a} They were separated from each other by distance of place, and equally so, by all the peculiarities which distinguish the interests of one State from those of another. No combination therefore could be dreaded. In the second place, as there was a gradation in the States from V^{a} the largest down to Delaware the smallest, it would always happen that ambitious combinations among a few States might & w^{d} be counteracted by defensive combinations of greater extent among the rest. No combination has been seen among [1] large Counties merely as such, agst lesser Counties. The more close the Union of the States, and the more compleat the authority of the whole: the less opportunity will be allowed [2] the stronger States to injure the weaker.

Adj^{d}

Wednesday June 20. 1787.[3] In Convention

Mr William Blount from N. Carolina took his seat.

1st propos: [4] of the Report of Com^{e} of the whole [5] before the House.

Mr Elseworth 2^{ded} by Mr Gorham, moves to alter it so as to run "that the Government of the United States ought to consist of a supreme legislative, Executive and Judiciary." This alteration he

---

[1] The word "the" is here inserted in the transcript.

[2] The word "to" is here inserted in the transcript.

[3] The year "1787" is omitted in the transcript.

[4] The words "The first Resolution" are substituted in the transcript for "1st propos."

[5] The word "being" is here inserted in the transcript.

said would drop the word *national*, and retain the proper title "the United States." He could not admit the doctrine that a breach of any of the federal articles could dissolve the whole. It would be highly dangerous not to consider the Confederation as still subsisting. He wished also the plan of the Convention to go forth as an amendment to [1] the articles of [2] Confederation, since under this idea the authority of the Legislatures could ratify it. If they are unwilling, the people will be so too. If the plan goes forth to the people for ratification several succeeding Conventions within the States would be unavoidable. He did not like these conventions. They were better fitted to pull down than to build up Constitutions.

Mᵣ RANDOLPH, did not object to the change of expression, but apprised the gentlemen [3] who wished for it that he did not admit it for the reasons assigned; particularly that of getting rid of a reference to the people for ratification. The motion of Mᵣ Ellsewᵗʰ was acquiesced in nem: con:

The 2ᵈ Resol: "that the national Legislature ought to consist of two branches" [4] taken up, the word "national" struck out as of course.

Mᵣ LANSING, observed that the true question here was, whether the Convention would adhere to or depart from the foundation of the present Confederacy; and moved instead of the 2ᵈ Resolution, "that the powers of Legislation be vested in the U. States in Congress." He had already assigned two reasons agˢᵗ such an innovation as was proposed: 1.[5] the want of competent powers in the Convention.—2.[5] the state of the public mind. It had been observed by [Mᵣ Madison] in discussing the first point, that in two States the Delegates to Congˢ were chosen by the people. Notwithstanding the first appearance of this remark, it had in fact no weight, as the Delegates however chosen, did not represent the people merely as so many individuals; but as forming a Sovereign State. [Mᵣ Randolph] put it, he said, on its true footing namely that the public safety superseded the scruple arising from the review of our powers. But in order to feel the force of this consideration, the same impression must be had of the public danger. He had not himself the same impression, and could not therefore dismiss his scruple. [Mᵣ Wilson] contended that as the Convention were only to recommend, they might recommend

---

[1] The word "of" is substituted in the transcript for "to."
[2] The word "the" is here inserted in the transcript.
[3] The word "gentlemen" is used in the singular in the transcript.
[4] The word "being" is here inserted in the transcript.
[5] The figures "1" and "2" are changed to "first" and "secondly" in the transcript.

what they pleased. He differed much from him. Any act whatever of so respectable a body must have a great effect, and if it does not succeed, will be a source of great dissentions. He admitted that there was no certain criterion of the public mind on the subject. He there-fore recurred to the evidence of it given by the opposition in the States to the scheme of an Impost. It could not be expected that those possessing Sovereignty could ever voluntarily part with it. It was not to be expected from any one State, much less from thirteen. He proceeded to make some observations on the plan itself and the argum^{ts} urged in support of it. The point of Representation could receive no elucidation from the case of England. The corruption of the boroughs did not proceed from their comparative smallness: but from the actual fewness of the inhabitants, some of them not having more than one or two. A great inequality existed in the Counties of England. Yet the like complaint of peculiar corruption in the small ones had not been made. It had been said that Congress rep-resent the State prejudices: will not any other body whether chosen by the Legislatures or people of the States, also represent their prejudices? It had been asserted by his colleague [Col. Hamilton] that there was no coincidence of interests among the large States that ought to excite fears of oppression in the smaller. If it were true that such a uniformity of interests existed among the States, there was equal safety for all of them, whether the representation remained as heretofore, or were proportioned as now proposed. It is proposed that the Genl Legislature shall have a negative on the laws of the States. Is it conceivable that there will be leisure for such a task? there will on the most moderate calculation, be as many Acts sent up from the States as there are days in the year. Will the members of the general Legislature be competent Judges? Will a gentleman from Georgia be a Judge of the expediency of a law which is to operate in N. Hamshire. Such a Negative would be more injurious than that of Great Britain heretofore was. It is said that the National Gov^t must have the influence arising from the grant of offices and honors. In order to render such a Government effectual he believed such an influence to be necessary. But if the States will not agree to it, it is in vain, worse than in vain to make the proposition. If this influence is to be attained, the States must be entirely abolished. Will any one say this would ever be agreed to? He doubted whether any Genl Government equally beneficial to all can be attained. That now under consideration he is sure, must be utterly unattainable. He had another objection. The system was too novel & complex. No man could foresee what its operation will be either with respect to the Gen! Gov! or the State Gov!: One or other it has been surmised must absorb the whole.

Col. MASON, did not expect this point would have been reagitated. The essential differences between the two plans, had been clearly stated. The principal objections ag!! that of M! R. were the *want of power* & the *want of practicability*. There can be no weight in the first as the fiat is not to be *here*, but in the people. He thought with his colleague M! R. that there were besides certain crisises, in which all the ordinary cautions yielded to public necessity. He gave as an example, the eventual Treaty with G. B. in forming which the Comrs. of the U. S. had boldly disregarded the improvident shackles of Cong! had given to their Country an honorable & happy peace, and instead of being censured for the transgression of their powers, had raised to themselves a monument more durable than brass. The *impracticability* of gaining the public concurrence he thought was still more groundless. [M! Lansing] had cited the attempts of Congress to gain an enlargement of their powers, and had inferred from the miscarriage of these attempts, the hopelessness of the plan which he [M! L] opposed. He thought a very different inference ought to have been drawn; viz that the plan which [M! L] espoused, and which proposed to augment the powers of Congress, never could be expected to succeed. He meant not to throw any reflections on Cong! as a body, much less on any particular members of it. He meant however to speak his sentiments without reserve on this subject; it was a privilege of Age, and perhaps the only compensation which nature had given for the privation of so many other enjoyments: and he should not scruple to exercise it freely. Is it to be thought that the people of America, so watchful over their interests; so jealous of their liberties, will give up their all, will surrender both the sword and the purse, to the same body, and that too not chosen immediately by themselves? They never will. They never ought. Will they trust such a body, with the regulation of their trade, with the regulation of their taxes; with all the other great powers, which are in contemplation? Will they give unbounded confidence to a secret Journal—to the intrigues—to the factions which in the nature of things appertain to such an Assembly? If any man doubts the existence of these characters of Congress, let him consult their Journals for the years 78, 79, & 80.—It will be said, that if the people are averse to parting with power, why is it hoped that they will part with it to a National Legislature. The proper answer is that in this case they do not part with power: they only transfer it from one sett of immediate Representatives to another sett.—Much has been said of the unsettled state of the mind of the people, he believed the mind of the people of America, as elsewhere, was unsettled as to some points; but settled as to others. In two points he was sure it was well settled. 1.[1] in an attachment to Republican Government. 2.[1] in an attachment to more than one branch in the Legislature. Their constitutions accord so generally in both these circumstances, that they seem almost to have been preconcerted. This must either have been a miracle, or have resulted from the genius of the people. The only exceptions to the establishm[t] of two branches in the Legislatures are the State of P[a]. & Cong[s] and the latter the only single one not chosen by the people themselves. What has been the consequence? The people have been constantly averse to giving that Body further powers—It was acknowledged by [M[r] Patterson] that his plan could not be enforced without military coertion. Does he consider the force of this concession. The most jarring elements of Nature; fire & water themselves are not more incompatible that[2] such a mixture of civil liberty and military execution. Will the militia march from one State to[3] another, in order to collect the arrears of taxes from the delinquent members of the Republic? Will they maintain an army for this purpose? Will not the Citizens of the invaded State assist one another till they rise as one Man, and shake off the Union altogether. Rebellion is the only case, in which the military force of the State can be properly exerted ag[st] its Citizens. In one point of view he was struck with horror at the prospect of recurring to this expedient. To punish the non-payment of taxes with death, was a severity not yet adopted by despotism itself: yet this unexampled cruelty would be mercy compared to a military collection of revenue, in which the bayonet could make no discrimination between the innocent and the guilty. He took this occasion to repeat, that notwithstanding his solicitude to establish a national Government, he never would agree to abolish the State Gov[ts] or render them absolutely insignificant. They were as necessary as the Gen[l] Gov[t] and he would be equally careful to preserve them. He was aware of the difficulty of drawing the line between them, but hoped it was not insurmountable. The Convention, tho' comprising so many distinguished characters, could not be expected to make a faultless Gov[t] And he would prefer trusting to posterity the amendment of its defects, rather than to push the experiment too far.

---

[1] The figures " 1 " and " 2 " are changed to " first " and " secondly " in the transcript.

[2] The word " than " is substituted in the transcript for " that."

[3] The word " into " is substituted in the transcript for " in."

M: LUTHER MARTIN agreed with [Col Mason] as to the importance of the State Gov:^{ts} he would support them at the expence of the Genl Gov:^t which was instituted for the purpose of that support. He saw no necessity for two branches, and if it existed Congress might be organized into two. He considered Cong^s as representing the people, being chosen by the Legislatures who were chosen by the people. At any rate, Congress represented the Legislatures; and it was the Legislatures not the people who refused to enlarge their powers. Nor could the rule of voting have been the ground of objection, otherwise ten of the States must always have been ready, to place further confidence in Cong:^s The causes of repugnance must therefore be looked for elsewhere.—At the separation from the British Empire, the people of America preferred the establishment of themselves into thirteen separate sovereignties instead of incorporating themselves into one: to these they look up for the security of their lives, liberties & properties: to these they must look up. The federal Gov:^t they formed, to defend the whole ag:st foreign nations, in case of war, and to defend the lesser States ag:st the ambition of the larger: they are afraid of granting powers [1] unnecessarily, lest they should defeat the original end of the Union; lest the powers should prove dangerous to the sovereignties of the particular States which the Union was meant to support; and expose the lesser to being swallowed up by the larger. He conceived also that the people of the States having already vested their powers in their respective Legislatures, could not resume them without a dissolution of their Governments. He was ag:st Conventions in the States: was not ag:st assisting States ag:st rebellious subjects; thought the *federal* plan of M: Patterson did not require coercion more than the *National one*, as the latter must depend for the deficiency of its revenues on requisitions & quotas, and that a national Judiciary extended into the States would be ineffectual, and would be viewed with a jealousy inconsistent with its usefulness.

M: SHERMAN 2^{ded} & supported M: Lansings motion. He admitted two branches to be necessary in the State Legislatures, but saw no necessity for them in a Confederacy of States. The examples were all, of a single Council. Cong:^s carried us thro' the war, and perhaps as well as any Gov:^t could have done. The complaints at present are not that the views of Cong:^s are unwise or unfaithful; but that their powers are insufficient for the execution of their views. The national debt & the want of power somewhere to draw forth

---

[1] The transcript uses the word " powers " in the singular.

the National resources, are the great matters that press. All the States were sensible of the defect of power in Cong? He thought much might be said in apology for the failure of the State Legislatures to comply with the confederation. They were afraid of bearing too hard on the people, by accumulating taxes; no *constitutional* rule had been or could be observed in the quotas—the accounts also were unsettled & every State supposed itself in advance, rather than in arrears. For want of a general system, taxes to a due amount had not been drawn from trade which was the most convenient resource. As almost all the States had agreed to the recommendation of Cong? on the subject of an impost, it appeared clearly that they were willing to trust Cong? with power to draw a revenue from Trade. There is no weight therefore in the argument drawn from a distrust of Cong? for money matters being the most important of all, if the people will trust them with power as to them, they will trust them with any other necessary powers. Cong? indeed by the confederation have in fact the right of saying how much the people shall pay, and to what purpose it shall be applied: and this right was granted to them in the expectation that it would in all cases have its effect. If another branch were to be added to Cong? to be chosen by the people, it would serve to embarrass. The people would not much interest themselves in the elections, a few designing men in the large districts would carry their points, and the people would have no more confidence in their new representatives than in Cong? He saw no reason why the State Legislatures should be unfriendly as had been suggested, to Cong? If they appoint Cong? and approve of their measures, they would be rather favorable and partial to them. The disparity of the States in point of size he perceived was the main difficulty. But the large States had not yet suffered from the equality of votes enjoyed by the small ones. In all great and general points, the interests of all the States were the same. The State of Virg? notwithstanding the equality of votes, ratified the Confederation without, or [1] even proposing, any alteration. Mass? also ratified without any material difficulty &c. In none of the ratifications is the want of two branches noticed or complained of. To consolidate the States as some had proposed would dissolve our Treaties with foreign Nations, which had been formed with us, as *confederated* States. He did not however suppose that the creation of two branches in the Legislature would have such an effect. If the difficulty on the subject of representation can not be otherwise got over, he would agree

---

[1] The word " or " is stricken out in the transcript.

to have two branches, and a proportional representation in one of them; provided each State had an equal voice in the other. This was necessary to secure the rights of the lesser States; otherwise three or four of the large States would rule the others as they please. Each State like each individual had its peculiar habits usages and manners, which constituted its happiness. It would not therefore give to others a power over this happiness, any more than an individual would do, when he could avoid it.

M⸢ᵣ⸣ WILSON, urged the necessity of two branches; observed that if a proper model were [1] not to be found in other Confederacies it was not to be wondered at. The number of them was small & the duration of some at least short. The Amphyctionic & Achæan were formed in the infancy of political Science; and appear by their History & fate, to have contained radical defects. The Swiss & Belgic Confederacies were held together not by any vital principle of energy but by the incumbent pressure of formidable neighbouring nations: The German owed its continuance to the influence of the H. of Austria. He appealed to our own experience for the defects of our Confederacy. He had been 6 years in [2] the 12 since the commencement of the Revolution, a member of Congress, and had felt all its weaknesses. He appealed to the recollection of others whether on many important occasions, the public interest had not been obstructed by the small members of the Union. The success of the Revolution was owing to other causes, than the Constitution of Congress. In many instances it went on even ag⸢ˢᵗ⸣ the difficulties arising from Cong⸢ˢ⸣ themselves. He admitted that the large States did accede as had been stated, to the Confederation in its present form. But it was the effect of necessity not of choice. There are other instances of their yielding from the same motive to the unreasonable measures of the small States. The situation of things is now a little altered. He insisted that a jealousy would exist between the State Legislatures & the General Legislature: observing that the members of the former would have views & feelings very distinct in this respect from their constituents. A private Citizen of a State is indifferent whether power be exercised by the Gen⸢ˡ⸣ or State Legislatures, provided it be exercised most for his happiness. His representative has an interest in its being exercised by the body to which he belongs. He will therefore view the National Legisl: with the eye of a jealous rival. He observed that the addresses of Cong⸢ˢ⸣ to the people at

---

[1] The word "was" is substituted in the transcript for "were."
[2] The word "of" is substituted in the transcript for "in."

large, had always been better received & produced greater effect, than those made to the Legislatures.

On the question for postponing in order to take up Mʳ Lansings proposition " to vest the powers of Legislation in Congᵃ "

Massᵗ no. Conᵗ ay. N. Y. ay. N. J. ay. Pᵃ no. Del. ay Mᵈ divᵈ Vᵃ no. N. C. no. S. C. no. Geo. no ¹

On motion of the Deputies from Delaware, the question on the 2ᵈ Resolution in the Report from the Committee of the whole was postponed till tomorrow.

Adjᵈ

THURSDAY JUNE 21. IN CONVENTION

Mʳ Jonathan Dayton from N. Jersey took his seat.*

³ Docʳ JOHNSON. On a comparison of the two plans which had been proposed from Virginia & N. Jersey, it appeared that the peculiarity which characterized the latter was its being calculated to preserve the individuality of the States.ᐧ The plan from Vᵃ did not profess to destroy this individuality altogether, but was charged with such a tendency. One Gentleman alone (Col. Hamilton) in his animadversions on the plan of N. Jersey, boldly and decisively contended for an abolition of the State Govᵗˢ Mʳ Wilson & the gentlemen from Virgᵃ who also were adversaries of the plan of N. Jersey held a different language. They wished to leave the States in possession of a considerable, tho' a subordinate jurisdiction. They had not yet however shewn how this cᵈ consist with, or be secured agˢᵗ the general sovereignty & jurisdiction, which they proposed to give to the national Government. If this could be shewn in such a manner as to satisfy the patrons of the N. Jersey propositions, that the individuality of the States would not be endangered, many of their objections would no doubt be removed. If this could not be shewn their objections would have their full force. He wished it therefore to be well considered whether in case the States, as was

* From June 21 to July 18 inclusive not copied by Mʳ Eppes.²

---

¹ In the transcript the vote reads: "Connecticut, New York, New Jersey, Delaware, aye—4; Massachusetts, Pennsylvania, Virginia, North Carolina, South Carolina, Georgia, no—6; Maryland divided."

² This footnote is omitted in the transcript. It refers to a copy of Madison's journal made by John W. Eppes, Jefferson's son-in-law, for Jefferson's use some time between 1799 and 1810. "The Writings of James Madison, Hunt, Editor, Vol. VI (1906), 329, n; Documentary History of the Constitution, Vol. V (1905), 294-296.

³ The transcript here inserts the following: "The second Resolution in the Report from the Committee of the Whole, being under consideration."

proposed, sh? retain some portion of sovereignty at least, this portion could be preserved, without allowing them to participate effectually in the Gen! Gov!, without giving them each a distinct and equal vote for the purpose of defending themselves in the general Councils.

M? WILSON's respect for Doc? Johnson, added to the importance of the subject led him to attempt, unprepared as he was, to solve the difficulty which had been started. It was asked how the Gen! Gov! and individuality of the particular States could be reconciled to each other; and how the latter could be secured agst the former? Might it not, on the other side be asked how the former was to be secured agst the latter? It was generally admitted that a jealousy & rivalship would be felt between the Gen! & particular Gov^{ts}? As the plan now stood, tho' indeed contrary to his opinion, one branch of the Gen! Gov! (the Senate or second branch) was to be appointed by the State Legislatures. The State Legislatures, therefore, by this participation in the Gen! Gov! would have an opportunity of defending their rights. Ought not a reciprocal opportunity to be given to the Gen! Gov! of defending itself by having an appointment of some one constituent branch of the State Gov^{ts}? If a security be necessary on one side, it w^d seem reasonable to demand it on the other. But taking the matter in a more general view, he saw no danger to the States from the Gen! Gov! In case a combination should be made by the large ones it w^d produce a general alarm among the rest; and the project w^d be frustrated. But there was no temptation to such a project. The States having in general a similar interest, in case of any proposition [1] in the National Legislature to encroach on the State Legislatures, he conceived a general alarm w^d take place in the National Legislature itself, that it would communicate itself to the State Legislatures, and w^d finally spread among the people at large. The Gen! Gov! will be as ready to preserve the rights of the States as the latter are to preserve the rights of individuals; all the members of the former, having a common interest, as representatives of all the people of the latter, to leave the State Gov^{ts} in possession of what the people wish them to retain. He could not discover, therefore any danger whatever on the side from which it had been [2] apprehended. On the contrary, he conceived that in spite of every precaution the general Gov! would be in perpetual danger of encroachments from the State Gov^{ts}?

---

[1] The transcript uses the word "proposition" in the plural.
[2] The word "was" is substituted in the transcript for "had been."

Mr MADISON was of opinion[1] that there was 1. less danger of encroachment from the Genl Gov.^{t} than from the State Gov.^{ts} 2.[2] that the mischief from encroachments would be less fatal if made by the former, than if made by the latter. 1. All the examples of other confederacies prove the greater tendency in such systems to anarchy than to tyranny; to a disobedience of the members than to[3] usurpations of the federal head. Our own experience had fully illustrated this tendency.—But it will be said that the proposed change in the principles & form of the Union will vary the tendency; that the Genl Gov.^{t} will have real & greater powers, and will be derived in one branch at least from the people, not from the Gov.^{ts} of the States. To give full force to this objection, let it be supposed for a moment that indefinite power should be given to the Genl Legislature, and the States reduced to corporations dependent on the Genl Legislature; Why sh.^{d} it follow that the Genl Gov.^{t} w.^{d} take from the States any branch of their power as far as its operation was beneficial, and its continuance desireable to the people? In some of the States, particularly in Connecticut, all the Townships are incorporated, and have a certain limited jurisdiction. Have the Representatives of the people of the Townships in the Legislature of the State ever endeavored to despoil the Townships of any part of their local authority? As far as this local authority is convenient to the people they are attached to it; and their representatives chosen by & amenable to them naturally respect their attachment to this, as much as their attachment to any other right or interest. The relation of a General Gov.^{t} to State Gov.^{ts} is parallel. 2. Guards were more necessary ag.st encroachments of the State Gov.^{ts} on the Genl Gov.^{t} than of the latter on the former. The great objection made ag.st an abolition of the State Gov.^{ts} was that the Genl Gov.^{t} could not extend its care to all the minute objects which fall under the cognizance of the local jurisdictions. The objection as stated lay not ag.st the probable abuse of the general power, but ag.st the imperfect use that could be made of it throughout so great an extent of country, and over so great a variety of objects. As far as as its operation would be practicable it could not in this view be improper; as far as it would be impracticable, the conveniency[4] of the Genl Gov.^{t} itself would concur with that of the people in the maintenance of subordinate Governments. Were it practicable for the Genl Gov.^{t} to extend its care to every

---

[1] The phrase " in the first place " is here inserted in the transcript and the figure " 1 " is omitted.

[2] The figure " 2 " is changed to " and in the second place " in the transcript.

[3] The word " to " is omitted in the transcript.

[4] The word " conveniency " is changed to " convenience " in the transcript.

requisite object without the cooperation of the State Gov^{ts} the people would not be less free as members of one great Republic than as members of thirteen small ones. A Citizen of Delaware was not more free than a Citizen of Virginia: nor would either be more free than a Citizen of America. Supposing therefore a tendency in the Gen! Government to absorb the State Gov^{ts} no fatal [1] consequence could result. Taking the reverse of [2] the supposition, that a tendency should be left in the State Gov^{ts} towards an independence on the General Gov^t and the gloomy consequences need not be pointed out. The imagination of them, must have suggested to the States the experiment we are now making to prevent the calamity, and must have formed the chief motive with those present to undertake the arduous task.

On the question for resolving " that the Legislature ought to consist of two Branches "

Mass. ay. Con^t ay. N. Y. no. N. Jersey no P^a ay. Del. no. M^d div^d V^a ay. N. C. ay. S. C. ay. Geo. ay.[3]

The *third* resolution of the Report [4] taken into consideration.

Gen! PINKNEY moved " that the 1st branch, instead of being elected by the people, sh^d be elected in such manner as the Legislature of each State should direct." He urged 1.[5] that this liberty would give more satisfaction, as the Legislatures could then accomodate the mode to the conveniency [6] & opinions of the people. 2.[5] that it would avoid the undue influence of large Counties which would prevail if the elections were to be made in districts as must be the mode intended by the Report of the Committee. 3.[5] that otherwise disputed elections must be referred to the General Legislature which would be attended with intolerable expence and trouble to the distant parts of the republic.

Mr L. MARTIN seconded the Motion.

Col. HAMILTON considered the motion as intended manifestly to transfer the election from the people to the State Legislatures, which would essentially vitiate the plan. It would increase that State influence which could not be too watchfully guarded agst All too must admit the possibility, in case the Gen! Gov^t sh^d maintain itself,

---

[1] The transcript italicizes the word "fatal."

[2] The word " as " is substituted in the transcript for " of."

[3] In the transcript the vote reads: " Massachusetts, Connecticut, Pennsylvania, Virginia, North Carolina, South Carolina, Georgia, aye—7; New York, New Jersey, Delaware, no—3; Maryland, divided."

[4] The word " being " is here inserted in the transcript.

[5] The figures " 1," " 2 " and " 3 " are changed to " first," " secondly " and " thirdly " in the transcript.

[6] The word " conveniency " is changed to " convenience " in the transcript.

that the State Gov^{ts} might gradually dwindle into nothing. The system therefore sh^d not be engrafted on what might possibly fail.

Mr Mason urged the necessity of retaining the election by the people. Whatever inconveniency [1] may attend the democratic principle, it must actuate one part of the Gov^t It is the only security for the rights of the people.

Mr Sherman, would like an election by the Legislatures best, but is content with [2] plan as it stands.

Mr Rutlidge could not admit the solidity of the distinction between a mediate & immediate election by the people. It was the same thing to act by oneself, and to act by another. An election by the Legislature would be more refined than an election immediately by the people: and would be more likely to correspond with the sense of the whole community. If this Convention had been chosen by the people in districts it is not to be supposed that such proper characters would have been preferred. The Delegates to Cong^s he thought had also been fitter men than would have been appointed by the people at large.

Mr Wilson considered the election of the 1st branch by the people not only as the corner Stone, but as the foundation of the fabric: and that the difference between a mediate & immediate election was immense. The difference was particularly worthy of notice in this respect: that the Legislatures are actuated not merely by the sentiment of the people; but have an official sentiment opposed to that of the Genl Gov^t and perhaps to that of the people themselves.

Mr King enlarged on the same distinction. He supposed the Legislatures w^d constantly choose men subservient to their own views as contrasted to the general interest; and that they might even devise modes of election that w^d be subversive of the end in view. He remarked several instances in which the views of a State might be at variance with those of the Genl Gov^t: and mentioned particularly a competition between the National & State debts, for the most certain & productive funds.

Genl Pinkney was for making the State Gov^{ts} a part of the General System. If they were to be abolished, or lose their agency, S. Carolina & other States would have but a small share of the benefits of Gov^t

On the question for Genl Pinkney motion to substitute election

---

[1] The word "inconveniency" is changed to "inconvenience" in the transcript.

[2] The word "the" is here inserted in the transcript.

of [1] 1st branch in such mode as the Legislatures should appoint, in stead of its being elected by the people.''

Mass^{ts} no. Con^t ay. N. Y. no. N. J. ay. P^a no. Del. ay. M^d div^d V^a no. N. C. no. S. C. ay Geo. no.[2]

General PINKNEY then moved that the 1st branch be elected *by the people* in such mode as the Legislatures should direct; but waved it on its being hinted that such a provision might be more properly tried in the detail of the plan.

On the question for ye election of the 1st branch by the *people*.''

Mass^{ts} ay. Con^t ay. N. Y. ay. N. J. no. P^a ay. Del. ay. M^d div^d V^a ay. N. C. ay. S. C. ay Geo. ay.[3]

[1] Election of the 1st branch '' for the term of three years,''[4] considered

Mr RANDOLPH moved to strike out, '' three years '' and insert '' two years ''—he was sensible that annual elections were a source of great mischiefs in the States, yet it was the want of such checks agst the popular intemperence as were now proposed, that rendered them so mischievous. He would have preferred annual to biennial, but for the extent of the U. S. and the inconveniency[5] which would result from them to the representatives of the extreme parts of the Empire. The people were attached to frequency of elections. All the Constitutions of the States except that of S. Carolina, had established annual elections.

Mr DICKENSON. The idea of annual elections was borrowed from the antient usage of England, a country much less extensive than ours. He supposed biennial would be inconvenient. He preferred triennial: and in order to prevent the inconveniency[5] of an entire change of the whole number at the same moment, suggested a rotation, by an annual election of one third.

Mr ELSEWORTH was opposed to three years, supposing that even one year was preferable to two years. The people were fond of frequent elections and might be safely indulged in one branch of the Legislature. He moved for 1 year.

Mr STRONG seconded & supported the motion.

---

[1] The word " the " is here inserted in the transcript.

[2] In the transcript the vote reads: " Connecticut, New Jersey, Delaware, South Carolina, aye—4; Massachusetts, New York, Pennsylvania, Virginia, North Carolina, Georgia, no—6; Maryland, divided."

[3] In the transcript the vote reads: " Massachusetts, Connecticut, New York, Pennsylvania, Delaware, Virginia, North Carolina, South Carolina, Georgia, aye—9; New Jersey, no—1; Maryland, divided."

[4] The word " being " is here inserted in the transcript.

[5] The word " inconveniency " is changed to " inconvenience " in the transcript.

M͏ͬ Wilson being for making the 1ˢᵗ branch an effectual representation of the people at large, preferred an annual election of it. This frequency was most familiar & pleasing to the people. It would be not [1] more inconvenient to them, than triennial elections, as the people in all the States have annual meetings with which the election of the National representatives might be made to co-incide. He did not conceive that it would be necessary for the Natˡ Legisl: to sit constantly; perhaps not half—perhaps not one fourth of the year.

M͏ͬ Madison was persuaded that annual elections would be extremely inconvenient and apprehensive that biennial would be too much so: he did not mean inconvenient to the electors; but to the representatives. They would have to travel seven or eight hundred miles from the distant parts of the Union; and would probably not be allowed even a reimbursement of their expences. Besides, none of those who wished to be re-elected would remain at the seat of Governmᵗ; confiding that their absence would not affect them. The members of Congˢ had done this with few instances of disappointment. But as the choice was here to be made by the people themselves who would be much less complaisant to individuals, and much more susceptible of impressions from the presence of a Rival candidate, it must be supposed that the members from the most distant States would travel backwards & forwards at least as often as the elections should be repeated. Much was to be said also on the time requisite for new members who would always form a large proportion, to acquire that knowledge of the affairs of the States in general without which their trust could not be usefully discharged.

M͏ͬ Sherman preferred annual elections, but would be content with biennial. He thought the Representatives ought to return home and mix with the people. By remaining at the seat of Govᵗ they would acquire the habits of the place which might differ from those of their Constituents.

Col. Mason observed that the States being differently situated such a rule ought to be formed as would put them as nearly as possible on a level. If elections were annual the middle States would have a great advantage over the extreme ones. He wished them to be biennial; and the rather as in that case they would coincide with the periodical elections of S. Carolina as well of the other States.

Col. Hamilton urged the necessity of 3 years. There ought to be neither too much nor too little dependence, on the popular senti-

---

[1] The words " be not " are transposed to read " not be " in the transcript.

ments. The checks in the other branches of Govern! would be but feeble, and would need every auxiliary principle that could be interwoven. The British House of Commons were elected septennially, yet the democratic spirit of y? Constitution had not ceased. Frequency of elections tended to make the people listless to them; and to facilitate the success of little cabals. This evil was complained of in all the States. In Virg? it had been lately found necessary to force the attendance & voting of the people by severe regulations.

On the question for striking out " three years "

Mass^{ts} ay. Con! ay. N. Y. no. N. J. div^d P^a. ay. Del. no. M^d no. V^a ay. N. C. ay. S. C. ay. Geo. ay.[1]

The motion for " two years " was then inserted nem. con.

Adj^d

FRIDAY JUNE 22. IN CONVENTION

The clause in Resol. 3.[2] " to receive fixed stipends to be paid out of the Nation! Treasury " [3] considered.

Mr ELSEWORTH, moved to substitute payment by the States out of their own Treasurys: observing that the manners of different States were very different in the Stile of living and in the profits accruing from the exercise of like talents. What would be deemed therefore a reasonable compensation in some States, in others would be very unpopular, and might impede the system of which it made a part.

Mr WILLIAMSON favored the idea. He reminded the House of the prospect of new States to the Westward. They would be [4] poor—would pay little into the common Treasury—and would have a different interest from the old States. He did not think therefore that the latter ought to pay the expences of men who would be employed in thwarting their measures & interests.

Mr GHORUM, wished not to refer the matter to the State Legislatures who were always paring down salaries in such a manner as to keep out of offices men most capable of executing the functions of them. He thought also it would be wrong to fix the compensations [5] by the constitutions,[5] because we could not venture to make it as liberal

---

[1] In the transcript the vote reads: "Massachusetts, Connecticut, Pennsylvania, Virginia, North Carolina, South Carolina, Georgia, aye—7; New York, Delaware, Maryland, no—3; New Jersey, divided."

[2] The words "the third Resolution" are substituted in the transcript for "Resol. 3."

[3] The word "being" is here inserted in the transcript.

[4] The word "too" is here inserted in the transcript.

[5] The transcript uses the words "conpensations" and "constitutions" in the singular.

as it ought to be without exciting an enmity ag.st the whole plan. Let the Nati.^{l} Legisl: provide for their own wages from time to time; as the State Legislatures do. He had not seen this part of their power abused, nor did he apprehend an abuse of it.

Mr RANDOLPH [1] feared we were going too far, in consulting popular prejudices. Whatever respect might be due to them, in lesser matters, or in cases where they formed the permanent character of the people, he thought it neither incumbent on nor honorable for the Convention, to sacrifice right & justice to that consideration. If the States were to pay the members of the Nat.^{l} Legislature, a dependence would be created that would vitiate the whole System. The whole nation has an interest in the attendance & services of the members. The Nation.^{l} Treasury therefore is the proper fund for supporting them.

Mr KING, urged the danger of creating a dependence on the States by leav.^{g} to them the payment of the members of the Nat.^{l} Legislature. He supposed it w.^{d} be best to be explicit as to the compensation to be allowed. A reserve on that point, or a reference to the Nat.^{l} Legislature of the quantum, would excite greater opposition than any sum that would be actually necessary or proper.

Mr SHERMAN contended for referring both the quantum and the payment of it to the State Legislatures.

Mr WILSON was ag.st *fixing* the compensation as circumstances would change and call for a change of the amount. He thought it of great moment that the members of the Nat.^{l} Gov.^{t} should be left as independent as possible of the State Gov.^{ts} in all respects.

Mr MADISON concurred in the necessity of preserving the compensations for the Nat.^{l} Gov.^{t} independent on the State Gov.^{ts} but at the same time approved of *fixing* them by the Constitution, which might be done by taking a standard which w.^{d} not vary with circumstances. He disliked particularly the policy suggested by Mr Wiliamson of leaving the members from the poor States beyond the Mountains, to the precarious & parsimonious support of their constituents. If the Western States hereafter arising should be admitted into the Union, they ought to be considered as equals & as brethren. If their representatives were to be associated in the Common Councils, it was of common concern that such provisions should be made as would invite the most capable and respectable characters into the service.

Mr HAMILTON apprehended inconveniency [2] from *fixing* the wages.

---

[1] The words " said he " are here inserted in the transcript.

[2] The word " inconveniency " is changed to " inconvenience " in the transcript.

He was strenuous agst making the National Council dependent on the Legislative rewards of the States. Those who pay are the masters of those who are paid. Payment by the States would be unequal as the distant States would have to pay for the same term of attendance and more days in travelling to & from the seat of the [1] Gov^t He expatiated emphatically on the difference between the feelings & views of the *people*—& the *Governments* of the States arising from the personal interest & official inducements which must render the latter unfriendly to the Genl Gov^t

Mr WILSON moved that the Salaries of the 1st branch " *be ascertained by the National Legislature,*" [2] and be paid out of the Nat^l Treasury.

Mr MADISON, thought the members of the Legis^l too much interested to ascertain their own compensation. It w^d be indecent to put their hands into the public purse for the sake of their own pockets.

On this question [3] Mas. no. Con^t no. N. Y. div^d N. J. ay. P^a ay. Del. no. M^d no. V^a no. N. C. no. S. C. no. Geo. div^d [4]

On the question for striking out " Nat^l Treasury " as moved by Mr Elseworth

Mr HAMILTON renewed his opposition to it. He pressed the distinction between [5] State Gov^{ts} & the people. The former w^d be the rivals of the Genl Gov^t The State legislatures ought not therefore to be the paymasters of the latter.

Mr ELSEWORTH. If we are jealous of the State Gov^{ts} they will be so of us. If on going home I tell them we gave the Gen: Gov^t such powers because we c^d not trust you, will they adopt it, and with^t y^r approbation it is a nullity.

[6] Mass^{ts} ay. Con^t ay. N. Y. div^d N. J. no Pen^a no. Del. no. M^d no. V^a no. N. C. ay. S. C. ay. Geo. div^d * [7]

* Note. [It appeared that Mass^{ts} concurred, not because they thought the State Treas^y ought to be substituted; but because they thought nothing should be said on the subject, in which case it w^d silently devolve on the Nat^l Treasury to support the National Legislature.]

---

[1] The word "the" is omitted in the transcript.
[2] The transcript does not italicize the phrase "*be ascertained by the National Legislature.*"
[3] The transcript here inserts the following: "shall the salaries of the first branch be ascertained by the National Legislature?"
[4] In the transcript the vote reads: "New Jersey, Pennsylvania, aye—2; Massachusetts, Connecticut, Delaware, Maryland, Virginia, North Carolina, South Carolina, no—7; New York, Georgia, divided."
[5] The word "the" is here inserted in the transcript.
[6] The words "On the question" are here inserted in the transcript.
[7] In the transcript the vote reads: "Massachusetts,* Connecticut, North Carolina, South Carolina, aye—4; New Jersey, Pennsylvania, Delaware, Maryland, Virginia, no—5; New York, Georgia, divided; so it passed in the negative."

On a question for substituting "adequate compensation" in place of "fixt stipends" it was agreed to nem. con. the friends of the latter being willing that the practicability of *fixing* the compensation should be considered hereafter in forming the details.

It was then moved by Mr BUTLER that a question be taken on both points jointly; to wit "adequate compensation to be paid out of the Nat^l Treasury." It was objected to as out of order, the parts having been separately decided on. The Presid^t refer^d the question of order to the House, and it was determined to be in order. Con. N. J. Del. M^d N. C. S. C.—ay—[1] N. Y. P^a V^a Geo. no—[1] Mass: divided. The question on the sentence was then postponed by S. Carolina in right of the State.

Col. MASON moved to insert "twenty-five years of age as a qualification for the members of the 1st branch." He thought it absurd that a man to day should not be permitted by the law to make a bargain for himself, and tomorrow should be authorized to manage the affairs of a great nation. It was the more extraordinary as every man carried with him in his own experience a scale for measuring the deficiency of young politicians; since he would if interrogated be obliged to declare that his political opinions at the age of 21. were too crude & erroneous to merit an influence on public measures. It had been said that Cong^s had proved a good school for our young men. It might be so for any thing he knew but if it were, he chose that they should bear the expence of their own education.

Mr WILSON was agst abridging the rights of election in any shape. It was the same thing whether this were done by disqualifying the objects of choice, or the persons chusing. The motion tended to damp the efforts of genius, and of laudable ambition. There was no more reason for incapacitating *youth* than *age*, where the requisite qualifications were found. Many instances might be mentioned of signal services rendered in high stations to the public before the age of 25: The present Mr Pitt and Lord Bolingbroke were striking instances.

On the question for inserting "25 years of age"

Mass^{ts} no. Con^t ay. N. Y. div^d N. J. ay. P^a no. Del. ay. M^d ay. V^a ay. N. C. ay. S. C. ay. Geo. no.[2]

---

[1] In the transcript the figures "6" and "4" are inserted after "ay" and "no" respectively.

[2] In the transcript the vote reads: "Connecticut, New Jersey, Delaware, Maryland, Virginia, North Carolina, South Carolina, aye—7; Massachusetts, Pennsylvania, Georgia, no—3; New York, divided."

M? GHORUM moved to strike out the last member of 3 Resol:[1] concerning ineligibility of members of the 1ˢᵗ branch to offices[2] during the term of their membership & for one year after. He considered it as[3] unnecessary & injurious. It was true abuses had been displayed in G. B. but no one cᵈ say how far they might have contributed to preserve the due influence of the Govᵗ nor what might have ensued in case the contrary theory had been tried.

M? BUTLER opposed it. This precaution agˢᵗ intrigue was necessary. He appealed to the example of G. B. where men got[4] into Parlᵗ that they might get offices for themselves or their friends. This was the source of the corruption that ruined their Govᵗ

M? KING, thought we were refining too much. Such a restriction on the members would discourage merit. It would also give a pretext to the Executive for bad appointments, as he might always plead this as a bar to the choice he wished to have made.

M? WILSON was agˢᵗ fettering elections, and discouraging merit. He suggested also the fatal consequence in time of war, of rendering perhaps the best Commanders ineligible: appealing[5] to our situation during the late war, and indirectly leading to a recollection of the appointment of the Commander in Chief out of Congress.

Col. MASON was for shutting the door at all events agˢᵗ corruption. He enlarged on the venality and abuses in this particular in G. Britain: and alluded to the multiplicity of foreign Embassies by Congˢ The disqualification he regarded as a corner stone in the fabric.

Col. HAMILTON. There are inconveniences on both sides. We must take man as we find him, and if we expect him to serve the public must interest his passions in doing so. A reliance on pure patriotism had been the source of many of our errors. He thought the remark of M? Ghorum a just one. It was impossible to say what wᵈ be[6] effect in G. B. of such a reform as had been urged. It was known that one of the ablest politicians [M? Hume,] had pronounced all that influence on the side of the crown, which went under the name of corruption,[7] an essential part of the weight which maintained the equilibrium of the Constitution.

---

[1] The words "the third Resolution" are substituted in the transcript for "3 Resol:"

[2] The letter "s" is stricken out of the word "offices" in the transcript.

[3] The word "as" is stricken out in the transcript.

[4] The word "get" is substituted in the transcript for "got."

[5] The word "appealed" is substituted in the transcript for "appealing."

[6] The word "the" is here inserted in the transcript.

[7] The transcript italicizes the word "corruption."

On M: Ghorum's Motion for striking out "ineligibility," [1]
Mas^{ts}. ay. Con^t no. N. Y. div^d N. J. ay. P^a. div^d Del. div^d.
Mar^d no. V^a no. N. C. ay. S. C. no. Geo. ay.[2]
Adj^d.

SATURDAY JUNE 23. IN CONVENTION

The 3. Resol: resumed.[3]
On [4] Question yesterday postponed by S. Carol: for agreeing to
the whole sentence "for allowing an adequate compensation to be
paid out of the Treasury of the U. States"
Mast^s ay. Con^t no. N. Y. no. N. J. ay. Pen^a ay Del. no.
M^d ay. V^a ay. N. C. no. S. C. no. Geo divided.[5] So the question
was lost, & the sentence not inserted:

Genl PINKNEY moves to strike out the ineligibility of members of
the 1st branch to offices established "by a particular State." He
argued from the inconveniency [6] to which such a restriction would
expose both the members of the 1st branch, and the States wishing
for their services; [7] from the smallness of the object to be attained
by the restriction.

It w^d seem from the ideas of some that we are erecting a Kingdom to be divided agst itself, he disapproved such a fetter on the
Legislature.

Mr SHERMAN seconds the motion. It w^d seem that we are erecting a Kingdom at war with itself. The Legislature ought not to [8]
fettered in such a case. on the question
Mast^s no. Con^t ay. N. Y. ay. N. J. ay. P^a no. Del. no.
M^d ay. V^a ay. N. C. ay. S. C. ay. Geo. ay.[9]

[1] The transcript here inserts the following: "it was lost by an equal
division of the votes."
[2] In the transcript the vote reads: "Massachusetts, New Jersey, North
Carolina, Georgia, aye—4; Connecticut, Maryland, Virginia, South Carolina,
no—4; New York, Pennsylvania, Delaware, divided."
[3] In the transcript this sentence reads: "The third Resolution being resumed."
[4] The word "the" is here inserted in the transcript.
[5] In the transcript the vote reads: "Massachusetts, New Jersey, Pennsylvania, Maryland, Virginia, aye—5; Connecticut, New York, Delaware, North
Carolina, South Carolina, no—5; Georgia, divided."
[6] The word "inconveniency" is changed to "inconvenience" in the transcript.
[7] The word "and" is here inserted in the transcript.
[8] The word "be" is here inserted in the transcript.
[9] In the transcript the vote reads: "Connecticut, New York, New Jersey,
Maryland, Virginia, North Carolina, South Carolina, Georgia, aye—8; Massachusetts, Pennsylvania, Delaware, no—3."

M: MADISON renewed his motion yesterday made & waved to render the members of the 1ˢᵗ branch "ineligible during their term of service, & for one year after—to such offices only as should be established, or the emoluments thereof, augmented by the Legislature of the U. States during the time of their being members." He supposed that the unnecessary creation of offices, and increase of salaries, were the evils most experienced, & that if the door was shut agˢᵗ them: it might properly be left open for the appoint: of members to other offices as an encouragem: to the Legislative service.

M: Alex: MARTIN seconded the motion.

M: BUTLER. The amend: does not go far eno' & wᵈ be easily evaded

M: RUTLIDGE, was for preserving the Legislature as pure as possible, by shutting the door against appointments of its own members to offices,[1] which was one source of its corruption.

M: MASON. The motion of my colleague is but a partial remedy for the evil. He appealed to him as a witness of the shameful partiality of the Legislature of Virginia to its own members. He enlarged on the abuses & corruption in the British Parliament, connected with the appointment of its members. He cᵈ not suppose that a sufficient number of Citizens could not be found who would be ready, without the inducement of eligibility to offices, to undertake the Legislative service. Genius & virtue it may be said, ought to be encouraged. Genius, for aught he knew, might, but that virtue should be encouraged by such a species of venality, was an idea, that at least had the merit of being new.

M: KING remarked that we were refining too much in this business; and that the idea of preventing intrigue and solicitation of offices was chimerical. You say that no member shall himself be eligible to any office. Will this restrain him from from availing himself of the same means which would gain appointments for himself, to gain them for his son, his brother, or any other object of his partiality. We were losing therefore the advantages on one side, without avoiding the evils on the other.

M: WILSON supported the motion. The proper cure he said for corruption in the Legislature was to take from it the power of appointing to offices. One branch of corruption would indeed remain, that of creating unnecessary offices, or granting unnecessary salaries, and for that the amendment would be a proper remedy. He animadverted on the impropriety of stigmatizing with the name

---

[1] The transcript uses the word "offices" in the singular.

of venality the laudable ambition of rising into the honorable offices of the Government; an ambition most likely to be felt in the early & most incorrupt period of life, & which all wise & free Gov^{ts}. had deemed it sound policy, to cherish, not to check. The members of the Legislature have perhaps the hardest & least profitable task of any who engage in the service of the state. Ought this merit to. be made a disqualification?

M^r. SHERMAN, observed that the motion did not go far enough. It might be evaded by the creation of a new office, the translation to it of a person from another office, and the appointment of a member of the Legislature to the latter. A new Embassy might be established to a new Court, & an ambassador taken from another, in order to *create* a vacancy for a favorite member. He admitted that inconveniencies lay on both sides. He hoped there w^d. be sufficient inducements to the public service without resorting to the prospect of desireable offices, and on the whole was rather agst the motion of Mr Madison.

Mr GERRY thought there was great weight in the objection of Mr Sherman. He added as another objection agst admitting the eligibility of members in any case that it would produce intrigues of ambitious men for displacing proper officers, in order to create vacancies for themselves. In answer to M^r. King he observed that although members, if disqualified themselves might still intrigue & cabal for their sons, brothers &c, yet as their own interest would be dearer to them, than those of their nearest connections, it might be expected they would go greater lengths to promote it.

Mr MADISON had been led to this motion as a middle ground between an eligibility in all cases, and an absolute disqualification. He admitted the probable abuses of an eligibility of the members, to offices, particularly within the gift of the Legislature He had witnessed the partiality of such bodies to their own members, as had been remarked of the Virginia assembly by his colleague [Col. Mason]. He appealed however to him, in turn to vouch another fact not less notorious in Virginia, that the backwardness of the best citizens to engage in the Legislative service gave but too great success to unfit characters. The question was not to be viewed on one side only. The advantages & disadvantages on both ought to be fairly compared. The objects to be aimed at were to fill all offices with the fittest characters, & to draw the wisest & most worthy citizens into the Legislative service. If on one hand, public bodies were partial to their own members; on the other they were as apt to be misled by taking characters on report, or the authority of patrons and dependents. All who had been concerned in the appointment of strangers on those recommedations must be sensible of this truth. Nor w⁴ the partialities of such Bodies be obviated by disqualifying their own members. Candidates for office would hover round the seat of Gov⁴ or be found among the residents there, and practise all the means of courting the favor of the members. A great proportion of the appointments made by the States were evidently brought about in this way. In the general Gov⁴ the evil must be still greater, the characters of distant states, being much less known throughout the U. States than those of the distant parts of the same State. The elections by Congress had generally turned on men living at the seat of the fed¹ Gov⁴ or in its neighbourhood.—As to the next object, the impulse to the Legislative service, was evinced by experience to be in general too feeble with those best qualified for it. This inconveniency ¹ w⁴ also be more felt in the Nat¹ Gov⁴ than in the State Gov⁴ˢ as the sacrifices req⁴ from the distant members, w⁴ be much greater, and the pecuniary provisions, probably, more disproportiate. It w⁴ therefore be impolitic to add fresh objections to the Legislative service by an absolute disqualification of its members. The point in question was whether this would be an objection with the most capable citizens. Arguing from experience he concluded that it would. The Legislature of Virg⁴ would probably have been without many of its best members, if in that situation, they had been ineligible to Cong⁴ to the Gov⁴ & other honorable offices of the State.

M⁴ BUTLER thought Characters fit for office w⁴ never be unknown.

Col. MASON. If the members of the Legislature are disqualified, still the honors of the State will induce those who aspire to them to enter that service, as the field in which they can best display & improve their talents, & lay the train for their subsequent advancement.

M⁴ JENIFER remarked that in Maryland, the Senators chosen for five years, c⁴ hold no other office & that this circumstance gained them the greatest confidence of the people.

On the question for agreeing to the motion of M⁴ Madison.

Mass⁴ˢ div⁴ C⁴ ay. N. Y. no. N. J. ay. P⁴ no. Del. no. M⁴ no. V⁴ no. N. C. no. S. C. no. Geo. no.²

M⁴ SHERMAN mov⁴ to insert the words " and incapable of hold-

---

¹ The word " inconveniency " is changed to " inconvenience " in the transcript.

² In the transcript the vote reads: " Connecticut, New Jersey, aye—2; New York, Pennsylvania, Delaware, Maryland, Virginia, North Carolina, South Carolina, Georgia, no—8; Massachusetts, divided."

ing " after the words " eligible to offices " [1] wch was agreed to without opposition.

The word " established " & the words " [2] Nat! Gov^t " were struck out of Resolution 3^d: [3]

Mr SPAIGHT called for a division of the question, in consequence of which it was so put, as that it turned in [4] the first member of it, " on the ineligibility of the [5] members *during the term for which they were elected* "—whereon the States were,

Mass^{ts} div^d C^t ay. N. Y. ay. N. J. ay. P^a no. Del. ay. M^d ay. V^a ay. N. C. ay. S. C. ay. Geo. no.[6]

On the 2^d member of the sentence extending ineligibility of members to one year after the term for which they were elected Col MASON thought this essential to guard agst evasions by resignations, and stipulations for office to be fulfilled at the expiration of the legislative term. Mr GERRY, had known such a case. Mr HAMILTON. Evasions c^d not be prevented—as by proxies—by friends holding for a year, & them [7] opening the way &c. Mr RUTLIDGE admitted the possibility of evasions but was for controuling them as possible.[8]

[9] Mass. no. C^t no. N. Y. ay. N. J. no. P^a div^d Del. ay. Mar^d ay V^a no. N. C. no. S. C. ay. Geo. no [10]

Adj^d

MONDAY. JUNE 25. IN CONVENTION.

Resolution 4.[11] being taken up.

Mr PINKNEY [12] spoke as follows— The efficacy of the System will

---

[1] The words " ineligible to any office " are substituted in the transcript for " eligible to offices."

[2] The words " under the " are here inserted in the transcript.

[3] The words " the third Resolution " are substituted in the transcript for " Resolution 3d "

[4] The word " on " is substituted in the transcript for " in."

[5] The word " the " is omitted in the transcript.

[6] In the transcript the vote reads: " Connecticut, New York, New Jersey, Delaware, Maryland, Virginia, North Carolina, South Carolina, aye—8; Pennsylvania, Georgia, no—2; Massachusetts, divided."

[7] The word " then " is substituted in the transcript for " them."

[8] The phrase " contracting them as far as possible " is substituted in the transcript for " controuling them as possible."

[9] The words " On the question " are here inserted in the transcript.

[10] In the transcript the vote reads: " New York, Delaware, Maryland, South Carolina, aye—4; Massachusetts, Connecticut, New Jersey, Virginia, North Carolina, Georgia, no—6; Pennsylvania, divided."

[11] The words " The fourth Resolution " are substituted in the transcript for " Resolution 4."

[12] Pinckney furnished Madison with a copy of this speech which he transcribed, but apparently not with the whole of it, as Madison's note at the end

depend on this article. In order to form a right judgm! in the case, it will be proper to examine the situation of this Country more accurately than it has yet been done. The people of the U. States are perhaps the most singular of any we are acquainted with. Among them there are fewer distinctions of fortune & less of rank, than among the inhabitants of any other nation. Every freeman has a right to the same protection & security; and a very moderate share of property entitles them to the possession of all the honors and privileges the public can bestow: hence arises a greater equality, than is to be found among the people of any other country, and an equality which is more likely to continue—I say this equality is likely to continue, because in a new Country, possessing immense tracts of uncultivated lands, where every temptation is offered to emigration & where industry must be rewarded with competency, there will be few poor, and few dependent—Every member of the Society almost, will enjoy an equal power of arriving at the supreme offices & consequently of directing the strength & sentiments of the whole Community. None will be excluded by birth, & few by fortune, from voting for proper persons to fill the offices of Government— the whole community will enjoy in the fullest sense that kind of political liberty which consists in the power the members of the State reserve to themselves, of arriving at the public offices, or at least, of having votes in the nomination of those who fill them.

If this State of things is true & the prospect of its continuing [1] probable, it is perhaps not politic to endeavour too close an imitation of a Government calculated for a people whose situation is, & whose views ought to be extremely different

Much has been said of the Constitution of G. Britain. I will confess that I believe it to be the best Constitution in existence; but at the same time I am confident it is one that will not or can not be introduced into this Country, for many centuries.—If it were proper to go here into a historical dissertation on the British Constitution, it might easily be shewn that the peculiar excellence, the distinguishing feature of that Governm! can not possibly be introduced into our System—that its balance between the Crown & the people can not be made a part of our Constitution.—that we neither have or can have the members to compose it, nor the rights, privileges & properties of so distinct a class of Citizens to guard.—that the materials for form-

---

indicates. The original Pinckney draft is among the Madison papers, and shows Madison's copying to have been accurate.

[1] The word "continuance" is substituted in the transcript for "continuing."

ing this balance or check do not exist, nor is there a necessity for having so permanent a part of our Legislative, until the Executive power is so constituted as to have something fixed & dangerous in its principle—By this I mean a sole, hereditary, though limited Executive.

That we cannot have a proper body for forming a Legislative balance between the inordinate power of the Executive and the people, is evident from a review of the accidents & circumstances which gave rise to the peerage of Great Britain—I believe it is well ascertained that the parts which compose the British Constitution arose immediately from the forests of Germany; but the antiquity of the establishment of nobility is by no means clearly defined. Some authors are of opinion that the dignity denoted by the titles of dux et [1] comes, was derived from the old Roman to the German Empire; while others are of opinion that they existed among the Germans long before the Romans were acquainted with them. The institution however of nobility is immemorial among the nations who may probably be termed the ancestors of [2] Britain.—At the time they were summoned in England to become a part of the National Council, and [3] the circumstances which have [3] contributed to make them a constituent part of that constitution, must be well known to all gentlemen who have had industry & curiosity enough to investigate the subject— The nobles with their possessions & and dependents composed a body permanent in their nature and formidable in point of power. They had a distinct interest both from the King and the people; an interest which could only be represented by themselves, and the guardianship [4] could not be safely intrusted to others.—At the time they were originally called to form a part of the National Council, necessity perhaps as much as other cause, induced the Monarch to look up to them. It was necessary to demand the aid of his subjects in personal & pecuniary services. The power and possessions of the Nobility would not permit taxation from any assembly of which they were not a part: & the blending [5] the deputies of the Commons with them, & thus forming what they called their parler-ment [6] was perhaps as much the effect of chance as of any thing else. The Commons were at that time compleatly subordinate to the nobles, whose

---

[1] The word " and " is substituted in the transcript for " et."
[2] The word " Great " is here inserted in the transcript.
[3] The words " and " and " have " are crossed out in the transcript.
[4] The words " of which " are here inserted in the transcript.
[5] The word " of " is here inserted in the transcript.
[6] The transcript italicizes the word " parler-ment."

consequence & influence seem to have been the only reasons for their superiority; a superiority so degrading to the Commons that in the first Summons we find the peers are called upon to consult,[1] the commons to consent.[1] From this time the peers have composed a part of the British Legislature, and notwithstanding their power and influence have diminished & those of the Commons have increased, yet still they have always formed an excellent balance ag.st either the encroachments of the Crown or the people.

I have said that such a body cannot exist in this Country for ages, and that untill the situation of our people is exceedingly changed no necessity will exist for so permanent a part of the Legislature. To illustrate this I have remarked that the people of the United States are more equal in their circumstances than the people of any other Country—that they have very few rich men among them,—by rich men I mean those whose riches may have a dangerous influence, or such as are esteemed rich in Europe—perhaps there are not one hundred such on the Continent; that it is not probable this number will be greatly increased: that the genius of the people, their mediocrity of situation & the prospects which are afforded their industry in a Country which must be a new one for centuries are unfavorable to the rapid distinction of ranks. The destruction of the right of primogeniture & the equal division of the property of Intestates will also have an effect to preserve this mediocrity; for laws invariably affect the manners of a people. On the other hand that vast extent of unpeopled territory which opens to the frugal & industrious a sure road to competency & independence will effectually prevent for a considerable time the increase of the poor or discontented, and be the means of preserving that equality of condition which so eminently distinguishes us.

If equality is as I contend the leading feature of the U. States, where then are the riches & wealth whose representation & protection is the peculiar province of this permanent body. Are they in the hands of the few who may be called rich; in the possession of less than a hundred citizens? certainly not. They are in the great body of the people, among whom there are no men of wealth, and very few of real poverty.—Is it probable that a change will be created, and that a new order of men will arise? If under the British Government, for a century no such change was probable,[2] I think it

---

[1] The transcript italicizes the words " consult " and " consent."
[2] The word " produced " is substituted for the word " probable " in the transcript.

may be fairly concluded it will not take place while even the semblance of Republicanism remains.—How is this change to be effected? Where are the sources from whence it is to flow? From the landed interest? No. That is too unproductive & too much divided in most of the States. From the Monied interest? If such exists at present, little is to be apprehended from that source. Is it to spring from commerce? I believe it would be the first instance in which a nobility sprang from merchants. Besides, Sir, I apprehend that on this point the policy of the U. States has been much mistaken. We have unwisely considered ourselves as the inhabitants of an old instead of a new country. We have adopted the maxims of a State full of people & manufactures & established in credit. We have deserted our true interest, and instead of applying closely to those improvements in domestic policy which would have ensured the future importance of our commerce, we have rashly & prematurely engaged in schemes as extensive as they are imprudent. This however is an error which daily corrects itself & I have no doubt that a few more severe trials will convince us, that very different commercial principles ought to govern the conduct of these States.

The people of this country are not only very different from the inhabitants of any State we are acquainted with in the modern world; but I assert that their situation is distinct from either the people of Greece or Rome, or of any State we are acquainted with among the antients.—Can the orders introduced by the institution of Solon, can they be found in the United States? Can the military habits & manners of Sparta be resembled to our habits & manners? Are the distinctions of Patrician & Plebeian known among us? Can the Helvetic or Belgic confederacies, or can the unwieldy, unmeaning body called the Germanic Empire, can they be said to possess either the same or a situation like ours? I apprehend not.—They are perfectly different, in their distinctions of rank, their Constitutions, their manners & their policy.

Our true situation appears to me to be this.—a new extensive Country containing within itself the materials for forming a Government capable of extending to its citizens all the blessings of civil & religious liberty—capable of making them happy at home. This is the great end of Republican Establishments. We mistake the object of our Government, if we hope or wish that it is to make us respectable abroad. Conquest or superiority among other powers is not or ought not ever to be the object of republican systems. If they are sufficiently active & energetic to rescue us from contempt & preserve our domestic happiness & security, it is all we can expect from them,—it is more than almost any other Government ensures to its citizens.

I believe this observation will be found generally true:—that no two people are so exactly alike in their situation or circumstances as to admit the exercise of the same Government with equal benefit: that a system must be suited to the habits & genius of the people it is to govern, and must grow out of them.

The people of the U. S. may be divided into three classes— *Professional men* who must from their particular pursuits always have a considerable weight in the Government while it remains popular—*Commercial men,* who may or may not have weight as a wise or injudicious commercial policy is pursued.—If that commercial policy is pursued which I conceive to be the true one, the merchants of this Country will not or ought not for a considerable time to have much weight in the political scale.—The third is the *landed interest,* the owners and cultivators of the soil, who are and ought ever to be the governing spring in the system.—These three classes, however distinct in their pursuits are individually equal in the political scale, and may be easily proved to have but one interest. The dependence of each on the other is mutual. The merchant depends on the planter. Both must in private as well as public affairs be connected with the professional men; who in their turn must in some measure depend upon [1] them. Hence it is clear from this manifest connection, & the equality which I before stated exists, & must for the reasons then assigned, continue, that after all there is one, but one great & equal body of citizens composing the inhabitants of this Country among whom there are no distinctions of rank, and very few or none of fortune.

For a people thus circumstanced are we then to form a government & the question is what kind [2] of Government is best suited to them.

Will it be the British Govt? No. Why? Because G. Britain contains three orders of people distinct in their situation, their possessions & their principles.—These orders combined form the great body of the Nation, and as in national expences the wealth of the whole community must contribute, so ought each component part to be properly & duly [3] represented—No other combination of power could form this due representation, but the one that exists.—Neither

---

[1] The word "on" is substituted in the transcript for "upon."
[2] The word "sort" is substituted in the transcript for "kind."
[3] The words "properly & duly" are transposed in the transcript to read "duly and properly."

the peers or the people could represent the royalty, nor could the Royalty & the people form a proper representation for the Peers.— Each therefore must of necessity be represented by itself, or the sign of itself; and this accidental mixture has certainly formed a Government admirably well balanced.

But the U. States contain but one order that can be assimilated to the British Nation,—this is the order of Commons. They will not surely then attempt to form a Government consisting of three branches, two of which shall have nothing to represent. They will not have an Executive & Senate [hereditary] because the King & Lords of England are so. The same reasons do not exist and therefore the same provisions are not necessary.

We must as has been observed suit our Governm.^{t} to the people it is to direct. These are I believe as active, intelligent & susceptible of good Governm.^{t} as any people in the world. The Confusion which has produced the present relaxed State is not owing to them. It is owing to the weakness & [defects] of a Gov.^{t} incapable of combining the various interests it is intended to unite, and destitute of energy.— All that we have to do then is to distribute the powers of Gov.^{t} in such a manner, and for such limited periods, as while it gives a proper degree of permanency to the Magistrate, will reserve to the people, the right of election they will not or ought not frequently to part with.— I am of opinion that this may be easily [1] done; and that with some amendments the propositions before the Committee will fully answer this end.

No position appears to me more true than this; that the General Gov.^{t} can not effectually exist without reserving to the States the possession of their local rights. They are the instruments upon which the Union must frequently depend for the support & execution of their powers, however immediately operating upon the people, and not upon the States.

Much has been said about the propriety of abolishing the distinction of State Governments, & having but one general System. Suffer me for a moment to examine this question.*

* The residue of this speech was not furnished like the above by Mr Pinckney.[2]

[1] The words "be easily" are transposed in the transcript to "easily be."

[2] "The residue" of Pinckney's speech, according to Robert Yates was as follows:

"The United States include a territory of about 1500 miles in length, and in breadth about 400; the whole of which is divided into states and districts. While we were dependent on the crown of Great Britain, it was in contemplation to have formed the whole into one—but it was found impracticable. No legislature could make good laws for the whole, nor can it now be done. It would

The mode of constituting the 2^d branch being under consideration. The word " national " was struck out and " United States " inserted.

Mr Ghorum, inclined to a compromise as to the rule of proportion. He thought there was some weight in the objections of the small States. If V^a should have 16. votes & Del^{re} with several other States together 16. those from Virg^a would be more likely to unite than the others, and would therefore have an undue influence. This remark was applicable not only to States, but to Counties or other districts of the same State. Accordingly the Constitution of Mass^{ts} had provided that the representatives of the larger districts should not be in an exact ratio to their numbers. And experience he thought had shewn the provision to be expedient.

Mr Read. The States have heretofore been in a sort of partnership. They ought to adjust their old affairs before they open [1] a new account. He brought into view the appropriation of the common interest in the Western lands, to the use of particular States. Let justice be done on this head; let the fund be applied fairly & equally to the discharge of the general debt, and the smaller States who had been injured; would listen then perhaps to those ideas of just representation which had been held out.

Mr Ghorum. did [2] not see how the Convention could interpose in the case. Errors he allowed had been committed on the subject. But Cong^s were now using their endeavors to rectify them. The best remedy would be such a Government as would have vigor enough to do justice throughout. This was certainly the best chance that could be afforded to the smaller States.

Mr Wilson. the question is shall the members of the 2^d branch be chosen by the Legislatures of the States? When he considered the amazing extent of Country—the immense population which is to fill it, the influence which [3] the Gov^t we are to form will have, not only on the present generation of our people & their multiplied posterity,

---

necessarily place the power in the hands of the few, nearest the seat of government. State governments must therefore remain, if you mean to prevent confusion. The general negative powers will support the general government. Upon these considerations I am led to form the second branch differently from the report. Their powers are important and the number not too large, upon the principle of proportion. I have considered the subject with great attention; and I propose this plan (reads it) and if no better plan is proposed, I will then move its adoption." *Secret Proceedings and Debates of the Convention Assembled at Philadelphia, in the year 1787, for the purpose of forming the Constitution of the United States of America*, by Robert Yates (1821), p. 163.

[1] The word " opened " is substituted in the transcript for " open."
[2] The word " could " is substituted in the transcript for " did."
[3] The word " of " is substituted in the transcript for " which."

but on the whole Globe, he was lost in the magnitude of the object. The project of Henry the 4.ᵗʰ & his Statesmen was but the picture in miniature of the great portrait to be exhibited. He was opposed to an election by the State Legislatures. In explaining his reasons it was necessary to observe the twofold relation in which the people would stand. 1.¹ as Citizens of the Genˡ Govᵗ 2.¹ as Citizens of their particular State. The Genˡ Govᵗ was meant for them in the first capacity: the State Govᵗˢ in the second. Both Govᵗˢ were derived from the people—both meant for the people—both therefore ought to be regulated on the same principles. The same train of ideas which belonged to the relation of the Citizens to their State Govᵗˢ were applicable to their relation to the Genˡ Govᵗ and in forming the latter, we ought to proceed, by abstracting as much as possible from the idea of ² State Govᵗˢ With respect to the province & objects ³ of the Genˡ Govᵗ they should be considered as having no existence. The election of the 2ᵈ branch by the Legislatures, will introduce & cherish local interests & local prejudices. The Genˡ Govᵗ is not an assemblage of States, but of individuals for certain political purposes— it is not meant for the States, but for the individuals composing them; the *individuals* therefore not the *States,* ought to be represented in it: A proportion in this representation can be preserved in the 2ᵈ as well as in the 1ˢᵗ branch; and the election can be made by electors chosen by the people for that purpose. He moved an amendment to that effect which was not seconded.

Mᵣ ELSEWORTH saw no reason for departing from the mode contained in the Report. Whoever chooses the member, he will be a Citizen of the State he is to represent & will feel the same spirit & act the same part whether he be appointed by the people or the Legislature. Every State has its particular views & prejudices, which will find their way into the general councils, through whatever channel they may flow. Wisdom was one of the characteristics which it was in contemplation to give the second branch. Would not more of it issue from the Legislatures; than from an immediate election by the people. He urged the necessity of maintaining the existence & agency of the States. Without their co-operation it would be impossible to support a Republican Govᵗ over so great an extent of Country. An army could scarcely render it practicable. The largest States are the worst Governed. Virgᵃ is obliged to

---

[1] The figure " 1 " is changed in the transcript to " first," and the figure " 2 " to " and secondly."

[2] The word " the " is here inserted in the transcript.

[3] The word " objects " is used in the singular in the transcript.

acknowledge her incapacity to extend her Gov! to Kentucky. Mas^{ts} can not keep the peace one hundred miles from her capitol and is now forming an army for its support. How long Pen^a may be free from a like situation can not be foreseen. If the principles & materials of our Gov! are not adequate to the extent of these single States; how can it be imagined that they can support a single Gov! throughout the U. States. The only chance of supporting a Gen! Gov! lies in engrafting [1] it on that [2] of the individual States.

Doc^r JOHNSON urged the necessity of preserving the State Gov^{ts} which would be at the mercy of the Gen! Gov! on Mr Wilson's plan.

Mr MADISON thought it w^d obviate difficulty if the present resol: were postponed. & the 8th taken up, which is to fix the right of suffrage in the 2^d branch.

Doc^r [3] WILLIAMSON professed himself a friend to such a system as would secure the existence of the State Gov^{ts} The happiness of the people depended on it. He was at a loss to give his vote as to the Senate untill he knew the number of its members. In order to ascertain this, he moved to insert these words [4] after " 2^d branch of the Nat! Legislature "—[5] " who shall bear such proportion to the n^o of the 1st branch as 1 to   ." He was not seconded.

Mr MASON. It has been agreed on all hands that an efficient Gov! is necessary that to render it such it ought to have the faculty of self-defence, that to render its different branches effectual each of them ought to have the same power of self defence. He did not wonder that such an agreement should have prevailed in [6] these points. He only wondered that there should be any disagreement about the necessity of allowing the State Gov^{ts} the same self-defence. If they are to be preserved as he conceived to be essential, they certainly ought to have this power, and the only mode left of giving it to them, was by allowing them to appoint the 2^d branch of the Nat! Legislature.

Mr BUTLER observing that we were put to difficulties at every step by the uncertainty whether an equality or a ratio of representation w^d prevail finally in the 2^d branch, moved to postpone the 4th Resol: & to proceed to the [7] Resol: on that point. Mr MADISON seconded him.

---

[1] The word " grafting " is substituted in the transcript for " engrafting."
[2] The word " those " is substituted in the transcript for " that."
[3] The word " Mr." is substituted in the transcript for " Doc^r "
[4] The words " these words " are omitted in the transcript.
[5] The words " the words " are here inserted in the transcript.
[6] The word " on " is substituted in the transcript for " in."
[7] The word " eighth " is here inserted in the transcript.

On the question

Mass^{ts} no. Con^t no. N. Y. ay. N. J. no. P^a no. Del. no. M^d no. V^a ay. N. C. no. S. C. ay. Geo. ay.[1]

On a question to postpone the 4 and take up the 7. Resol: ays [2] — Mar^d V^a N. C. S. C. Geo:—Noes [3] Mas. C^t N. Y. N. J. P^a Del: [3]

On the question to agree "that the members of the 2^d branch be chosen by the indiv! Legislatures" Mas^{ts} ay. Con^t ay. N. Y. ay. N. J. ay. P^a no. Del. ay. M^d ay. V^a no. N. C. ay. S. C. ay. Geo. ay.*[4]

On a question on the clause requiring the age of 30 years at least—" it was agreed to unanimously: [5]

On a question to strike out—the words " sufficient to ensure their independency [6] " after the word " term " it was agreed to.

[7] That the 2^d branch hold their offices for [8] term of seven years,[9] considered

Mr GHORUM suggests a term of " 4 years," ¼ to be elected every year.

Mr RANDOLPH. supported the idea of rotation, as favorable to the wisdom & stability of the Corps, which might possibly be always sitting, and aiding the Executive. And moves after " 7 years " to add, " to go out in fixt proportion " which was agreed to.

Mr WILLIAMSON. suggests " 6 years," as more convenient for Rotation than 7 years.

Mr SHERMAN seconds him.

Mr REED proposed that they s^d hold their offices " during good " behaviour. Mr R. MORRIS seconds him.

* It must be kept in view that the largest States particularly Pennsylvania & Virginia always considered the choice of the 2^d Branch by the State Legislatures as opposed to a proportional Representation to which they were attached as a fundamental principle of just Government. The smaller States who had opposite views, were reinforced by the members from the large States most anxious to secure the importance of the State Governments.

---

[1] In the transcript the vote reads: "New York, Virginia, South Carolina, Georgia, aye—4; Massachusetts, Connecticut, New Jersey, Pennsylvania, Delaware, Maryland, North Carolina, no—7."
[2] The word "ays" is omitted in the transcript.
[3] The word "noes" is omitted in the transcript; "aye—5" being inserted after "Georgia" and "no—6" after "Delaware."
[4] In the transcript this vote reads: "Massachusetts, Connecticut, New York, New Jersey, Delaware, Maryland, North Carolina, South Carolina, Georgia, aye—9; Pennsylvania, Virginia, no—2."
[5] The words "agreed to unanimously" are transposed in the transcript to read "unanimously agreed to."
[6] The word "independency" is changed to "independence" in the transcript.
[7] The words "The clause" are here inserted in the transcript.
[8] The word "a" is here inserted in the transcript.
[9] The word "being" is here inserted in the transcript.

Gen! Pinkney proposed "4 years." A longer term [1] w⁴ fix them at the seat of Gov⁴ They w⁴ acquire an interest there, perhaps transfer their property & lose sight of the States they represent. Under these circumstances the distant States w⁴ labour under great disadvantages.

M⁵ Sherman moved to strike out "7 years" in order to take questions on the several propositions.

On the question to strike out "seven"

Mas⁵ ay. Con⁴ ay. N. Y. ay. N. J. ay. P⁰ no. Del. no. M⁴ div⁴ V⁰ no. N. C. ay. S. C. ay. Geo. ay.[2]

On the question to insert "6 years, which failed 5 St⁵ being ay. 5 no. & 1 divided

Mas⁵ no. Con⁴ ay. N. Y. no. N. J. no. P⁰ ay. Del ay. M⁴ div⁴ V⁰ ay. N. C. ay. S. C. no. Geo. no.[3]

On a motion to adjourn, the votes were 5 for 5 ag⁵⁴ it & 1 divided, —Con. N. J. P⁰ Del. V⁰ —ay.[4] Mass⁵ N. Y. N. C. S. C. Geo: no.[4] Mary⁴ divided.

On the question for "5 years" it was lost.

Mas⁵ no. Con⁴ ay. N. Y. no. N. J. no. P⁰ ay. Del. ay. M⁴ div⁴ V⁰ ay. N. C. ay. S. C. no. Geo no.[5]

Adj⁴

Tuesday. June 26. in Convention

The duration of the 2⁴ branch [6] under consideration.

M⁵ Ghorum moved to fill the blank with "six years," one third of the members to go out every second year.

M⁵ Wilson 2ᵈᵉᵈ the motion.

Gen! Pinkney opposed six years in favor of four years. The States he said had different interests. Those of the Southern, and of S. Carolina in particular were different from the Northern. If the

---

[1] The word "time" is substituted in the transcript for "term."
[2] In the transcript the vote reads: "Massachusetts, Connecticut, New York, New Jersey, North Carolina, South Carolina, Georgia, aye—7; Pennsylvania, Delaware, Virginia, no—3; Maryland, divided."
[3] In the transcript the vote reads: "Connecticut, Pennsylvania, Delaware, Virginia, North Carolina, aye—5; Massachusetts, New York, New Jersey, South Carolina, Georgia, no—5; Maryland, divided."
[4] The figure "5" is here inserted in the transcript.
[5] In the transcript the vote reads: "Connecticut, Pennsylvania, Delaware, Virginia, North Carolina, aye—5; Massachusetts, New York, New Jersey, South Carolina, Georgia, no—5; Maryland, divided."
[6] The word "being" is here inserted in the transcript.

Senators should be appointed for a long term, they w^d settle in the State where they exercised their functions; and would in a little time be rather the representatives of that than of the State appoint^g them.

M^r. READ mov^d that the term be nine years. This w^d admit of a very convenient rotation, one third going out triennially. He w^d still prefer " during good behaviour," but being little supported in that idea, he was willing to take the longest term that could be obtained.

M^r. BROOME 2^{ded} the motion.

M^r. MADISON. In order to judge of the form to be given to this institution, it will be proper to take a view of the ends to be served by it. These were first to protect the people agst their rulers: secondly to protect the people agst the transient impressions into which they themselves might be led. A people deliberating in a temperate moment, and with the experience of other nations before them, on the plan of Gov^t most likely to secure their happiness, would first be aware, that those charg^d with the public happiness, might betray their trust. An obvious precaution agst this danger w^d be to divide the trust between different bodies of men, who might watch & check each other. In this they w^d be governed by the same prudence which has prevailed in organizing the subordinate departments of Gov^t, where all business liable to abuses is made to pass thro' separate hands, the one being a check on the other. It w^d next occur to such a people, that they themselves were liable to temporary errors, thro' want of information as to their true interest, and that men chosen for a short term, & employed but a small portion of that in public affairs, might err from the same cause. This reflection w^d naturally suggest that the Gov^t be so constituted, as that one of its branches might have an opp^y of acquiring a competent knowledge of the public interests. Another reflection equally becoming a people on such an occasion, w^d be that they themselves, as well as a numerous body of Representatives, were liable to err also, from fickleness and passion. A necessary fence agst this danger would be to select a portion of enlightened citizens, whose limited number, and firmness might seasonably interpose agst impetuous councils. It ought finally to occur to a people deliberating on a Gov^t for themselves, that as different interests necessarily result from the liberty meant to be secured, the major interest might under sudden impulses be tempted to commit injustice on the minority. In all civilized Countries the people fall into different classes hav^g a real or supposed difference of interests. There will be creditors & debtors, farmers, merch^{ts} & manufacturers.

There will be particularly the distinction of rich & poor. It was true as had been observ⁴ [by M⁴ Pinkney] we had not among us those hereditary distinctions, of rank which were a great source of the contests in the ancient Gov⁴⁵ as well as the modern States of Europe, nor those extremes of wealth or poverty which characterize the latter. We cannot however be regarded even at this time, as one homogeneous mass, in which every thing that affects a part will affect in the same manner the whole. In framing a system which we wish to last for ages, we sh⁴ not lose sight of the changes which ages will produce. An increase of population will of necessity increase the proportion of those who will labour under all the hardships of life, & secretly sigh for a more equal distribution of its blessings. These may in time outnumber those who are placed above the feelings of indigence. According to the equal laws of suffrage, the power will slide into the hands of the former. No agrarian attempts have yet been made in in this Country, but symtoms, of a leveling spirit, as we have understood, have sufficiently appeared in a certain quarters to give notice of the future danger. How is this danger to be guarded ag⁴ on republican principles?. How is the danger in all cases of interested coalitions to oppress the minority to be guarded ag⁴⁴? Among other means by the establishment of a body in the Gov⁴ sufficiently respectable for its wisdom & virtue, to aid on such emergences, the preponderance of justice by throwing its weight into that scale. Such being the objects of the second branch in the proposed Gov⁴ he thought a considerable duration ought to be given to it. He did not conceive that the term of nine years could threaten any real danger; but in pursuing his particular ideas on the subject, he should require that the long term allowed to the 2⁴ branch should not commence till such a period of life, as would render a perpetual disqualification to be re-elected little inconvenient either in a public or private view. He observed that as it was more than probable we were now digesting a plan which in its operation w⁴ decide for ever the fate of Republican Gov⁴ we ought not only to provide every guard to liberty that its preservation c⁴ require, but be equally careful to supply the defects which our own experience had particularly pointed out.

M⁴ SHERMAN. Gov⁴ is instituted for those who live under it. It ought therefore to be so constituted as not to be dangerous to their liberties. The more permanency it has the worse if it be a bad Gov⁴ Frequent elections are necessary to preserve the good behavior of rulers. They also tend to give permanency to the Government, by preserving that good behavior, because it ensures their re-election.

In Connecticut elections have been very frequent, yet great stability & uniformity both as to persons & measures have been experienced from its original establishm.ᵗ to the present time; a period of more than 130 years. He wished to have provision made for steadiness & wisdom in the system to be adopted; but he thought six or four years would be sufficient. He sh.ᵈ be content with either.

M.ʳ READ wished it to be considered by the small States that it was their interest that we should become one people as much as possible; that State attachments sh.ᵈ be extinguished as much as possible; that the Senate sh.ᵈ be so constituted as to have the feelings of Citizens of the whole.

M.ʳ HAMILTON. He did not mean to enter particularly into the subject. He concurred with M.ʳ Madison in thinking we were now to decide for ever the fate of Republican Government; and that if we did not give to that form due stability and wisdom, it would be disgraced & lost among ourselves, disgraced & lost to mankind for ever. He acknowledged himself not to think favorably of Republican Government; but addressed his remarks to those who did think favorably of it, in order to prevail on them to tone their Government as high as possible. He professed himself to be as zealous an advocate for liberty as any man whatever, and trusted he should be as willing a martyr to it though he differed as to the form in which it was most eligible.—He concurred also in the general observations of [M.ʳ Madison] on the subject, which might be supported by others if it were necessary. It was certainly true: that nothing like an equality of property existed: that an inequality would exist as long as liberty existed, and that it would unavoidably result from that very liberty itself. This inequality of property constituted the great & fundamental distinction in Society. When the Tribunitial power had levelled the boundary between the *patricians* & *plebeians,* what followed? The distinction between rich & poor was substituted. He meant not however to enlarge on the subject. He rose principally to remark that [M.ʳ Sherman] seemed not to recollect that one branch of the proposed Gov.ᵗ was so formed, as to render it particularly the guardians of the poorer orders of Citizens; nor to have adverted to the true causes of the stability which had been exemplified in Con.ᵗ Under the British system as well as the federal, many of the great powers appertaining to Gov.ᵗ particularly all those relating to foreign Nations were not in the hands of the Gov.ᵗ there. Their internal affairs also were extremely simple, owing to sundry causes many of which were peculiar to that Country. Of late the Goverm.ᵗ had entirely given way to the people, and had in fact suspended many of its ordinary functions in order to prevent those turbulent scenes which had appeared elsewhere. He asks M: S. whether the State at this time, dare impose & collect a tax on y° people? To these causes & not to the frequency of elections, the effect, as far as it existed ought to be chiefly ascribed.

M: GERRY. wished we could be united in our ideas concerning a permanent Gov: All aim at the same end, but there are great differences as to the means. One circumstance He thought should be carefully attended to. There were not 1/1000 part of our fellow citizens who were not ag:ˢᵗ every approach towards Monarchy. Will they ever agree to a plan which seems to make such an approach. The Convention ought to be extremely cautious in what they hold out to the people. Whatever plan may be proposed will be espoused with warmth by many out of respect to the quarter it proceeds from as well as from an approbation of the plan itself. And if the plan should be of such a nature as to rouse a violent opposition, it is easy to foresee that discord & confusion will ensue, and it is even possible that we may become a prey to foreign powers. He did not deny the position of M: Madison, that the majority will generally violate justice when they have an interest in so doing; But did not think there was any such temptation in this Country. Our situation was different from that of G. Britain: and the great body of lands yet to be parcelled out & settled would very much prolong the difference. Notwithstanding the symtoms of injustice which had marked many of our public Councils, they had not proceeded so far as not to leave hopes, that there would be a sufficient sense of justice & virtue for the purpose of Gov: He admitted the evils arising from a frequency of elections: and would agree to give the Senate a duration of four or five years. A longer term would defeat itself. It never would be adopted by the people.

M: WILSON did not mean to repeat what had fallen from others, but w:ᵈ add an observation or two which he believed had not yet been suggested. Every nation may be regarded in two relations 1.[1] to its own citizens. 2 [1] to foreign nations. It is therefore not only liable to anarchy & tyranny within, but has wars to avoid & treaties to obtain from abroad. The Senate will probably be the depositary of the powers concerning the latter objects. It ought therefore to be made respectable in the eyes of foreign Nations. The true reason why G. Britain has not yet listened to a commercial treaty with us has been, because she had no confidence in the stability or

---

[1] The figures "1" and "2" are changed to "first" and "secondly" in the transcript.

efficacy of our Government. 9 years with a rotation, will provide these desirable qualities; and give our Gov.^t an advantage in this respect over Monarchy itself. In a monarchy much must always depend on the temper of the man. In such a body, the personal character will be lost in the political. He w^d add another observation. The popular objection ag.^st appointing any public body for a long term was that it might by gradual encroachments prolong itself first into a body for life, and finally become a hereditary one. It would be a satisfactory answer to this objection that as ⅓ would go out triennially, there would be always three divisions holding their places for unequal terms,[1] and consequently acting under the influence of different views, and different impulses—On the question for 9 years, ⅓ to go out triennially

Mass.^ts no.   Con.^t no.   N. Y. no.   N. J. no.   P.^a ay.   Del. ay. M.^d no.   V.^a ay.   N. C. no.   S. C. no.   Geo. no.[2]

On the question for 6 years ⅓ to go out biennially

Mass.^ts ay.   Con.^t ay.   N. Y. no.   N. J. no.   P.^a ay.   Del. ay. M.^d ay.   V.^a ay.   N. C. ay.   S. C. no.   Geo. no.[3]

[4] "To receive fixt stipends by which they may be compensated for their services." [5] considered

General PINKNEY proposed "that no Salary should be allowed." As this [the Senatorial] branch was meant to represent the wealth of the Country, it ought to be composed of persons of wealth; and if no allowance was to be made the wealthy alone would undertake the service. He moved to strike out the clause.

Doct.^r FRANKLIN seconded the motion. He wished the Convention to stand fair with the people. There were in it a number of young men who would probably be of the Senate. If lucrative appointments should be recommended we might be chargeable with having carved out places for ourselves. On the question, Mas.^ts Connecticut * P.^a M.^d S. Carolina ay.[7] N. Y. N. J. Del. Virg.^a N. C. Geo. no.[8]

* Quer. whether Connecticut should not be—no, & Delaware, ay.[6]

---

[1] The word "times" is substituted in the transcript for "terms."
[2] In the transcript the vote reads: "Pennsylvania, Delaware, Virginia, aye—3; Massachusetts, Connecticut, New York, New Jersey, Maryland, North Carolina, South Carolina, Georgia, no—8."
[3] In the transcript the vote reads: "Massachusetts, Connecticut, Pennsylvania, Delaware, Maryland, Virginia, North Carolina, aye—7; New York, New Jersey, South Carolina, Georgia, no—4."
[4] The words "The clause of the fourth Resolution" are here inserted in the transcript.
[5] The word "being" is here inserted in the transcript.
[6] An interrogation mark and the initials "J.M." are here inserted in the transcript. According to the Journal, Connecticut was "ay" and Delaware "no."
[7] The figure "5" is here inserted in the transcript.
[8] The figure "6" is here inserted in the transcript.

M⁼ WILLIAMSON moved to change the expression into these words towit " to receive a compensation for the devotion of their time to the public Service." The motion was seconded by M⁼ Elseworth. And was [1] agreed to by all the States except S. Carol⁼ It seemed to be meant only to get rid of the word " fixt " and leave greater room for modifying the provision on this point.

M⁼ ELSEWORTH moved to strike out " to be paid out of the nati! Treasury " and insert " to be paid by their respective States." If the Senate was meant to strengthen the Gov⁺ it ought to have the confidence of the States. The States will have an interest in keeping up a representation, and will make such provision for supporting the members as will ensure their attendance.

M⁼ MADISON considered this [2] a departure from a fundamental principle, and subverting the end intended by allowing the Senate a duration of 6 years. They would if this motion should be agreed to, hold their places during pleasure; during the pleasure of the State Legislatures. One great end of the institution was, that being a firm, wise and impartial body, it might not only give stability to the Gen! Gov⁺ in its operations on individuals, but hold an even balance among different States. The motion would make the Senate like Congress, the mere Agents & Advocates of State interests & views, instead of being the impartial umpires & Guardians of justice and [3] general Good. Cong⁵ had lately by the establishment of a board with full powers to decide on the mutual claims be- between the U. States & the individual States, fairly acknowledged themselves to be unfit for discharging this part of the business referred to them by the Confederation.

M⁼ DAYTON considered the payment of the Senate by the States as fatal to their independence. he was decided for paying them out of the Nat! Treasury.

On the question for payment of the Senate to be left to the States as moved by M⁼ Elseworth.[4]

Mass⁺ˢ no. Con⁺ ay. N. Y. ay. N. J. ay. P⁼ no. Del. no. M⁼ no. V⁼ no. N. C. no. S. C. ay. Geo. ay.[5]

Col. MASON. He did not rise to make any motion, but to hint an idea which seemed to be proper for consideration. One impor-

---

[1] The word "was" is omitted in the transcript.
[2] The word "as" is here inserted in the transcript.
[3] The word "the" is here inserted in the transcript.
[4] The phrase "it passed in the negative" is here inserted in the transcript.
[5] In the transcript the vote reads: "Connecticut, New York, New Jersey, South Carolina, Georgia, aye—5; Massachusetts, Pennsylvania, Delaware, Maryland, Virginia, North Carolina, no—6."

tant object in constituting the Senate was to secure the rights of property. To give them weight & firmness for this purpose, a considerable duration in office was thought necessary. But a longer term than 6 years, would be of no avail in this respect, if needy persons should be appointed. He suggested therefore the propriety of annexing to the office a qualification of property. He thought this would be very practicable; as the rules of taxation would supply a scale for measuring the degree of wealth possessed by every man.

A question was then taken whether the words " to be paid out of the public ¹ treasury," should stand."

Mass.^{ts} ay. Con^t no. N. Y. no. N. J. no. P.^{a} ay. Del. ay. M.^{d} ay. V.^{a} ay. N. C. no. S. C. no. Geo. no.²

Mr Butler moved to strike out the ineligibility of Senators to *State offices.*

Mr Williamson seconded the motion.

Mr Wilson remarked the additional dependence this w^d create in the Senators on the States. The longer the time he observed allotted to the officer, the more compleat will be the dependance, if it exists at all.

Genl Pinkney was for making the States as much as could be conveniently done, a part of the Genl Gov.^{t}: If the Senate was to be appointed by the States, it ought in pursuance of the same idea to be paid by the States: and the States ought not to be barred from the opportunity of calling members of it into offices at home. Such a restriction would also discourage the ablest men from going into the Senate.

Mr Williamson moved a resolution so penned as to admit of the two following questions. 1.³ whether the members of the Senate should be ineligible to & incapable of holding offices *under the U. States*

2.³ Whether &c. under the *particular States.*

On the Question to postpone in order to consider ⁴ Williamson's Resol.^{n} Mas^{ts} no. Con^t ay. N. Y. no. N. J. no. P.^{a} ay. Del. ay. M.^{d} ay. V.^{a} ay. N. C. ay. S. C. ay. Geo. ay.⁵

Mr Gerry & Mr Madison—move to add to Mr Williamsons 1,³ Quest: " and for 1 year thereafter." On this amend^t

---

¹ The word "public" is changed to "national" in the transcript.

² In the transcript the vote reads: " Massachusetts, Pennsylvania, Delaware, Maryland, Virginia, aye—5; Connecticut, New York, New Jersey, North Carolina, South Carolina, Georgia, no—6."

³ The figures " 1 " and " 2 " are changed to "first" and "secondly" in the transcript.

⁴ The word "Mr." is here inserted in the transcript.

⁵ In the transcript the vote reads: " Connecticut, Pennsylvania, Delaware, Maryland, Virginia, North Carolina, South Carolina, Georgia, aye—8; Massachusetts, New York, New Jersey, no—3."

Mas.^{ts} no. Con.^{t} ay. N. Y. ay. N. J. no. P. no. Del. ay. M.^{d} ay. V.^{a} ay. N. C. ay. S. C. ay. Geo. no.^{1}

On Mr Will-son's 1 Question as amend.^{ed} vz. inelig: & incapable &c. &c for 1 year &c. ag.^{d} ^{2} unanimously.

On the 2.^{3} question as to ineligibility &c. to State offices.^{4}

Mas. ay. C.^{t} no. N. Y. no. N. J. no. P. ay. Del. no. M.^{d} no. V.^{a} ay. N. C. no. S. C. no. Geo. no.^{5}

The 5.^{6} Resol: ''that each branch have the right of originating acts '' was agreed to nem: con:

Adj.^{d}

WEDNESDAY JUNE 27. IN CONVENTION

Mr RUTLIDGE moved to postpone the 6th Resolution, defining the powers of Cong.^{s} in order to take up the 7 & 8 which involved the most fundamental points; the rules of suffrage in the 2 branches which was agreed to nem. con.

A question being proposed on Resol: 7^7: declaring that the suffrage in the first branch s.^{d} be according to an equitable ratio.

Mr L. MARTIN contended at great length and with great eagerness that the General Gov.^{t} was meant merely to preserve the State Govern.^{ts}: not to govern individuals: that its powers ought to be kept within narrow limits; that if too little power was given to it, more might be added; but that if too much, it could never be resumed: that individuals as such have little to do but with their own States; that the Genl Gov.^{t} has no more to apprehend from the States composing the Union, while it pursues proper measures, that^8 a Gov.^{t} over individuals has to apprehend from its subjects: that to resort to the Citizens at large for their sanction to a new Govern.^{t} will be throwing them back into a State of Nature: that the dissolution of the State Gov.^{ts} is involved in the nature of the process: that the

---

^{1} In the transcript the vote reads: "Connecticut, New York, Delaware, Maryland, Virginia, North Carolina, South Carolina, aye—7; Massachusetts, New Jersey, Pennsylvania, Georgia, no—4."

^{2} The word "to" is here inserted in the transcript.

^{3} The figure "2" is changed to "second" in the transcript.

^{4} The transcript italicizes the words "State offices."

^{5} In the transcript the vote reads: "Massachusetts, Pennsylvania, Virginia, aye—3; Connecticut, New York, New Jersey, Delaware, Maryland, North Carolina, South Carolina, Georgia, no—8."

^{6} The figure "5" is changed to "fifth" in the transcript.

^{7} The words "the seventh Resolution" are substituted in the transcript for "Resol: 7."

^{8} The word "than" is substituted in the transcript for "that."

people have no right to do this without the consent of those to whom
they have delegated their power for State purposes: through their
tongue only they can speak, through their ears, only, can hear: that
the States have shewn a good disposition to comply with the Acts, of
Cong^s. weak, contemptibly weak as that body has been; and have
failed through inability alone to comply: that the heaviness of the
private debts, and the waste of property during the war, were the
chief causes of this inability: that he did not conceive the instances
mentioned by M^r. Madison of compacts between V^a. & M^d. between
P^a. & N. J. or of troops raised by Mass^ts for defence against the Rebels,
to be violations of the articles of confederation—that an equal vote in
each State was essential to the federal idea, and was founded in justice
& freedom, not merely in policy: that tho' the States may give up this
right of sovereignty, yet they had not, and ought not: that the States
like individuals were in a State of nature equally sovereign & free. In
order to prove that individuals in a State of nature are equally free
& independent he read passages from Locke, Vattel, Lord Summers—
Priestly. To prove that the case is the same with States till they surrender their equal sovereignty, he read other passages in Locke &
Vattel, and also Rutherford: that the States being equal cannot treat
or confederate so as to give up an equality of votes without giving
up their liberty: that the propositions on the table were a system
of slavery for 10 States: that as V^a. Mas^ts & P^a. have ⁴²⁄₉₀ of the votes
they can do as they please without a miraculous Union of the other
ten: that they will have nothing to do, but to gain over one of the
ten to make them compleat masters of the rest: that they can then
appoint an Execut^e & Judiciary & legislate [1] for them as they please:
that there was & would continue a natural predilection & partiality
in men for their own States; that the States, particularly the smaller,
would never allow a negative to be exercised over their laws: that
no State in ratifying the Confederation had objected to the equality
of votes; that the complaints at present run not ag^st this equality
but the want of power; that 16 members from V^a. would be more
likely to act in concert than a like number formed of members from
different States; that instead of a junction of the small States as a
remedy, he thought a division of the large States would be more
eligible.—This was the substance of a speech which was continued
more than three hours. He was too much exhausted he said to
finish his remarks, and reminded the House that he should tomorrow,
resume them.

Adj^d

---

[1] The word " legislature " is substituted in the transcript for " legislate."

THURSDAY JUNE 28ᵀᴴ IN CONVENTION

Mᵣ L. MARTIN resumed his discourse, contending that the Genˡ Govᵗ ought to be formed for the States, not for individuals: that if the States were to have votes in proportion to their numbers of people, it would be the same thing whether their representatives were chosen by the Legislatures or the people; the smaller States would be equally enslaved; that if the large States have the same interest with the smaller as was urged, there could be no danger in giving them an equal vote; they would not injure themselves, and they could not injure the large ones on that supposition without injuring themselves and if the interests, were not the same, the inequality of suffrage wᵈ be dangerous to the smaller States: that it will be in vain to propose any plan offensive to the rulers of the States, whose influence over the people will certainly prevent their adopting it: that the large States were weak at present in proportion to their extent: & could only be made formidable to the small ones, by the weight of their votes; that in case a dissolution of the Union should take place, the small States would have nothing to fear from their power; that if in such a case the three great States should league themselves together, the other ten could do so too: & that he had rather see partial confederacies take place, than the plan on the table.

This was the substance of the residue of his discourse which was delivered with much diffuseness & considerable vehemence.

Mᵣ LANSING & Mᵣ DAYTON moved to strike out "not." so that the 7 art: might read that the rights [1] of suffrage in the 1ˢᵗ branch ought to be according to the rule established by the Confederation."

Mᵣ DAYTON expressed great anxiety that the question might not be put till tomorrow; Governᵣ Livingston being kept away by indisposition, and the representation of N. Jersey thereby suspended.

Mᵣ WILLIAMSON. thought that if any political truth could be grounded on mathematical demonstration, it was that if the States were equally sovereign now, and parted with equal proportions of sovereignty, that they would remain equally sovereign. He could not comprehend how the smaller States would be injured in the case, and wished some Gentleman would vouchsafe a solution of it. He observed that the small States, if they had a plurality of votes would have an interest in throwing the burdens off their own shoul-

---

[1] The transcript uses the word "rights" in the singular.

ders on those of the large ones. He begged that the expected addition of new States from the Westward might be kept in [1] view. They would be small States, they would be poor States, they would be unable to pay in proportion to their numbers; their distance from market rendering the produce of their labour less valuable; they would consequently be tempted to combine for the purpose of laying burdens on commerce & consumption which would fall with greatest [2] weight on the old States.

M̲ᴿ Mᴀᴅɪsᴏɴ, s̲ᵈ he was much disposed to concur in any expedient not inconsistent with fundamental principles, that could remove the difficulty concerning the rule of representation. But he could neither be convinced that the rule contended for was just, nor [3] necessary for the safety of the small States ag̲ˢᵗ the large States. That it was not just, had been conceded by M̲ᴿ Breerly & M̲ᴿ Patterson themselves. The expedient proposed by them was a new partition of the territory of the U. States. The fallacy of the reasoning drawn from the equality of Sovereign States in the formation of compacts, lay in confounding mere Treaties, in which were specified certain duties to which the parties were to be bound, and certain rules by which their subjects were to be reciprocally governed in their intercourse, with a compact by which an authority was created paramount to the parties, & making laws for the government of them. If France, England & Spain were to enter into a Treaty for the regulation of commerce &c with the Prince of Monacho & 4 or 5 other of the smallest sovereigns of Europe, they would not hesitate to treat as equals, and to make the regulations perfectly reciprocal. W̲ᵈ the case be the same, if a Council were to be formed of deputies from each with authority and discretion, to raise money, levy troops, determine the value of coin &c? Would 30 or 40. million [4] of people submit their fortunes into the hands, of a few thousands? If they did it would only prove that they expected more from the terror of their superior force, than they feared from the selfishness of their feeble associates. Why are Counties of the same states represented in proportion to their numbers? Is it because the representatives are chosen by the people themselves? So will be the representatives in the Nation! Legislature. Is it because, the larger have more at stake than the smaller? The case will be the same with the larger & smaller States. Is it because the laws are to operate immediately

---

[1] The words "taken into" are substituted in the transcript for "kept in."
[2] The word "greater" is substituted in the transcript for "greatest."
[3] The words "that it was" are here inserted in the transcript.
[4] The transcript uses the word "million" in the plural.

on their persons & properties? The same is the case in some degree as the articles of confederation stand; the same will be the case in a far greater degree under the plan proposed to be substituted. In the cases of captures, of piracies, and of offences in a federal army; the property & persons of individuals depend on the laws of Cong[s] By the plan proposed a compleat power of taxation, the highest prerogative of supremacy is proposed to be vested in the National Gov[t] Many other powers are added which assimilate it to the Gov[t] of individual States. The negative proposed on the State laws, will make it an essential branch of the State Legislatures & of course will require that it should be exercised by a body established on like principles with the other [1] branches of those Legislatures.—That it is not necessary to secure the small States ag[st] the large ones he conceived to be equally obvious: Was a combination of the large ones dreaded? this must arise either from some interest common to V[a] Mas[ts] & P[a] & distinguishing them from the other States or from the mere circumstance of similarity of size. Did any such common interest exist? In point of situation they could not have been more effectually separated from each other by the most jealous citizen of the most jealous State. In point of manners, Religion, and the other circumstances which sometimes beget affection between different communities, they were not more assimilated than the other States.—In point of the staple productions they were as dissimilar as any three other States in the Union. The Staple of Mas[ts] was *fish*, of P[a] *flower*, of V[a] *Tob?* Was a combination to be apprehended from the mere circumstance of equality of size? Experience suggested no such danger. The journals of Cong[s] did not present any peculiar association of these States in the votes recorded. It had never been seen that different Counties in the same State, conformable in extent, but disagreeing in other circumstances, betrayed a propensity to such combinations. Experience rather taught a contrary lesson. Among individuals of superior eminence & weight in Society, rivalships were much more frequent than coalitions. Among independent nations, pre-eminent over their neighbours, the same remark was verified. Carthage & Rome tore one another to pieces instead of uniting their forces to devour the weaker nations of the Earth. The Houses of Austria & France were hostile as long as they remained the greatest powers of Europe. England & France have succeeded to the pre-eminence & to the enmity. To this principle we owe perhaps our liberty. A coalition between those powers would have

---

[1] The word "other" is omitted in the transcript.

been fatal to us. Among the principal members of antient & Modern confederacies, we find the same effect from the same cause. The contintions, not the Coalitions of Sparta, Athens & Thebes, proved fatal to the smaller members of the Amphyctionic Confederacy. The contentions, not the combinations of Prussia & Austria, have distracted & oppressed the Germanic [1] empire. Were the large States formidable *singly* to their smaller neighbours? On this supposition the latter ought to wish for such a general Gov^t as will operate with equal energy on the former as on themselves. The more lax the band, the more liberty the larger will have to avail themselves of their superior force. Here again Experience was an instructive monitor. What is ye situation of the weak compared with the strong in those stages of civilization in which the violence of individuals is least controuled by an efficient Government? The Heroic period of Antient Greece the feudal licentiousness of the middle ages of Europe, the existing condition of the American Savages, answer this question. What is the situation of the minor sovereigns in the great society of independent nations, in which the more powerful are under no controul but the nominal authority of the law of Nations? Is not the danger to the former exactly in proportion to their weakness. But there are cases still more in point. What was the condition of the weaker members of the Amphyctionic Confederacy. Plutarch [[2] life of Themistocles] will inform us that it happened but too often that the strongest cities corrupted & awed the weaker, and that Judgment went in favor of the more powerful party. What is the condition of the lesser states in the German Confederacy? We all know that they are exceedingly trampled upon; and that they owe their safety as far as they enjoy it, partly to their enlisting themselves, under the rival banners of the pre-eminent members, partly to alliances with neighbouring Princes which the Constitution of the Empire does not prohibit. What is the state of things in the lax system of the Dutch Confederacy? Holland contains about ½ the people, supplies about ½ of [3] the money, and by her influence, silently & indirectly governs the whole republic. In a word; the two extremes before us are a perfect separation & a perfect incorporation, of the 13 States. In the first case they would be independent nations subject to no law, but the law of nations. In the last, they would be mere counties of one entire republic, subject to one common law. In the first case the smaller States would have every thing to fear

---

[1] The word " German " is substituted in the transcript for " Germanic."
[2] The word " see " is here inserted in the transcript.
[3] The word " of " is omitted in the transcript.

from the larger. In the last they would have nothing to fear. The true policy of the small States therefore lies in promoting those principles & that form of Gov^t which will most approximate the States to the condition of counties. Another consideration may be added. If the Genl Gov^t be feeble, the large States distrusting its continuance, and foreseeing that their importance & security may depend on their own size & strength, will never submit to a partition. Give to the Genl Gov^t sufficient energy & permanency, & you remove the objection. Gradual partitions of the large, & junctions of the small States will be facilitated, and time may effect that equalization, which is wished for by the small States now, but can never be accomplished at once.

Mr WILSON. The leading argument of those who contend for equality of votes among the States is that the States as such being equal, and being represented not as districts of individuals, but in their political & corporate capacities, are entitled to an equality of suffrage. According to this mode of reasoning the representation of the boroughs in Eng^{ld} which has been allowed on all hands to be the rotten part of the Constitution, is perfectly right & proper. They are like the States represented in their corporate capacity like the States therefore they are entitled to equal voices, old Sarum to as many as London. And instead of the injury supposed hitherto to be done to London, the true ground of complaint lies with old Sarum: for London instead of two which is her proper share, sends four representatives to Parliament.

Mr SHERMAN. The question is not what rights naturally belong to men [1]; but how they may be most equally & effectually guarded in Society. And if some give up more than others in order to attain [2] this end, there can be no room for complaint. To do otherwise, to require an equal concession from all, if it would create danger to the rights of some, would be sacrificing the end to the means. The rich man who enters into Society along with the poor man, gives up more than the poor man, yet with an equal vote he is equally safe. Were he to have more votes than the poor man in proportion to his superior stake, the rights of the poor man would immediately cease to be secure. This consideration prevailed when the articles of Confederation were formed.

The determination of the question from [3] striking out the word " not " was put off till tomorrow at the request of the Deputies of

---

[1] The word "men" is used in the singular in the transcript.
[2] The word "obtain" is substituted in the transcript for "attain."
[3] The word "from" is changed to "for" in the transcript.

N. York.   See opposite page & insert the Speech of Doct! F in this place.[1]

M! President

The small progress we have made after 4 or five weeks close attendance & continual reasonings with each other—our different sentiments on almost every question, several of the last producing as many noes as ays, is methinks a melancholy proof of the imperfection of the Human Understanding. We indeed seem to feel our own want of political wisdom, since we have been running about in search of it. We have gone back to ancient history for models of Government, and examined the different forms of those Republics which having been formed with the seeds of their own dissolution now no longer exist. And we have viewed Modern States all round Europe, but find none of their Constitutions suitable to our circumstances.

In this situation of this Assembly, groping as it were in the dark to find political truth, and scarce able to distinguish it when presented to us, how has it happened, Sir, that we have not hitherto once thought of humbly applying to the Father of lights to illuminate our understandings? In the beginning of the Contest with G. Britain, when we were sensible of danger we had daily prayer in this room for the divine protection.—Our prayers, Sir, were heard, & they were graciously answered. All of us who were engaged in the struggle must have observed frequent instances of a superintending providence in our favor. To that kind providence we owe this happy opportunity of consulting in peace on the means of establishing our future national felicity. And have we now forgotten that powerful friend? or do we imagine that we no longer need his assistance? I have lived, Sir, a long time, and the longer I live, the more convincing proofs I see of this truth—*that God Governs in the affairs of men.* And if a sparrow cannot fall to the ground without his notice, is it probable that an empire can rise without his aid? We have been assured, Sir, in the sacred writings, that "except the Lord build the House they labour in vain that build it." I firmly believe this; and I also believe that without his concurring aid we shall succeed in this political building no better, than the Builders of Babel: We shall be divided by our little partial local interests; our projects will be confounded, and we ourselves shall become a reproach and bye word down to future ages. And what is worse, mankind may hereafter from this unfortunate instance, despair of establishing

---

[1] Madison's direction is omitted in the transcript and the words "Doctor Franklin" are inserted.

Governments by Human wisdom and leave it to chance, war and conquest.

I therefore beg leave to move—that henceforth prayers imploring the assistance of Heaven, and its blessings on our deliberations, be held in this Assembly every morning before we proceed to business, and that one or more of the Clergy of this City be requested to officiate in that Service—

M: SHARMAN seconded the motion.

M: HAMILTON & several others expressed their apprehensions that however proper such a resolution might have been at the beginning of the convention, it might at this late day, 1.[1] bring on it some disagreeable animadversions. & 2.[2] lead the public to believe that the embarrassments and dissensions within the Convention, had suggested this measure. It was answered by Doc: F. M: SHERMAN & others, that the past omission of a duty could not justify a further omission—that the rejection of such a proposition would expose the Convention to more unpleasant animadversions than the adoption of it: and that the alarm out of doors that might be excited for the state of things within, would at least be as likely to do good as ill.

M: WILLIAMSON, observed that the true cause of the omission could not be mistaken. The Convention had no funds.

M: RANDOLPH proposed in order to give a favorable aspect to y: measure, that a sermon be preached at the request of the convention on [3] 4th of July, the anniversary of Independence; & thenceforward prayers be used [4] in y: Convention every morning. D: FRANK: 2ded this motion After several unsuccessful attempts for silently postponing the [5] matter by adjourn: the adjournment was at length carried, without any vote on the motion.

FRIDAY JUNE 29TH IN CONVENTION

Doct: JOHNSON. The controversy must be endless whilst Gentlemen differ in the grounds of their arguments; Those on one side considering the States as districts of people composing one political Society; those on the other considering them as so many political

---

[1] The figure " 1 " is changed to " in the first place " in the transcript.
[2] The figure " 2 " is changed to " in the second place " in the transcript.
[3] The word " the " is here inserted in the transcript.
[4] The words " &c to be read " are substituted in the transcript for " be used."
[5] The word " this " is substituted in the transcript for " the."

societies. The fact is that the States do exist as political Societies, and a Gov͡t is to be formed for them in their political capacity, as well as for the individuals composing them. Does it not seem to follow, that if the States as such are to exist they must be armed with some power of self-defence. This is the idea of [Col. Mason] who appears to have looked to the bottom of this matter. Besides the Aristocratic and other interests, which ought to have the means of defending themselves, the States have their interests as such, and are equally entitled to likes means. On the whole he thought that as in some respects the States are to be considered in their political capacity, and in others as districts of individual citizens, the two ideas embraced on different sides, instead of being opposed to each other, ought to be combined; that in *one* branch the *people,* ought to be represented; in the *other* the *States.*

M͡r. GHORUM. The States as now confederated have no doubt a right to refuse to be consolidated, or to be formed into any new system. But he wished the small States which seemed most ready to object, to consider which are to give up most, they or the larger ones. He conceived that a rupture of the Union w͡d be an event unhappy for all, but surely the large States would be least unable to take care of themselves, and to make connections with one another. The weak therefore were most interested in establishing some general system for maintaining order. If among individuals, composed partly of weak, and partly of strong, the former most need the protection of law & Government, the case is exactly the same with weak & powerful States. What would be the situation of Delaware (for these things he found must be spoken out, & it might as well be done [1] first as last) what w͡d be the situation of Delaware in case of a separation of the States? Would she not lie [2] at the mercy of Pennsylvania? would not her true interest lie in being consolidated with her, and ought she not now to wish for such a union with P͡a under one Gov͡t as will put it out of the power of Pen͡a to oppress her? Nothing can be more ideal than the danger apprehended by the States, from their being formed into one nation. Mass͡ts was originally three colonies, viz old Mass͡ts Plymouth—& the province of Mayne. These apprehensions existed then. An incorporation took place; all parties were safe & satisfied; and every distinction is now forgotten. The case was similar with Connecticut & Newhaven. The dread of union was reciprocal; the consequence of it equally salutary and satisfactory. In like manner N. Jersey has been made

---

[1] The word "at" is here inserted in the transcript.
[2] The word "be" is substituted in the transcript for "lie."

one society out of two parts. Should a separation of the States take place, the fate of N. Jersey w.ᵈ be worst of all. She has no foreign commerce & can have but little. P.ᵃ & N. York will continue to levy taxes on her consumption. If she consults her interest she w.ᵈ beg of all things to be annihilated. The apprehensions of the small States ought to be appeased by another reflection. Mass.ᵗˢ will be divided. The province of Maine is already considered as approaching the term of its annexation to it; and P.ᵃ will probably not increase, considering the present state of her population, & other events that may happen. On the whole he considered a Union of the States as necessary to their happiness, & a firm Gen.ˡ Gov.ᵗ as necessary to their Union. He sh.ᵈ consider it as [1] his duty if his colleagues viewed the matter in the same light he did to stay here as long as any other State would remain with them, in order to agree on some plan that could with propriety be recommended to the people.

M.ʳ ELSWORTH, did not despair. He still trusted that some good plan of Gov.ᵗ w.ᵈ be divised & adopted.

M.ʳ READ. He sh.ᵈ have no objection to the system if it were truly national, but it has too much of a federal mixture in it. The little States he thought had not much to fear. He suspected that the large States felt their want of energy, & wished for a Gen.ˡ Gov.ᵗ to supply the defect. Mass.ᵗˢ was evidently labouring under her weakness and he believed Delaware w.ᵈ not be in much danger if in her neighbourhood. Delaware had enjoyed tranquility & he flattered himself w.ᵈ continue to do so. He was not however so selfish as not to wish for a good Gen.ˡ Gov.ᵗ In order to obtain one the whole States must be incorporated. If the States remain, the representatives of the large ones will stick together, and carry every thing before them. The Executive also will be chosen under the influence of this partiality, and will betray it in his administration. These jealousies are inseparable from the scheme of leaving the States in existence. They must be done away. The ungranted lands also which have been assumed by particular States must also [2] be given up. He repeated his approbation of the plan of M.ʳ Hamilton, & wished it to be substituted in place of [3] that on the table.

M.ʳ MADISON agreed with Doc.ʳ Johnson, that the mixed nature of the Gov.ᵗ ought to be kept in view; but thought too much stress was laid on the rank of the States as political societies. There was a gradation, he observed from the smallest corporation, with the most

---

[1] The word " as " is omitted in the transcript.
[2] The word " also " is stricken out in the transcript.
[3] The word " for " is substituted in the transcript for " in place of."

limited powers, to the largest empire with the most perfect sovereignty. He pointed out the limitations on the sovereignty of the States, as now confederated their laws in relation to the paramount law of the Confederacy were analogous to that of bye laws to the supreme law within a State. Under the proposed Gov.ᵗ the powers of the States will be much farther reduced. According to the views of every member, the Gen.ˡ Gov.ᵗ will have powers far beyond those exercised by the British Parliament, when the States were part of the British Empire. It will in particular have the power, without the consent of the State Legislatures, to levy money directly on [1] the people themselves; and therefore not to divest such *unequal* portions of the people as composed the several States, of an *equal* voice, would subject the system to the reproaches & evils which have resulted from the vicious representation in G. B.

He entreated the gentlemen representing the small States to renounce a principle w.ᶜʰ was confessedly unjust, which c.ᵈ never be admitted, & [2] if admitted must infuse mortality into a Constitution which we wished to last forever. He prayed them to ponder well the consequences of suffering the Confederacy to go to pieces. It had been s.ᵈ that the want of energy in the large states w.ᵈ be a security to the small. It was forgotten that this want of energy proceeded from the supposed security of the States ag.ˢᵗ all external danger. Let each state depend on itself for its security, & let apprehensions arise arise of danger, from distant powers or from neighbouring States, & the languishing condition of all the States, large as well as small, w.ᵈ soon be transformed into vigorous & high toned Gov.ᵗˢ His great fear was that their Gov.ᵗˢ w.ᵈ then have too much energy, that these [3] might not only be formidable in the large to the small States, but fatal to the internal liberty of all. The same causes which have rendered the old world the Theatre of incessant wars, & have banished liberty from the face of it, w.ᵈ soon produce the same effects here. The weakness & jealousy of the small States w.ᵈ quickly introduce some regular military force ag.ˢᵗ sudden danger from their powerful neighbours. The example w.ᵈ be followed by others, and w.ᵈ soon become universal. In time of actual war, great discretionary powers are constantly given to the Executive Magistrate. Constant apprehension of war, has the same tendency to render the head too large for the body. A standing military force, with an overgrown

---

[1] The word "from" is substituted in the transcript for "on."

[2] The word "which" is here inserted in the transcript.

[3] The word "these" is stricken out in the transcript and "this" is written above it.

Executive will not long be safe companions to liberty. The means of defence ag:ˢᵗ foreign danger, have been always the instruments of tyranny at home. Among the Romans it was a standing maxim to excite a war, whenever a revolt was apprehended. Throughout all Europe, the armies kept up under the pretext of defending, have enslaved the people. It is perhaps questionable, whether the best concerted system of absolute power in Europe cᵈ maintain itself, in a situation, where no alarms of external danger cᵈ tame the people to the domestic yoke. The insular situation of G. Britain was the principal cause of her being an exception to the general fate of Europe. It has rendered less defence necessary, and admitted a kind of defence wᶜʰ cᵈ not be used for the purpose of oppression.— These consequences he conceived ought to be apprehended whether the States should run into a total separation from each other, or shᵈ enter into partial confederacies. Either event wᵈ be truly deplorable; & those who might be accessary to either, could never be forgiven by their Country, nor by themselves.

* Mᴿ HAMILTON observed that individuals forming political Societies modify their rights differently, with regard to suffrage. Examples of it are found in all the States. In all of them some individuals are deprived of the right altogether, not having the requisite qualification of property. In some of the States the right of suffrage is allowed in some cases and refused in others. To vote for a member in one branch, a certain quantum of property, to vote for a member in another branch of the Legislature, a higher quantum of property is required. In like manner States may modify their right of suffrage differently, the larger exercising a larger, the smaller a smaller share of it. But as States are a collection of individual men which ought we to respect most, the rights of the people composing them, or of the artificial beings resulting from the composition. Nothing could be more preposterous or absurd than to sacrifice the former to the latter. It has been sᵈ that if the smaller States renounce their *equality*, they renounce at the same time their *liberty*. The truth is it is a contest for power, not for liberty. Will the men composing the small States be less free than those composing the larger. The State of Delaware having 40,000 souls will *lose* ² *power*, if she has ¹⁄₁₀ only of the votes allowed to Pᵃ having 400,000: but will the people of Del: *be less free*, if each citizen

* From this date he was absent till the   of ¹

---

¹ The date, "13th of August," is supplied in the transcript.
² The transcript does not italicize the word "*lose*."

has an equal vote with each citizen of P? He admitted that common residence within the same State would produce a certain degree of attachment; and that this principle might have a certain influence in [1] public affairs. He thought however that this might by some precautions be in a great measure excluded: and that no material inconvenience could result from it, as there could not be any ground for combination among the States whose influence was most dreaded. The only considerable distinction of interests, lay between the carrying & non-carrying States, which divide [2] instead of uniting the largest States. No considerable inconvenience had been found from the division of the State of N. York into different districts of different sizes.

Some of the consequences of a dissolution of the Union, and the establishment of partial confederacies, had been been pointed out. He would add another of a most serious nature. Alliances will immediately be formed with different rival & hostile nations of Europes, who will foment disturbances among ourselves, and make us parties to all their own quarrels. Foreign Nations having American dominions [3] are & must be jealous of us. Their representatives betray the utmost anxiety for our fate, & for the result of this meeting, which must have an essential influence on it.—It had been said that respectability in the eyes of foreign Nations was not the object at which we aimed; that the proper object of republican Government was domestic tranquility & happiness. This was an ideal distinction. No Governm? could give us tranquility & happiness at home, which did not possess sufficient stability and strength to make us respectable abroad. This was the critical moment for forming such a Government. We should run every risk in trusting to future amendments. As yet we retain the habits of union. We are weak & sensible of our weakness. Henceforward the motives will become feebler, and the difficulties greater. It is a miracle that we were [4] now here exercising our tranquil & free deliberations on the subject. It would be madness to trust to future miracles. A thousand causes must obstruct a reproduction of them.

M? Pierce considered the equality of votes under the Confederation as the great source of the public difficulties. The members of Cong? were advocates for local advantages. State distinctions must be sacrificed as far as the general good required, but without destroy-

---

[1] The word "on" is substituted in the transcript for "in."
[2] The word "divides" is substituted in the transcript for "divide."
[3] The transcript uses the word "dominions" in the singular.
[4] The word "are" is substituted in the transcript for "were."

ing the States. Tho' from a small State he felt himself a Citizen of the U. S.

M̃ GERRY, urged that we never were independent States, were not such now, & never could be even on the principles of the Confederation. The States & the advocates for them were intoxicated with the idea of their *sovereignty.* He was a member of Congress at the time the federal articles were formed. The injustice of allowing each State an equal vote was long insisted on. He voted for it, but it was ag̃ᵗ his Judgment, and under the pressure of public danger, and the obstinacy of the lesser States. The present confederation he considered as dissolving. The fate of the Union will be decided by the Convention. If they do not agree on something, few delegates will probably be appointed to Cong̃ If they do Cong̃ will probably be kept up till the new System should be adopted. He lamented that instead of coming here like a band of brothers, belonging to the same family, we seemed to have brought with us the spirit of political negociators.

M̃ L. MARTIN. remarked that the language of the States being *sovereign & independent,* was once familiar & understood; though it seemed now so strange & obscure. He read those passages in the articles of Confederation, which describe them in that language.

On the question as moved by M̃ Lansing. Shall the word " not " be struck out.

Massᵗˢ. no. Conᵗ ay. N. Y. ay. N. J. ay. Pᵃ no. Del. ay. M̃ᵈ divᵈ Vᵃ no. N. C. no. S. C. no. Geo. no.[1]

On the motion to agree to the clause as reported, " that the rule of suffrage in the 1ˢᵗ branch ought not to be according to that established by the articles of [2] Confederation.

Mass. ay. Conᵗ no. N. Y. no. N. J. no. Pᵃ ay. Del. no. M̃ᵈ divᵈ Vᵃ ay. N. C. ay. S. C. ay. Geo. ay.[3]

Docᵗ JOHNSON & M̃ ELSEWORTH moved to postpone the residue of the clause, & take up—y̧ 8—Resol:

On [2] question.

Mas. no. Conᵗ ay. N. Y. ay. N. J. ay. Pᵃ ay. Del. no. M̃ᵈ ay. Vᵃ ay. N. C. ay. S. C. ay. Geo. ay.[4]

---

[1] In the transcript the vote reads: " Connecticut, New York, New Jersey, Delaware, aye—4; Massachusetts, Pennsylvania, Virginia, North Carolina, South Carolina, Georgia, no—6; Maryland, divided."

[2] The word "the" is here inserted in the transcript.

[3] In the transcript the vote reads: " Massachusetts, Pennsylvania, Virginia, North Carolina, South Carolina, Georgia, aye—6; Connecticut, New York, New Jersey, Delaware, no—4; Maryland, divided."

[4] In the transcript the vote reads: " Connecticut, New York, New Jersey, Pennsylvania, Maryland, Virginia, North Carolina, South Carolina, Georgia, aye—9; Massachusetts, Delaware, no—2."

Mr ELSEWORTH moved that the rule of suffrage in the 2^d branch be the same with that established by the articles of confederation." He was not sorry on the whole he said that the vote just passed, had determined against this rule in the first branch. He hoped it would become a ground of compromise with regard to the 2^d branch. We were partly national; partly federal. The proportional representation in the first branch was conformable to the national principle & would secure the large States agst the small. An equality of voices was conformable to the federal principle and was necessary to secure the Small States agst the large. He trusted that on this middle ground a compromise would take place. He did not see that it could on any other. And if no compromise should take place, our meeting would not only be in vain but worse than in vain. To the Eastward he was sure Mass^{ts} was the only State that would listen to a proposition for excluding the States as equal political Societies, from an equal voice in both branches. The others would risk every consequence rather than part with so dear a right. An attempt to deprive them of it, was at once cutting the body of America in two, and as he supposed would be the case, somewhere about this part of it. The large States he conceived would notwithstanding the equality of votes, have an influence that would maintain their superiority. Holland, as had been admitted [by Mr Madison] had, notwithstanding a like equality in the Dutch Confederacy, a prevailing influence in the public measures. The power of self-defence was essential to the small States. Nature had given it to the smallest insect of the creation. He could never admit that there was no danger of combinations among the large States. They will like individuals find out and avail themselves of the advantage to be gained by it. It was true the danger would be greater, if they were contiguous and had a more immediate [1] common interest. A defensive combination of the small States was rendered more difficult by their greater number. He would mention another consideration of great weight. The existing confederation was founded on the equality of the States in the article of suffrage: was it meant to pay no regard to this antecedent plighted faith. Let a strong Executive, a Judiciary & Legislative power be created; but Let not too much be attempted; by which all may be lost. He was not in general a half-way man, yet he preferred doing half the good we could, rather than do nothing at all. The other half may be added, when the necessity shall be more fully experienced.

---

[1] The word " and " is here inserted in the transcript.

M: BALDWIN could have wished that the powers of the General Legislature had been defined, before the mode of constituting it had been agitated. He should vote against the motion of M: Elseworth, tho' he did not like the Resolution as it stood in the Report of the Committee of the whole. He thought the second branch ought to be the representation of property, and that in forming it therefore some reference ought to be had to the relative wealth of their Constituents, and to the principles on which the Senate of Mass^ts was constituted. He concurred with those who thought it w^d be impossible for the Gen! Legislature to extend its cares to the local matters of the States.

Adj^d

SATURDAY JUNE 30. 1787.[1]   IN CONVENTION

M: BREARLY moved that the Presid: write to the Executive of N. Hamshire, informing it that the business depending before the Convention was of such a nature as to require the immediate attendance of the deputies of that State. In support of his motion he observed that the difficulties of the subject and the diversity of opinions called for all the assistance we could possibly obtain. [it was well understood that the object was to add N. Hamshire to the n.° of States opposed to the doctrine of proportional representation, which it was presumed from her relative size she must be adverse to].

M: PATTERSON seconded the motion

M: RUTLIDGE could see neither the necessity nor propriety of such a measure. They are not unapprized of the meeting, and can attend if they choose. Rho. Island might as well be urged to appoint & send deputies. Are we to suspend the business until the deputies arrive? if we proceed he hoped all the great points would be adjusted before the letter could produce its effect.

M: KING. said he had written more than once as a private correspondent, & the answers[2] gave him every reason to expect that State would be represented very shortly, if it sh^d be so at all. Circumstances of a personal nature had hitherto prevented it. A letter c^d have no effect.

M: WILSON wished to know whether it would be consistent with the rule or reason of secresy, to communicate to N. Hamshire that

---

[1] The year " 1787 " is omitted in the transcript.
[2] The transcript uses the word " answers " in the singular.

the business was of such a nature as the motion described. It w^d spread a great alarm. Besides he doubted the propriety of soliciting any State on the subject; the meeting being merely voluntary—on the [1] motion of Mr Brearly Mas^{ts} no. Con^t no. N. Y. ay. N. J. ay. P^a not on ye floor. Del. not on floor. M^d div^d V^a no. N. C. no. S. C. no. Geo. not on floor.[2]

The motion of Mr Elseworth [3] resumed for allowing each State an equal vote in ye 2^d branch.

Mr WILSON did not expect such a motion after the establishment of ye contrary principle in the 1st branch; and considering the reasons which would oppose it, even if an equal vote had been allowed in the 1st branch. The Gentleman from Connecticut [Mr Elseworth] had pronounced that if the motion should not be acceded to, of all the States North of Pen^a one only would agree to any Genl Government. He entertained more favorable hopes of Conn^t and of the other Northern States. He hoped the alarms exceeded their cause, and that they would not abandon a Country to which they were bound by so many strong and endearing ties. But should the deplored event happen, it would neither stagger his sentiments nor his duty. If the minority of the people of America refuse to coalesce with the majority on just and proper principles, if a separation must take place, it could never happen on better grounds. The votes of yesterday agst the just principle of representation, were as 22 to 90 of the people of America. Taking the opinions to be the same on this point, and he was sure if there was any room for change, it could not be on the side of the majority, the question will be shall less than ¼ of the U. States withdraw themselves from the Union; or shall more than ¾. renounce the inherent, indisputable, and unalienable rights of men, in favor of the artificial systems of States. If issue must be joined, it was on this point he would chuse to join it. The gentleman from Connecticut in supposing that the prepondenancy [4] secured to the majority in the 1st branch had removed the objections to an equality of votes in the 2^d branch for the security of the minority, narrowed the case extremely. Such an equality will enable the minority to controul in all cases whatsoever, the sentiments and interests of the majority. Seven States will controul six: Seven

---

[1] The word "the" is omitted in the transcript.

[2] In the transcript the vote reads: "New York, New Jersey, aye—2; Massachusetts, Connecticut, Virginia, North Carolina, South Carolina, no—5; Maryland, divided; Pennsylvania, Delaware, Georgia, not on the floor."

[3] The word "being" is here inserted in the transcript.

[4] The word "prepondenancy" is changed to "preponderance" in the transcript.

States, according to the estimates that had been used, composed $^{24}\!\!/\!90$. of the whole people. It would be in the power then of less than ⅓ to overrule ⅔ whenever a question should happen to divide the States in that manner. Can we forget for whom we are forming a Government? Is it for *men*, or for the imaginary beings called *States?* Will our honest Constituents be satisfied with metaphysical distinctions? Will they, ought they to be satisfied with being told that the one third compose the greater number of States? The rule of suffrage ought on every principle to be the same in the 2^d as in the 1st branch. If the Government be not laid on this foundation, it can be neither solid nor lasting. Any other principle will be local, confined & temporary. This will expand with the expansion, and grow with the growth of the U. States.—Much has been said of an imaginary combination of three States. Sometimes a danger of monarchy, sometimes of aristocracy, has been charged on it. No explanation however of the danger has been vouchsafed. It would be easy to prove both from reason & history that rivalships would be more probable than coalitions; and that there are no coinciding interests that could produce the latter. No answer has yet been given to the observations of [Mr Madison] on this subject. Should the Executive Magistrate be taken from one of the large States would not the other two be thereby thrown into the scale with the other States? Whence then the danger of monarchy? Are the people of the three large States more aristocratic than those of the small ones? Whence then the danger of aristocracy from their influence? It is all a mere illusion of names. We talk of States, till we forget what they are composed of. Is a real & fair majority, the natural hot-bed of aristocracy? It is a part of the definition of this species of Gov^t or rather of tyranny, that the smaller number governs the greater. It is true that a majority of States in the 2^d branch can not carry a law ag^{st} a majority of the people in the 1st But this removes half only of the objection. Bad $Govern^{ts}$ are of two sorts. $1.^1$ that which does too little. $2.^1$ that which does too much: that which fails thro' weakness; and that which destroys thro' oppression. Under which of these evils do the U. States at present groan? under the weakness and inefficiency of its $Govern^t$. To remedy this weakness we have been sent to this Convention. If the motion should be agreed to, we shall leave the U. S. fettered precisely as heretofore; with the additional mortification of seeing the good purposes of y^e fair

---

¹ The figures " 1 " and " 2 " are changed to " first " and " secondly " in the transcript.

represention of the people in the 1ˢᵗ branch, defeated in [1] 2ᵈ. Twenty four will still controul sixty six. He lamented that such a disagreement should prevail on the point of representation, as he did not foresee that it would happen on the other point most contested, the boundary between the Genˡ & the local authorities. He thought the States necessary & valuable parts of a good system.

Mʳ ELSEWORTH. The capital objection of Mʳ Wilson " that the minority will rule the majority " is not true. The power is given to the few to save them from being destroyed by the many. If an equality of votes had been given to them in both branches, the objection might have had weight. Is it a novel thing that the few should have a check on the many? Is it not the case in the British Constitution the wisdom of which so many gentlemen have united in applauding? Have not the House of Lords, who form so small a proportion of the nation a negative on the laws, as a necessary defence of their peculiar rights agˢᵗ the encroachmᵗˢ of the Commons. No instance of a Confederacy has existed in which an equality of voices has not been exercised by the members of it. We are running from one extreme to another. We are razing the foundations of the building, when we need only repair the roof. No salutary measure has been lost for want of *a majority of the States,* to favor it. If security be all that the great States wish for the 1ˢᵗ branch secures them. The danger of combinations among them is not imaginary. Altho' no particular abuses could be foreseen by him, the possibility of them would be sufficient to alarm him. But he could easily conceive cases in which they might result from such combinations. Suppose that in pursuance of some commercial treaty or arrangement, three or four free ports & no more were to be established would not combinations be formed in favor of Boston—Philadᵃ & & some port in [2] Chesapeak? A like concert might be formed in the appointment of the great officers. He appealed again to the obligations of the federal pact which was still in force, and which had been entered into with so much solemnity; persuading himself that some regard would still be paid to the plighed faith under which each State small as well as great, held an equal right of suffrage in the general Councils. His remarks were not the result of partial or local views. The State he represented [Connecticut] held a middle rank.

Mʳ MADISON did justice to the able & close reasoning of Mʳ E. but must observe that it did not always accord with itself. On

---

[1] The word " the " is here inserted in the transcript.
[2] The words " of the " are substituted in the transcript for " in."

another occasion, the large States were described by him as the Aristocratic States, ready to oppress the small. Now the small are the House of Lords requiring a negative to defend them agst the more numerous commons. M^{r}. E. had also erred in saying that no instance had existed in which confederated States had not retained to themselves a perfect equality of suffrage. Passing over the German system in which the K. of Prussia has nine voices, he reminded Mr E. of the Lycian confederacy, in which the component members had votes proportioned to their importance, and which Montesquieu recommends as the fittest model for that form of Government. Had the fact been as stated by Mr E. it would have been of little avail to him, or rather would have strengthened the arguments agst him; the History & fate of the several confederacies modern as well as Antient, demonstrating some radical vice in their structure. In reply to the appeal of Mr E. to the faith plighted in the existing federal compact, he remarked that the party claiming from others an adherence to a common engagement ought at least to be guiltless itself of a violation. Of all the States however Connecticut was perhaps least able to urge this plea. Besides the various omissions to perform the stipulated acts from which no State was free, the Legislature of that State had by a pretty recent vote, *positively, refused* to pass a law for complying with the Requisitions of Cong^{s} and had transmitted a copy of the vote to Cong^{s} It was urged, he said, continually that an equality of votes in the 2^{d} branch was not only necessary to secure the small, but would be perfectly safe to the large ones whose majority in the 1st branch was an effectual bulwark. But notwithstanding this apparent defence, the majority of States might still injure the majority of [1] people. 1.[2] they could *obstruct* the wishes and interests of the majority. 2.[2] they could *extort* measures repugnant to the wishes & interest of the Majority. 3.[2] they could *impose* measures adverse thereto;˙as the 2^{d} branch will probly exercise some great powers, in which the 1st will not participate. He admitted that every peculiar interest whether in any class of citizens, or any description of States, ought to be secured as far as possible. Wherever there is danger of attack there ought[3] be given a constitutional power of defence. But he contended that the States were divided into different interests not by their difference of size, but by other circumstances; the most material of which resulted partly

---

[1] The word "the" is here inserted in the transcript.
[2] The figures "1," "2" and "3" are changed to "In the first place," "Secondly" and "Thirdly."
[3] The word "to" is here inserted in the transcript.

from climate, but principally from the effects of their having or not having slaves. These two causes concurred in forming the great division of interests in the U. States. It did not lie between the large & small States: It lay between the Northern & Southern, and if any defensive power were necessary, it ought to be mutually given to these two interests. He was so strongly impressed with this important truth that he had been casting about in his mind for some expedient that would answer the purpose. The one which had occurred was that instead of proportioning the votes of the States in both branches, to their respective numbers of inhabitants computing the slaves in the ratio of 5 to 3, they should be represented in one branch according to the number of free inhabitants only; and in the other according to the whole n? counting the slaves as if [1] free. By this arrangement the Southern Scale would have the advantage in one House, and the Northern in the other. He had been restrained from proposing this expedient by two considerations: one was his unwillingness to urge any diversity of interests on an occasion where it is but too apt to arise of itself—the other was, the inequality of powers that must be vested in the two branches, and which w⁵ destroy the equilibrium of interests.

M⁵ Elseworth assured the House that whatever might be thought of the Representatives of Connecticut the State was entirely federal in her disposition. He appealed to her great exertions during the war, in supplying both men & money. The muster rolls would show she had more troops in the field than Virg⁴ If she had been Delinquent, it had been from inability, and not more so than other States.

M⁵ Sherman. M⁵ Madison has [2] animadverted on the delinquency of the States, when his object required him to prove that the Constitution of Cong⁵ was faulty. Cong⁵ is not to blame for the faults of the States. Their measures have been right, and the only thing wanting has been, a further power in Cong⁵ to render them effectual.

M⁵ Davy was much embarrassed and wished for explanations. The Report of the Committee allowing the Legislatures to choose the Senate, and establishing a proportional representation in it, seemed to be impracticable. There will according to this rule be ninety members in the outset, and the number will increase as new States are added. It was impossible that so numerous a body could possess the activity and other qualities required in it. Were he to vote on the comparative merits of the report as it stood, and the amendment, he

---

[1] The word " if " is omitted in the transcript.
[2] The word " has " is omitted in the transcript.

should be constrained to prefer the latter. The appointment of the Senate by electors chosen by the people for that purpose was he conceived liable to an insuperable difficulty. The larger Counties or districts thrown into a general district, would certainly prevail over the smaller Counties or districts, and merit in the latter would be excluded altogether. The report therefore seemed to be right in referring the appointment to the Legislatures, whose agency in the general System did not appear to him objectionable as it did to some others. The fact was that the local prejudices & interests which could not be denied to exist, would find their way into the national councils whether the Representatives should be chosen by the Legislatures or by the people themselves. On the other hand, if a proportional representation was attended with insuperable difficulties, the making the Senate the Representative of the States, looked like bringing us back to Cong⁵ again, and shutting out all the advantages expected from it. Under this view of the subject he could not vote for any plan for the Senate yet proposed. He thought that in general there were extremes on both sides. We were partly federal, partly national in our Union, and he did not see why the Govᵗ might not in some respects operate on the States, in others on the people.

Mʳ WILSON admitted the question concerning the number of Senators, to be embarrassing. If the smallest States be allowed one, and the others in proportion, the Senate will certainly be too numerous. He looked forward to the time when the smallest States will contain 100,000 souls at least. Let there be then one Senator in each for every 100,000 souls and let the States not having that nᵒ of inhabitants be allowed one. He was willing himself to submit to this temporary concession to the small States; and threw out the idea as a ground of compromise.

Docᵗ FRANKLIN The diversity of opinions turns on two points. If a proportional representation takes place, the small States contend that their liberties will be in danger. If an equality of votes is to be put in its place, the large States say their money will be in danger. When a broad table is to be made, and the edges of planks do not fit, the artist takes a little from both, and makes a good joint. In like manner here both sides must part with some of their demands, in order that they may join in some accomodating proposition. He had prepared one which he would read, that it might lie on the table for consideration. The proposition was in the words following "

"That the Legislatures of the several States shall choose & send an equal number of Delegates, namely   who are to compose the 2ᵈ branch of the General Legislature—

That in all cases or questions wherein the Sovereignty of individual States may be affected, or whereby their authority over their own Citizens may be diminished, or the authority of the General Government within the several States augmented, each State shall have equal suffrage.

That in the appointment of all Civil officers of y.ᵉ Gen! Govᵗ in the election of whom the 2ᵈ branch may by the Constitution have part, each State shall have equal suffrage.

That in fixing the Salaries of such officers, and in all allowances for public services, and generally in all appropriations & dispositions of money to be drawn out of the General Treasury; and in all laws for supplying that Treasury, the Delegates of the several States shall have suffrage in proportion to the Sums which their respective States do actually contribute to the Treasury." Where a Ship had many owners this was the rule of deciding on her expedition. He had been one of the Ministers from this Country to France during the joint war and wᵈ have been very glad if allowed a vote in distributing the money to carry it on.

Mʳ KING observed that the simple question was whether each State should have an equal vote in the 2ᵈ branch; that it must be apparent to those gentlemen who liked neither the motion for this equality, nor the report as it stood, that the report was as susceptible of melioration as the motion; that a reform would be nugatory & nominal only if we should make another Congress of the proposed Senate: that if the adherence to an equality of votes was fixed & unalterable, there could not be less obstinacy on the other side, & that we were in fact cut insunder [1] already, and it was in vain to shut our eyes against it: that he was however filled with astonishment that if we were convinced that every *man* in America was secured in all his rights, we should be ready to sacrifice this substantial good to the phantom of *State* sovereignty: that his feelings were more harrowed & his fears more agitated for his Country than he could express, that he conceived this to be the last opportunity of providing for its liberty & happiness: that he could not therefore but repeat his amazement that when a just Governᵗ founded on a fair representation of the *people* of America was within our reach, we should renounce the blessing, from an attachment to the ideal freedom & importance of *States*: that should this wonderful illusion continue to prevail, his mind was prepared for every event, rather than to [2] sit down under a Govᵗ founded in [3] a vicious principle of representation, and which must be as short lived as it would be unjust. He

---

[1] The word "asunder" is substituted in the transcript for "insunder."
[2] The word "to" is omitted in the transcript.
[3] The word "on" is substituted in the transcript for "in."

might prevail on himself to accede to some such expedient as had been hinted by M! Wilson: but he never could listen to an equality of votes as proposed in the motion.

M! DAYTON. When assertion is given for proof, and terror substituted for argument, he presumed they would have no effect however eloquently spoken. It should have been shewn that the evils we have experienced have proceeded from the equality now objected to: and that the seeds of dissolution for the State Governments are not sown in the Gen! Government. He considered the system on the table as a novelty, an amphibious monster; and was persuaded that it never would be rec⁴ by the people.

M! MARTIN, w⁴ never confederate if it could not be done on just principles

M! MADISON would acquiesce in the concession hinted by M! Wilson, on condition that a due independence should be given to the Senate. The plan in its present shape makes the Senate absolutely dependent on the States. The Senate therefore is only another edition of Cong.ˢ He knew the faults of that Body & had used a bold language ag.ˢᵗ it. Still he w⁴ preserve the State rights, as carefully as the trials by jury.

M! BEDFORD, contended that there was no middle way between a perfect consolidation and a mere confederacy of the States. The first is out of the question, and in the latter they must continue if not perfectly, yet equally sovereign. If political Societies possess ambition avarice, and all the other passions which render them formidable to each other, ought we not to view them in this light here? Will not the same motives operate in America as elsewhere? If any gentleman doubts it let him look at the votes. Have they not been dictated by interest, by ambition? Are not the large States evidently seeking to aggrandize themselves at the expense of the small? They think no doubt that they have right on their side, but interest had blinded their eyes. Look at Georgia. Though a small State at present, she is actuated by the prospect of soon being a great one. S. Carolina is actuated both by present interest & future prospects. She hopes too to see the other States cut down to her own dimensions. N. Carolina has the same motives of present & future interest. Virg.ᵃ follows. Mary⁴ is not on that side of the Question. Pen.ᵃ has a direct and future interest. Mass.ᵗˢ has a decided and palpable interest in the part she takes. Can it be expected that the small States will act from pure disinterestedness. Look at G. Britain. Is the Representation there less unequal? But we shall be told again that that is the rotten part of the Constitution. Have not the boroughs however held fast their constitutional rights? and are we to act with greater purity than the rest of mankind. An exact proportion in the Representation is not preserved in any one of the States. Will it be said that an inequality of power will not result from an inequality of votes. Give the opportunity, and ambition will not fail to abuse it. The whole History of mankind proves it. The three large States have a common interest to bind them together in commerce. But whether a combination as we suppose, or a competition as others suppose, shall take place among them, in either case, the smaller[1] States must be ruined. We must like Solon make such a Govern.t as the people will approve. Will the smaller States ever agree to the proposed degradation of them. It is not true that the people will not agree to enlarge the powers of the present Cong.s The Language of the people has been that Cong.s ought to have the power of collecting an impost, and of coercing the States when[2] it may be necessary. On The first point they have been explicit &, in a manner, unanimous in their declarations. And must they not agree to this & similar measures if they ever mean to discharge their engagements. The little States are willing to observe their engagements, but will meet the large ones on no ground but that of the Confederation. We have been told with a dictatorial air that this is the last moment for a fair trial in favor of a good Governm.t It will be the last indeed if the propositions reported from the Committee go forth to the people. He was under no apprehensions. The Large States dare not dissolve the Confederation. If they do the small ones will find some foreign ally of more honor and good faith, who will take them by the hand and do them justice. He did not mean by this to intimidate or alarm. It was a natural consequence; which ought to be avoided by enlarging the federal powers not annihilating the federal system. This is what the people expect. All agree in the necessity of a more efficient Gov.t and why not make such an one; as they desire.

M.r ELSEWORTH,. Under a National Gov.t he should participate in the National Security, as remarked by [M.r King] but that was all. What he wanted was domestic happiness. The Nat.l Gov.t could not descend to the local objects on which this depended. It could only embrace objects of a general nature. He turned his eyes therefore for the preservation of his rights to the State Gov.ts From these alone he could derive the greatest happiness he expects in this life. His

---

[1] The word "small" is substituted in the transcript for "smaller."
[2] The word "where" is substituted in the transcript for "when."

happiness depends on their existence, as much as a new born infant on its mother for nourishment. If this reasoning was not satisfactory, he had nothing to add that could be so.

M! KING was for preserving the States in a subordinate degree, and as far as they could be necessary for the purposes stated by M! Elsewth. He did not think a full answer had been given to those who apprehended a dangerous encroachment on their jurisdictions. Expedients might be devised as he conceived that would give them all the security the nature of things would admit of. In the establishm! of Societies the Constitution was to the Legislature what the laws were to individuals. As the fundamental rights of individuals are secured by express provisions in the State Constitutions; why may not a like security be provided for the Rights of States in the National Constitution. The articles of Union between Engl! & Scotland furnish an example of such a provision in favor of sundry rights of Scotland. When that Union was in agitation, the same language of apprehension which has been heard from the smaller States, was in the mouths of the Scotch patriots. The articles however have not been violated and the Scotch have found an increase of prosperity & happiness. He was aware that this will be called a mere *paper security*. He thought it a sufficient answer to say that if fundamental articles of compact, are no sufficient defence against physical power, neither will there be any safety ag!t it if there be no compact. He could not sit down, without taking some notice of the language of the honorable gentleman from Delaware [M! Bedford]. It was not he that had uttered a dictatorial language. This intemperance had marked the honorabl gentleman himself. It was not he who with a vehemence unprecedented in that House, had declared himself ready to turn his hopes from our common Country, and court the protection of some foreign hand. This too was the language of the Honbl member himself. He was grieved that such a thought had entered into[1] his heart. He was more grieved that such an expression had dropped from his lips. The gentleman c! only excuse it to himself on the score of passion. For himself whatever might be his distress, he w! never court relief from a foreign power.

Adjourned

---

[1] The word " into " is omitted in the transcript.

Monday July 2D. in Convention

On the question for allowing each State one vote in the second branch as moved by Mr Elseworth,[1] Massts no. Cont ay. N. Y. ay. N. J. ay. Pa. no. Del. ay. Md. ay. Mr Jenifer being not present Mr Martin alone voted Va no. N. C. no. S. C. no. Geo. divd. Mr. Houston no. Mr Baldwin ay.

Mr. Pinkney thought an equality of votes in the 2d. branch inadmissible. At the same time candor obliged him to admit that the large States would feel a partiality for their own Citizens & give them a preference, in appointments: that they might also find some common points in their commercial interests, and promote treaties favorable to them. There is a real distinction [2] the Northern & Southn. interests. N. Carola. S. Carol: & Geo. in their Rice & Indigo had a peculiar interest which might be sacrificed. How then shall the larger States be prevented from administering the Genl. Govt. as they please, without being themselves unduly subjected to the will of the smaller? By allowing them some but not a full proportion. He was extremely anxious that something should be done, considering this as the last appeal to a regular experiment. Congs. have failed in almost every effort for an amendment of the federal System. Nothing has prevented a dissolution of it, but the appointmt. of this Convention; & he could not express his alarms for the consequences of such an event He read his motion, to form the States into classes, with an apportionment of Senators among them, [see art. 4, of his plan].[3]

General Pinkney. was willing the motion might be considered. He did not entirely approve it. He liked better the motion of Docr. Franklin [which see Saturday June 30]. Some compromise seemed to be necessary: the States being exactly divided on the question for an equality of votes in the 2d. branch. He proposed that a Committee consisting of a member from each State should be appointed to devise & report some compromise.

Mr L. Martin had no objection to a commitment, but no modifications whatever could reconcile the Smaller States to the least diminution of their equal Sovereignty.

---

[1] The phrase "it was lost by an equal division of votes," is here inserted in the transcript and the vote reads: "Connecticut, New York, New Jersey, Delaware, Maryland,* aye—5; Massachusetts, Pennsylvania, Virginia, North Carolina, South Carolina, no—5; Georgia, divided [Mr. Baldwin, aye, Mr. Houston, no]." The footnote referring to Maryland reads: "Mr. Jenifer not being present, Mr. Martin alone voted."

[2] The word "between" is here inserted in the transcript.

[3] See Appendix to Debates, IV, No. 3, p. 600.

M? SHARMAN. We are now at a full stop, and nobody he supposed meant that we shᵈ break up without doing something. A committee he thought most likely to hit on some expedient.

* M? Gov? MORRIS. thought a Comᵉ adviseable as the Convention had been equally divided. He had a stronger reason also. The mode of appointing the 2ᵈ branch tended he was sure to defeat the object of it. What is this object? to check the precipitation, changeableness, and excesses of the first branch. Every man of observation had seen in the democratic branches of the State Legislatures, precipitation—in Congress changeableness, in every department excesses agˢᵗ personal liberty private property & personal safety. What qualities are necessary to constitute a check in this case? *Abilities* and *virtue*, are equally necessary in both branches. Something more then is now wanted. 1.² the checking branch must have a personal interest in checking the other branch, one interest must be opposed to another interest. Vices as they exist, must be turned agˢᵗ each other. 2.³ It must have great personal property, it must have the aristocratic spirit; it must love to lord it thro' pride, pride is indeed the great principle that actuates both the poor & the rich. It is this principle which in the former resists, in the latter abuses authority. 3.⁴ It should be independent. In Religion the Creature is apt to forget its Creator. That it is otherwise in political affairs, the late debates here are an unhappy proof. The aristocratic body, should be as independent & as firm as the democratic. If the members of it are to revert to a dependence on the democratic choice, the democratic scale will preponderate. All the guards contrived by America have not restrained the Senatorial branches of the Legislatures from a servile complaisance to the democratic. If the 2ᵈ branch is to be dependent we are better without it. To make it independent, it should be for life. It will then do wrong, it will be said. He believed so: He hoped so. The Rich will strive to establish their dominion & enslave the rest. They always did. They always will. The proper security agˢᵗ them is to form them into a separate interest. The two forces will then controul each other. Let the rich mix with the poor and in a Commercial Country, they will establish an oligarchy. Take away commerce, and the democracy will triumph. Thus it has been

* Transfer hither the marginal note.¹
* He had just returned from N. Y. havᵍ left yᵉ Convention a few days after it commenced business.

---

¹ Madison's direction concerning the footnote is omitted in the transcript.
² The figure " 1 " is changed to " In the first place " in the transcript.
³ The figure " 2 " is changed to " In the second place " in the transcript.
⁴ The figure " 3 " is changed to " In the third place " in the transcript.

all the world over. So it will be among us. Reason tells us we are
but men: and we are not to expect any particular interference of
Heaven in our favor. By thus combining & setting apart, the aristocratic interest, the popular interest will be combined ag.st it. There
will be a mutual check and mutual security. 4.[1] An independence
for life, involves the necessary permanency. If we change our
measures no body will trust us: and how avoid a change of measures,
but by avoiding a change of men. Ask any man if he confides in
Cong.^{s} if he confides in the State of Pen.^{a} if he will lend his money
or enter into contract? He will tell you no. He sees no stability.
He can repose no confidence. If G. B. were to explain her refusal to
treat with us, the same reasoning would be employed.—He disliked
the exclusion of the 2^d branch from holding offices. It is dangerous.
It is like the imprudent exclusion of the military officers during
the war, from civil appointments. It deprives the Executive of the
principal source of influence. If danger be apprehended from the
Executive what a lift-handed way is this of obviating it? If the
son, the brother or the friend can be appointed, the danger may be
even increased, as the disqualified father &c. can then boast of a
disinterestedness which he does not possess. Besides shall the best,
the most able, the most virtuous citizens not be permitted to hold
offices? Who then are to hold them? He was also agst paying the
Senators. They will pay themselves if they can. If they can not
they will be rich and can do without it. Of such the 2^d branch
ought to consist; and none but such can compose it if they are not
to be paid—He contended that the Executive should appoint the
Senate & fill up vacancies. This gets rid of the difficulty in the
present question. You may begin with any ratio you please; it will
come to the same thing. The members being independ^t & for life,
may be taken as well from one place as from another.—It should be
considered too how the scheme could be carried through the States.
He hoped there was strength of mind eno' in this House to look
truth in the face. He did not hesitate therefore to say that loaves
& fishes must bribe the Demagogues. They must be made to expect
higher offices under the general than the State Gov^{ts}. A Senate for
life will be a noble bait. Without such captivating prospects, the
popular leaders will oppose & defeat the plan. He perceived that
the 1st branch was to be chosen by the people of the States: the 2^d
by those chosen by the people. Is not here a Gov^t by the States. A
Govern^t by Compact between Virg^a in the 1st & 2^d branch; Mas^{ts} in

---

[1] The figure " 4 " is changed to " In the fourth place " in the transcript.

the 1ˢᵗ & 2ᵈ branch &c. This is going back to mere treaty. It is no Govᵗ at all. It is altogether dependent on the States, and will act over again the part which Congˢ has acted. A firm Governᵗ alone can protect our liberties. He fears the influence of the rich. They will have the same effect here as elsewhere if we do not by such a Govᵗ keep them within their proper sphere.[1] We should remember that the people never act from reason alone. The Rich will take[2] advantage of their passions & make these the instruments for oppressing them. The Result of the Contest will be a violent aristocracy, or a more violent despotism. The schemes of the Rich will be favored by the extent of the Country. The people in such distant parts can not communicate & act in concert. They will be the dupes of those who have more knowledge & intercourse. The only security agˢᵗ encroachments will be a select & sagacious body of men, instituted to watch agˢᵗ them on all sides. He meant only to hint these observations, without grounding any motion on them

Mʳ RANDOLPH favored the commitment though he did not expect much benefit from the expedient. He animadverted on the warm & rash language of Mʳ Bedford on Saturday; reminded the small States that if the large States should combine some danger of which he did not deny there would be a check in the revisionary power of the Executive, and intimated that in order to render this still more effectual, he would agree that in the choice of the[3] Executive each State should have an equal vote. He was persuaded that two such opposite bodies as Mʳ Morris had planned, could never long co-exist. Dissentions would arise as has been seen even between the Senate and H. of Delegates in Maryland, appeals would be made to the people; and in a little time, commotions would be the result—He was far from thinking the large States could subsist of themselves any more than the small; an avulsion would involve the whole in ruin, and he was determined to pursue such a scheme of Government as would secure us agˢᵗ such a calamity.

Mʳ STRONG was for the Commitment; and hoped the mode of constituting both branches would be referred. If they should be established on different principles, contentions would prevail, and there would never be a concurrence in necessary measures.

Docʳ WILLIAMSON. If we do not concede on both sides, our business must soon be at an end. He approved of the Commitment,

---

[1] The transcript uses the word " sphere " in the plural.
[2] The word " the " is here inserted in the transcript.
[3] The word " an " is substituted in the transcript for " the."

supposing that as the Com^e w^d be a smaller body, a compromise would be pursued with more coolness

Mr WILSON objected to the Committee, because it would decide according to that very rule of voting which was opposed on one side. Experience in Cong^s had also proved the inutility of Committees consisting of members from each State

Mr LANSING w^d not oppose the commitment, though expecting little advantage from it.

Mr MADISON opposed the Commitment. He had rarely seen any other effect than delay from *such* Committees in Cong^s Any scheme of compromise that could be proposed in the Committee might as easily be proposed in the House; and the report of the Committee when [1] it contained merely the *opinion* of the Com^e would neither shorten the discussion, nor influence the decision of the House.

Mr GERRY was for the Commitm^t Something must be done, or we shall disappoint not only America, but the whole world. He suggested a consideration of the State we should be thrown into by the failure of the Union. We should be without an Umpire to decide controversies and must be at the mercy of events. What too is to become of our treaties—what of our foreign debts, what of our domestic? We must make concessions on both sides. Without these the Constitutions of the several States would never have been formed.

On the question " for committing," generally:

Mass^s ay. Con^t ay. N. Y. ay. N. J. no. P. ay. Del. no. M^d ay. V^a ay. N. C. ay. S. C. ay. Geo. ay.[2]

On the question for committing [3] " to a member from each State."

Mass^{ts} ay. Con^t ay. N. Y. ay. N. J. ay. P^a no. Del. ay. M^d ay. V^a ay. N. C. ay. S. C. ay. Geo. ay.[4]

The Committee elected by ballot, were Mr Gerry, Mr Elseworth, Mr Yates, Mr Patterson, Dr Franklin, Mr Bedford, Mr Martin, Mr Mason, Mr Davy, Mr Rutledge, Mr. Baldwin.

That time might be given to the Committee, and to such as chose to attend to the celebrations on the anniversary of Independence, the Convention adjourned till Thursday.

---

[1] The word " where " is substituted in the transcript for " when."
[2] In the transcript the vote reads: " Massachusetts, Connecticut, New York, Pennsylvania, Maryland, Virginia, North Carolina, South Carolina, Georgia, aye—9; New Jersey, Delaware, no—2."
[3] The word " it " is here inserted in the transcript.
[4] In the transcript the vote reads: " Massachusetts, Connecticut, New York, New Jersey, Delaware, Maryland, Virginia, North Carolina, South Carolina, Georgia, aye—10; Pennsylvania, no—1."

THURSDAY JULY 5.TH IN CONVENTION

Mr GERRY delivered in from the Committee appointed on Monday last the following Report.

'' The Committee to whom was referred the 8.th Resol. of the Report from the Committee of the whole House, and so much of the 7.th as has not been decided on, submit the following Report: That the subsequent propositions be recommended to the Convention on condition that both shall be generally adopted. 1. that in the I.st branch of the Legislature each of the States now in the Union shall be allowed 1 member for every 40,000 inhabitants of the description reported in the 7.th Resolution of the Com.^e of the whole House: that each State not containing that number shall be allowed 1 member: that all bills for raising or appropriating money, and for fixing the Salaries of the officers of the Govern.^t of the U. States shall originate in the 1.st branch of of the Legislature, and shall not be altered or amended by the 2.^d branch: and that no money shall be drawn from the public Treasury. but in pursuance of appropriations to be originated in the 1.st branch '' II. That in the 2.^d branch each State shall have an equal vote.'' *

Mr GHORUM observed that as the report consisted of propositions mutually conditional he wished to hear some explanations touching the grounds on which the conditions were estimated.

Mr GERRY. The Committee were of different opinions as well as the Deputations from which the Com.^e were taken, and agreed to the Report merely in order that some ground of accomodation might be proposed. Those opposed to the equality of votes have only assented conditionally; and if the other side do not generally agree will not be under any obligation to support the Report.

Mr WILSON thought the Committee had exceeded their powers.

Mr MARTIN was for taking the question on the whole report.

* This report was founded on a motion in the Committe made by Dr Franklin. It was barely acquiesced in by the members from the States opposed to an equality of votes in the 2.^d branch and was evidently considered by the members on the other side, as a gaining of their point. A motion was made by Mr Sherman [he [1] acted in place of Mr Elseworth who was kept away by indisposition.] In the Committee to the following effect " that each State should have an equal vote in the 2.^d branch; provided that no decision therein should prevail unless the majority of States concurring should also comprize a majority of the inhabitants of the U. States." This motion was not much deliberated on nor approved in the Committee. A similar proviso had been proposed in the debates on the articles of Confederation in 1777, to the articles giving certain powers to " nine States." See Journals of Cong.^s for 1777, p. 462.

[1] The word " who " is substituted in the transcript for " he."

Mʳ WILSON was for a division of the question: otherwise it wᵈ be a leap in the dark.

Mʳ MADISON. could not regard the exclusive [1] privilege of originating money bills as any concession on the side of the small States. Experience proved that it had no effect. If seven States in the upper branch wished a bill to be originated, they might surely find some member from some of the same States in the lower branch who would originate it. The restriction as to amendments was of as little consequence. Amendments could be handed privately by the Senate to members in the other house. Bills could be negatived that they might be sent up in the desired shape. If the Senate should yield to the obstinacy of the 1ˢᵗ branch the use of that body as a check would be lost. If the 1ˢᵗ branch should yield to that of the Senate, the privilege would be nugatory. Experience had also shewn both in G. B. and the States having a similar regulation that it was a source of frequent & obstinate altercations. These considerations had produced a rejection of a like motion on a former occasion when judged by its own merits. It could not therefore be deemed any concession on the present, and left in force all the objections which had prevailed agˢᵗ allowing each State an equal voice. He conceived that the Convention was reduced to the alternative of either departing from justice in order to conciliate the smaller States, and the minority of the people of the U. S. or of displeasing these by justly gratifying the larger States and the majority of the people. He could not himself hesitate as to the option he ought to make. The Convention with justice & the majority of the people on their side, had nothing to fear. With injustice and the minority on their side they had every thing to fear. It was in vain to purchase concord in the Convention on terms which would perpetuate discord among their Constituents. The Convention ought to pursue a plan which would bear the test of examination, which would be espoused & supported by the enlightened and impartial part of America, & which they could themselves vindicate and urge. It should be considered that altho' at first many may judge of the system recommended, by their opinion of the Convention, yet finally all will judge of the Convention by the System. The merits of the System alone can finally & effectually obtain the public suffrage. He was not apprehensive that the people of the small States would obstinately refuse to accede to a Govᵗ founded on just principles, and promising them substantial protection. He could not suspect that Delaware would

---

[1] The word " exclusive " is omitted in the transcript.

brave the consequences of seeking her fortunes apart from the other States, rather than submit to such a Gov! much less could he suspect that she would pursue the rash policy of courting foreign support, which the warmth of one of her representatives [M! Bedford] had suggested, or if she sh? that any foreign nation w? be so rash as to hearken to the overture. As little could he suspect that the people of N. Jersey notwithstanding the decided tone of the gentlemen from that State, would choose rather to stand on their own legs, and bid defiance to events, than to acquiesce under an establishment founded on principles the justice of which they could not dispute, and absolutely necessary to redeem them from the exactions levied on them by the commerce of the neighbouring States. A review of other States would prove that there was as little reason to apprehend an inflexible opposition elsewhere. Harmony in the Convention was no doubt much to be desired. Satisfaction to all the States, in the first instance still more so. But if the principal States comprehending a majority of the people of the U. S. should concur in a just & judicious plan, he had the firmest hopes, that all the other States would by degrees accede to it.

M! BUTLER said he could not let down his idea of the people, of America so far as to believe they would from mere respect to the Convention adopt a plan evidently unjust. He did not consider the privilege concerning money bills as of any consequence. He urged that the 2? branch ought to represent the States according to their property.

M! Gov! MORRIS. thought the form as well as the matter of the Report objectionable. It seemed in the first place to render amendments impracticable. In the next place, it seemed to involve a pledge to agree to the 2? part if the 1st sh? be agreed to. He conceived the whole aspect of it to be wrong. He came here as a Representative of America; he flattered himself he came here in some degree as a Representative of the whole human race; for the whole human race will be affected by the proceedings of this Convention. He wished gentlemen to extend their views beyond the present moment of time; beyond the narrow limits of place from which they derive their political origin. If he were to believe some things which he had heard, he should suppose that we were assembled to truck and bargain for our particular States. He can-not descend to think that any gentlemen are really actuated by these views. We must look forward to the effects of what we do. These alone ought to guide us. Much has been said of the sentiments of the people. They were unknown. They could not be known. All that we can infer is that if the plan we recommend be reasonable & right; all who have reasonable minds and sound intentions will embrace it, notwithstanding what had been said by some gentlemen. Let us suppose that the larger States shall agree; and that the smaller refuse: and let us trace the consequences. The opponents of the system in the smaller States will no doubt make a party, and a noise for a time, but the ties of interest, of kindred & of common habits which connect them with the other States will be too strong to be easily broken. In N. Jersey particularly he was sure a great many would follow the sentiments of Penᵃ & N. York. This Country must be united. If persuasion does not unite it, the sword will. He begged that [1] this consideration might have its due weight. The scenes of horror attending civil commotion can not be described, and the conclusion of them will be worse than the term of their continuance. The stronger party will then make traytors of the weaker; and the Gallows & Halter will finish the work of the sword. How far foreign powers would be ready to take part in the confusions he would not say. Threats that they will be invited have it seems been thrown out. He drew the melancholy picture of foreign intrusions as exhibited in the History of Germany, & urged it as a standing lesson to other nations. He trusted that the Gentlemen who may have hazarded such expressions, did not entertain them till they reached their own lips. But returning to the Report he could not think it in any respect calculated for the public good. As the 2ᵈ branch is now constituted, there will be constant disputes & appeals to the States which will undermine the Genˡ Government & controul & annihilate the 1ˢᵗ branch. Suppose that the delegates from Massᵗˢ & Rho I. in the Upper House disagree, and that the former are outvoted. What Results? they will immediately declare that their State will not abide by the decision, and make such representations as will produce that effect. The same may happen as to Virgᵃ & other States. Of what avail then will be what is on paper. State attachments, and State importance have been the bane of this Country. We can not annihilate; but we may perhaps take out the teeth of the serpents. He wished our ideas to be enlarged to the true interest of man, instead of being circumscribed within the narrow compass of a particular Spot. And after all how little can be the motive yielded by selfishness for such a policy. Who can say whether he himself, much less whether his children, will the next year be an inhabitant of this or that State.

---

[1] The word " that " is omitted in the transcript.

M⸿ Bedford. He found that what he had said as to the small States being taken by the hand, had been misunderstood; and he rose to explain. He did not mean that the small States would court the aid & interposition of foreign powers. He meant that they would not consider the federal compact as dissolved untill it should be so by the Acts of the large States. In this case The consequence of the breach of faith on their part, and the readiness of the small States to fulfill their engagements, would be that foreign Nations having demands on this Country would find it their interest to take the small States by the hand, in order to do themselves justice. This was what he meant. But no man can foresee to what extremities the small States may be driven by oppression. He observed also in apology that some allowance ought to be made for the habits of his profession in which warmth was natural & sometimes necessary. But is there not an apology in what was said by [M⸿ Gov⸿ Morris] that the sword is to unite: by M⸿ Ghorum that Delaware must be annexed to Penn⸿ and N. Jersey divided between Pen⸿ and N. York. To hear such language without emotion, would be to renounce the feelings of a man and the duty of a Citizen—As to the propositions of the Committee, the lesser States have thought it necessary to have a security somewhere. This has been thought necessary for the Executive Magistrate of the proposed Gov⸿ who has a sort of negative on the laws; and is it not of more importance that the States should be protected, than that the Executive branch of the Gov⸿ sh⸿ be protected. In order to obtain this, the smaller States have conceded as to the constitution of the first branch, and as to money bills. If they be not gratified by correspondent concessions as to the 2⸿ branch is it to be supposed they will ever accede to the plan; and what will be the consequence if nothing should be done! The condition of the U. States requires that something should be immediately done. It will be better that a defective plan should be adopted, than that none should be recommended. He saw no reason why defects might not be supplied by meetings 10, 15, or 20 years hence.

M⸿ Elseworth said he had not attended the proceedings of the Committee, but was ready to accede to the compromise they had reported. Some compromise was necessary; and he saw none more convenient or reasonable.

M⸿ Williamson hoped that the expressions of individuals would not be taken for the sense of their colleagues, much less of their States which was not & could not be known. He hoped also that the meaning of those expressions would not be misconstrued or exaggerated. He did not conceive that [M⸿ Gov⸿ Morris] meant that the sword ought to be drawn agst the smaller States. He only pointed out the probable consequences of anarchy in the U. S. A similar exposition ought to be given of the expressions [of Mr Ghorum]. He was ready to hear the Report discussed; but thought the propositions contained in it, the most objectionable of any he had yet heard.

Mr PATTERSON said that he had when the Report was agreed to in the Com^e reserved to himself the right of freely discussing it. He acknowledged that the warmth complained of was improper; but he thought the Sword & the Gallows as [1] little calculated to produce conviction. He complained of the manner in which M^r M— & Mr Govr Morris had treated the small States.

Mr GERRY. Tho' he had assented to the Report in the Committee, he had very material objections to it. We were however in a peculiar situation. We were neither the same Nation nor different Nations. We ought not therefore to pursue the one or the other of these ideas too closely. If no compromise should take place what will be the consequence. A secession he foresaw would take place; for some gentlemen seem decided on it; two different plans will be proposed; and the result no man could foresee. If we do not come to some agreement among ourselves some foreign sword will probably do the work for us.

Mr MASON. The Report was meant not as specific propositions to be adopted; but merely as a general ground of accomodation. There must be some accomodation on this point, or we shall make little further progress in the work. Accomodation was the object of the House in the appointment of the Committee; and of the Committee in the Report they had made. And however liable the Report might be to objections, he thought it preferable to an appeal to the world by the different sides, as had been talked of by some Gentlemen. It could not be more inconvenient to any gentleman to remain absent from his private affairs, than it was for him: but he would bury his bones in this City rather than expose his Country to the Consequences of a dissolution of the Convention without any thing being done.

The 1st proposition in the report for fixing the representation in the 1st branch, one member for every 40,000 inhabitants, being taken up.

Mr Govr MORRIS objected to that scale of apportionment. He thought property ought to be taken into the estimate as well as the number of inhabitants. Life & liberty were generally said to be of

---

[1] The word " as " is crossed out in the transcript.

more value, than property. An accurate view of the matter would nevertheless prove that property was the main object of Society. The savage State was more favorable to liberty than the Civilized; and sufficiently so to life. It was preferred by all men who had not acquired a taste for property; it was only renounced for the sake of property which could only be secured by the restraints of regular Government. These ideas might appear to some new, but they were nevertheless just. If property then was the main object of Gov.ᵗ certainly it ought to be one measure of the influence due to those who were to be affected by the Governm.ᵗ He looked forward also to that range of New States which w.ᵈ soon be formed in the West.. He thought the rule of representation ought to be so fixed as to secure to the Atlantic States a prevalence in the National Councils. The new States will know less of the public interest than these, will have an interest in many respects different, in particular will be little scrupulous of involving the Community in wars the burdens & operations of which would fall chiefly on the maritime States. Provision ought therefore to be made to prevent the maritime States from being hereafter outvoted by them. He thought this might be easily done by irrevocably fixing the number of representatives which the Atlantic States should respectively have, and the number which each new State will have. This w.ᵈ not be unjust, as the Western settlers w.ᵈ previously know the conditions on which they were to possess their lands. It would be politic as it would recommend the plan to the present as well as future interest of the States which must decide the fate of it.

M.ʳ RUTLIDGE. The gentleman last up had spoken some of his sentiments precisely. Property was certainly the principal object of Society. If numbers should be made the rule of representation, the Atlantic States will [1] be subjected to the Western. He moved that the first proposition in the report be postponed in order to take up the following viz " that the suffrages of the several States be regulated and proportioned according to the sums to be paid towards the general revenue by the inhabitants of each State respectively. that an apportionment of suffrages, according to the ratio aforesaid shall be made and regulated at the end of   years from the 1.ˢᵗ meeting of the Legislature of the U. S. and at the end of every   years but that for the present, and until the period above mentioned, the suffrages shall be for N. Hampshire   [2] Massach.ᵗˢ   &c.—

---

[1] The word " would " is substituted in the transcript for " will."
[2] The word " for " is here inserted in the transcript.

Col. MASON said the case of new States was not unnoticed in the Committee; but it was thought and he was himself decidedly of opinion that if they made a part of the Union, they ought to be subject to no unfavorable discriminations. Obvious considerations required it.

M: RADOLPH concurred with Col.[1] Mason.

On[2] Question on M: Rutlidges motion.

Mas^{ts} no. Con^t no. N. Y. no. N. J. no. P^a no. Del. no. Mary^d no. V^a no. N. C. no. S. C. ay. Geo. not on floor.[3]

Adj^d

FRIDAY JULY 6TH IN CONVENTION

M: Govr MORRIS moved to commit so much of the Report as relates to "1 member for every 40,000 inhabitants" His view was that they might absolutely fix the number for each State in the first instance; leaving the Legislature at liberty to provide for changes in the relative importance of the States, and for the case of new States.

M: WILSON 2^{ded} the motion; but with a view of leaving the Committee under no implied shackles.

M: GHORUM apprehended great inconveniency[4] from fixing directly the number of Representatives to be allowed to each State. He thought the number of Inhabitants the true guide; tho' perhaps some departure might be expedient from the full proportion. The States also would vary in their relative extent by separations of parts of the largest States. A part of Virg^a is now on the point of a separation. In the province of Mayne a Convention is at this time deliberating on a separation from Mas^{ts}. In such events the number of representatives ought certainly to be reduced. He hoped to see all the States made small by proper divisions, instead of their becoming formidable as was apprehended, to the Small States. He conceived that let the Genl[5] Government be modified as it might, there would be a constant tendency in the State Governm^{ts} to

---

[1] The word " Mr." is substituted in the transcript for " Col."

[2] The word " the " is here inserted in the transcript.

[3] In the transcript the vote reads: " South Carolina, aye—1; Massachusetts, Connecticut, New York, New Jersey, Pennsylvania, Delaware, Maryland, Virginia, North Carolina, no—9; Georgia not on the floor."

[4] The word " inconveniency " is changed to " inconvenience " in the transcript.

[5] The word " Gen! " is omitted in the transcript.

encroach upon it: it was of importance therefore that the extent of the States sh!d be reduced as much & as fast as possible. The stronger the Gov! shall be made in the first instance the more easily will these divisions be effected; as it will be of less consequence in the opinion of the States whether they be of great or small extent.

M! GERRY did not think with his Colleague that the large States ought to be cut up. This policy has been inculcated by the middling and smaller States, ungenerously & contrary to the spirit of the Confederation. Ambitious men will be apt to solicit needless divisions, till the States be reduced to the size of Counties. If this policy should still actuate the small States, the large ones cou'd not confederate safely with them; but would be obliged to consult their safety by confederating only with one another. He favored the Commitment and thought that Representation ought to be in the Combined ratio of numbers of Inhabitants and of wealth, and not of either singly.

M! KING wished the clause to be committed chiefly in order to detach it from the Report with which it had no connection. He thought also that the Ratio of Representation proposed could not be safely fixed, since in a century & a half our computed increase of population would carry the number of representatives to an enormous excess; that y.e number of inhabitants was not the proper index of ability & wealth; that property was the primary object of Society; and that in fixing a ratio this ought not to [1] be excluded from the estimate. With regard to new States, he observed that there was something peculiar in the business which had not been noticed. The U. S. were now admitted to be proprietors of the Country N. West of the Ohio. Cong.s by one of their ordinances have impoliticly laid it out into ten States, and have made it a fundamental article of compact with those who may become settlers, that as soon as the number in any one State shall equal that of the smallest of the 13 original States, it may claim admission into the union. Delaware does not contain it is computed more than 35,000 souls, and for obvious reasons will not increase much for a considerable time. It is possible then that if this plan be persisted in by Cong.s 10 new votes may be added, without a greater addition of inhabitants than are represented by the single vote of Pen.a The plan as it respects one of the new States is already irrevocable, the sale of the lands having commenced, and the purchasers & settlers will immediately become entitled to all the privileges of the compact.

M! BUTLER agreed to the Commitment if the Committee were to

---

[1] The word " to " is omitted in the transcript.

be left at liberty. He was persuaded that the more the subject was examined, the less it would appear that the number of inhabitants would be a proper rule of proportion. If there were no other objection the changeableness of the standard would be sufficient. He concurred with those who thought some balance was necessary between the old & new States. He contended strenuously that property was the only just measure of representation. This was the great object of Govern^t: the great cause of war; the great means of carrying it on.

Mr PINKNEY saw no good reason for committing. The value of land had been found on full investigation to be an impracticable rule. The contributions of revenue including imports & exports, must be too changeable in their amount; too difficult to be adjusted; and too injurious to the non-commercial States. The number of inhabitants appeared to him the only just & practicable rule. He thought the blacks ought to stand on an equality with [1] whites: But w^d agree to the ratio settled by Cong^s He contended that Cong^s had no right under the articles of Confederation to authorize the admission of new States; no such case having been provided for.

Mr DAVY, was for committing the clause in order to get at the merits of the question arising on the Report. He seemed to think that wealth or property ought to be represented in the 2^d branch; and numbers in the 1st branch.

On the Motion for committing as made by Mr Govr Morris.

Mas^{ts} ay. Con^t ay. N. Y. no. N. J. no. P^a ay. Del. no. M^d div^d V^a ay. N. C. ay. S. C. ay. Geo. ay.[2]

The members app^d by Ballot were Mr Govr Morris, Mr Gorham Mr Randolph, Mr Rutlidge, Mr King.

Mr WILSON signified that his view in agreeing to the commitm^t was that the Com^e might consider the propriety of adopting a scale similar to that established by the Constitution of Mas^{ts} which w^d give an advantage to ye small States without substantially departing from a [3] rule of proportion.

Mr WILSON & Mr MASON moved to postpone the clause relating to money bills in order to take up the clause relating to an equality of votes in the second branch.

---

[1] The word "the" is here inserted in the transcript.

[2] In the transcript the vote reads: "Massachusetts, Connecticut, Pennsylvania, Virginia, North Carolina, South Carolina, Georgia, aye—7; New York, New Jersey, Delaware, no—3; Maryland, divided."

[3] The word "the" is substituted in the transcript for the word "a."

On the question [1] Mas.[ts] no. Con.[t] no. N. Y. ay. N. J. ay. P.[a] ay. Del. ay. M.[d] ay. V.[a] ay. N. C. no. S. C. ay. Geo. ay.

The clause relating to equality of votes being under consideration,

Doc.[t] FRANKLIN observed that this question could not be properly put by itself, the Committee having reported several propositions as mutual conditions of each other. He could not vote for it if separately taken, but should vote for the whole together.

Col. MASON perceived the difficulty & suggested a reference of the rest of the Report to y.[e] Committee just appointed, that the whole might be brought into one view.

M.[r] RANDOLPH disliked y.[e] reference to that Committee, as it consisted of members from States opposed to the wishes of the smaller States, and could not therefore be acceptable to the latter.

M.[r] MARTIN & M.[r] JENIFER moved to postpone the clause till the Com.[e] last appointed should report.

M.[r] MADISON observed that if the uncommitted part of the Report was connected with the part just committed, it ought also to be committed; if not connected, it need not be postponed till report should be made.

On the question for postponing moved by M.[r] Martin & M.[r] Jennifer   Con.[t] N. J. Del. M.[d] V.[a] Geo., ay [2]
P.[a] N. C. S. C..............no [3]
Mas. N. Y..............divided

The 1.st clause relating to the originating of money bills was then resumed.

M.[r] GOVERN.[r] MORRIS was opposed to a restriction of this right in either branch, considered merely in itself and as unconnected with the point of representation in the 2.[d] branch. It will disable the 2.[d] branch from proposing its own money plans, and giving the people an opportunity of judging by comparison of the merits of those proposed by the 1.st branch.

M.[r] WILSON could see nothing like a concession here on the part of the smaller States. If both branches were to say yes [4] or no,[4] it was of little consequence which should say yes [4] or no [4] first, which last. If either was indiscriminately to have the right of originating, the reverse of the Report, would he thought be most proper; since it

---

[1] The words "of postponement" are here inserted in the transcript and the vote reads: "New York, New Jersey, Pennsylvania, Delaware, Maryland, Virginia, South Carolina, Georgia, aye—8; Massachusetts, Connecticut, North Carolina, no—3."
[2] The figure "6" is here inserted in the transcript.
[3] The figure "3" is here inserted in the transcript.
[4] The transcript italicizes the words "yes" and "no."

was a maxim that the least numerous body was the fittest for deliberation; the most numerous for decision. He observed that this discrimination had been transcribed from the British into several American constitutions. But he was persuaded that on examination of the American experiments it would be found to be a trifle light as air. Nor could he ever discover the advantage of it in the Parliamentary history of G. Britain. He hoped if there was any advantage in the privilege, that it would be pointed out.

Mr WILLIAMSON thought that if the privilege were not common to both branches it ought rather to be confined to the 2^d as the bills in that case would be more narrowly watched, than if they originated with the branch having most of the popular confidence.

Mr MASON. The consideration which weighed with the Committee was that the 1st branch would be the immediate representatives of the people, the 2^d would not. Should the latter have the power of giving away the people's money, they might soon forget the source from whence they received it. We might soon have an aristocracy. He had been much concerned at the principles which had been advanced by some gentlemen, but had the satisfaction to find they did not generally prevail. He was a friend to proportional representation in both branches; but supposed that some points must be yielded for the sake of accomodation.

Mr WILSON. If he had proposed that the 2^d branch should have an independent disposal of public money, the observations of [Col Mason] would have been a satisfactory answer. But nothing could be farther from what he had said. His question was how is the power of the 1st branch increased or that of the 2^d diminished by giving the proposed privilege to the former? Where is the difference, in which branch it begins if both must concur, in the end?

Mr GERRY would not say that the concession was a sufficient one on the part of the small States. But he could not but regard it in the light of a concession. It w^d make it a constitutional principle that the 2^d branch were not possessed of the Confidence of the people in money matters, which w^d lessen their weight & influence. In the next place if the 2^d branch were dispossessed of the privilege, they w^d be deprived of the opportunity which their continuance in office 3 times as long as the 1st branch would give them of makig three successive essays in favor of a particular point.

Mr PINKNEY thought it evident that the Concession was wholly on one side, that of the large States, the privilege of originating money bills being of no account.

Mr Govr MORRIS had waited to hear the good effects of the restriction. As to the alarm sounded, of an aristocracy, his creed was that there never was, nor ever will be a civilized Society without an aristocracy. His endeavor was to keep it as much as possible from doing mischief. The restriction if it has any real operation will deprive us of the services of the 2ᵈ branch in digesting & proposing money bills of which it will be more capable than the 1ˢᵗ branch. It will take away the responsibility of the 2ᵈ branch, the great security for good behavior. It will always leave a plea, as to an obnoxious money bill that it was disliked, but could not be constitutionally amended; nor safely rejected. It will be a dangerous source of disputes between the two Houses. We should either take the British Constitution altogether or make one for ourselves. The Executive there has dissolved two Houses as the only cure for such disputes. Will our Executive be able to apply such a remedy? Every law directly or indirectly takes money out of the pockets of the people. Again What use may be made of such a privilege in case of great emergency? Suppose an Enemy at the door, and money instantly & absolutely necessary for repelling him, may not the popular branch avail itself of this duress, to extort concessions from the Senate destructive of the Constitution itself. He illustrated this danger by the example of the Long Parliament's expedᵗˢ for subverting the H. of Lords; concluding on the whole that the restriction would be either useless or pernicious.

Docᵗ FRANKLIN did not mean to go into a justification of the Report; but as it had been asked what would be the use of restraining the 2ᵈ branch from medling with money bills, he could not but remark that it was always of importance that the people should know who had disposed of their money, & how it had been disposed of. It was a maxim that those who feel, can best judge. This end would, he thought, be best attained, if money affairs were to be confined to the immediate representatives of the people. This was his inducement to concur in the report. As to the danger or difficulty that might arise from a negative in the 2ᵈ ¹ where the people wᵈ not be proportionally represented, it might easily be got over by declaring that there should be no such Negative: or if that will not do, by declaring that there shall be no such branch at all.

Mʳ MARTIN said that it was understood in the Committee that the difficulties and disputes which had been apprehended, should be guarded agˢᵗ in the detailing of the plan.

Mʳ WILSON. The difficulties & disputes will increase with the

---

¹ The word "branch" is here inserted in the transcript.

attempts to define & obviate them. Queen Anne was obliged to dissolve her Parliam^t in order to terminate one of these obstinate disputes between the two Houses. Had it not been for the mediation of the Crown, no one can say what the result would have been. The point is still *sub judice* in England. He approved of the principles laid down by the Hon'ble President[1] [Doct^r Franklin] his Colleague, as to the expediency of keeping the people informed of their money affairs. But thought they would know as much, and be as well satisfied, in one way as in the other.

Genl PINKNEY was astonished that this point should have been considered as a concession. He remarked that the restriction[2] to money bills had been rejected on the merits singly considered, by 8 States agst 3. and that the very States which now called it a concession, were then agst it as nugatory or improper in itself.

On the Question whether the clause relating to money bills in the Report of the Com^e consisting of a member from each State, sh^d stand as part of the Report—

Mass^{ts} divid^d Con^t ay. N. Y. div^d N. J. ay. P^a no. Del. ay. M^d ay. V^a no. N. C. ay. S. C. no. Geo. div^d [3]

A Question was then raised whether the question was carried in the affirmative: there being but 5 ays out of 11. States present. The words of the rule are[4] (see May 28).[5]

On the[6] question: Mas. Con^t N. J. P^a Del. M^d N. C. S. C. Geo ay[7]

N. Y. V^a.............................no [8]

[In several preceding instances like votes had *sub silentio* been entered as decided in the affirmative.]

Adjourned

---

[1] In the transcript after the word "President" reference is made to a footnote which reads: "He was at that time President of the State of Pennsylvania."

[2] The word "as" is here inserted in the transcript.

[3] In the transcript the vote reads: "Connecticut, New Jersey, Delaware, Maryland, North Carolina, aye—5; Pennsylvania, Virginia, South Carolina, no—3; Massachusetts, New York, Georgia, divided."

[4] The phrase "For the words of the Rule" is substituted in the transcript for "The words of the rule are."

[5] A House to do business shall consist of the Deputies of not less than seven States; and all questions shall be decided by the greater number of these which shall be fully represented: but a less number than seven may adjourn from day to day. See *ante*, p. 19.

[6] The word "this" is substituted in the transcript for "the."

[7] The figure "9" is here added in the transcript.

[8] The figure "2" is here added in the transcript.

END OF VOLUME ONE